EXCAVATIONS AT MILLA SKERRA, SANDWICK, UNST

EXCAVATIONS AT MILLA SKERRA, SANDWICK, UNST

RHYTHMS OF LIFE IN IRON AGE SHETLAND

Edited by

OLIVIA LELONG

with contributions by

Beverley Ballin Smith, Torben Bjarke Ballin, Ruby Cerón-Carrasco, Ann Clarke, Brendan Derhan, Paul Duffy, Katharina Dulias, Ceiridwen J. Edwards, Clare Ellis, Amanda Forster, Martin Goldberg, Fraser Hunter, Richard Jones, Jo McKenzie, Dawn McLaren, Jennifer Miller, Anthony Newton, Susan Ramsay and Catherine Smith

Illustrations by

Ingrid Shearer and Jill Sievewright

OXBOW | books
Oxford & Philadelphia

Published in the United Kingdom in 2019 by
OXBOW BOOKS
The Old Music Hall, 106–108 Cowley Road, Oxford, OX4 1JE

and in the United States by
OXBOW BOOKS
1950 Lawrence Road, Havertown, PA 19083

Hardback Edition: ISBN 978-1-78570-343-0
Digital Edition: ISBN 978-1-78570-344-7 (epub)

A CIP record for this book is available from the British Library

Library of Congress Control Number: 2018964658

Typeset in India by Versatile PreMedia Services. www.versatilepremedia.com

For a complete list of Oxbow titles, please contact:

UNITED KINGDOM
Oxbow Books
Telephone (01865) 241249
Email: oxbow@oxbowbooks.com
www.oxbowbooks.com

UNITED STATES OF AMERICA
Oxbow Books
Telephone (800) 791-9354, Fax (610) 853-9146
Email: queries@casemateacademic.com
www.casemateacademic.com/oxbow

Oxbow Books is part of the Casemate Group

Front cover: Main image: Excavation underway at Milla Skerra in 2005. Photo by Tom Dawson.
Top image, front cover: Sandwick, Easting from the south-west, with the excavation site at the centre of the image. Photo by Olivia Lelong.
Back cover: Top image: The medieval chapel site at Framgord, Easting. Photo by Olivia Lelong.
Bottom image: The house under excavation, with the hearth in the foreground. Photo by Olivia Lelong.

Contents

List of Figures

List of tables

Acknowledgements

The excavation of Milla Skerra was generously funded by Historic Environment Scotland, the Heritage Lottery Fund, the Russell Trust, the Hunter Archaeological Trust, Unst Community Council and Shetland Islands Council. Historic Environment Scotland funded the post-excavation analysis and publication.

I would like to thank the volunteers who devoted their time, effort, skill and enthusiasm to excavating the site: Shula Burns, Jean and Harry Edwards, Margaret Hunter, Davy Leask, Liam O'Neil, Jan Sandison, Les Smith and Andrew Magnus Thomson of the Unst Archaeology Group, along with Zoe Anderson, Florence Boisserie, Susan Campbell, Lucy Cooke, Pieterjan Deckers, Andy and Nadine Duffus, Joy French, Liz Gott, John Isbister, Carol Knott, Marie Lefere, Emily Mahon, John Pulley, Bernard Redman, Pat Thomson, Mike Tilley and Neil Wilkin. Especially warm thanks to the Unst folk for being so generous with their hospitality, home bakes, good humour and detailed knowledge of the island.

Ingrid Shearer directed the training aspects of the fieldwork (2004-6) and also produced the maps and site illustrations for this volume. Tom Dawson of the SCAPE (Scottish Coastal Archaeology and the Problem of Erosion) Trust set up and oversaw the fieldwork element, and Labhaoise McKenna of the SCAPE Trust facilitated and helped deliver the final season. The contributions of all three were vital to the success of the project.

Thanks also to the professional archaeologists who worked to excavate and record the site in conditions that ranged from rain and wind to killer midges to blazing sunshine: Andrew Baines, Amanda Brend, Sheelagh Conron, Charlotte Francoz, Martin Goldberg, Rowena Keane, Phil Kennedy, Carole Killeen, Labhaoise McKenna, Scott Macleod, Aoife Patterson, Roderick Regan, Pat Reid, Christine Rennie, Abigail Walsh and Brendon Wilkins.

The project was made possible through many other people's efforts and contributions, all gratefully acknowledged here. Val Turner, Shetland Islands Council Archaeologist, first brought the eroding site to the attention of Tom Dawson. Sir John Scott, former Lord Lieutenant of the Shetland Islands, who owns the site, and Dougal Fraser, who farms it, kindly allowed and facilitated access. Helen Bradley of the former Council for Scottish Archaeology (now Archaeology Scotland) worked with the Unst community to organise the Adopt-a-Monument reconstruction work, which was carried out by Ric Barton and Jim Keddie. Jill Sievewright executed the artefact illustrations. Robina Barton, Martin Carruthers, Carol Christiansen, Kate Coutts, Chris Dyer, Noel Fojut, Brian Hunter, RAF Corporal Ian Kitson-Hyde, Jenny Murray, Christopher Rich, Alice Roberts, Duncan Sandison, Rudi Saunders, RAF Warrant Officer Phil Stanley and Iain Thomason all provided practical and moral support in different ways. Finally, thank you to Paul Murtagh for commenting on earlier drafts of the chapters and Julie Gardiner at Oxbow Books for her editorial support and considerable patience.

Olivia Lelong

Summary

A seaside settlement at Sandwick, on the Shetland island of Unst, had been buried for about 1800 years when it was discovered by local people, after winter storms tore into the foreshore and exposed stone walls and thick layers of hearth waste, pottery and animal bones. Archaeologists and local volunteers excavated it over four seasons (2004–7), finding evidence for occupation across six main phases. A programme of post-excavation analysis and radiocarbon dating established a main sequence from the mid-1st millennium BC to the 2nd century AD, when the settlement was inundated with windblown sand, as well as earlier and later activity.

Throughout its lifetime, the settlement at Milla Skerra consisted of different configurations of conjoined buildings and yards on the same spot. Due to the windy conditions, the alkaline (shell-sand) environment and the inhabitants' complex uses of domestic waste (midden), the site built up like a miniature tell over hundreds of years. Midden heaps covered yards and walls and new buildings were constructed on top; one substantial stone wall was still being re-used centuries later, half-buried in the accumulated residues of generations.

A semi-circular or oval house, built in the 2nd century BC, had a paved floor with a thin radial wall extending to a central hearth, which was rebuilt twice as ashes and cooking waste piled up behind it. The yards were used at different times for craft work, including processing animal hides and possibly metalworking, for outdoor cooking and for storing midden. People were cultivating nutrient-rich midden heaps beside the settlement and also using midden in structured, symbolic ways in the buildings. In the 1st century AD, people ceased living in the house and spread midden over the floor; soon afterwards, the upper walls were pushed in or collapsed, perhaps representing its deliberate closure.

The excavated evidence was fleshed out by specialist analyses of painted pebbles, metalwork, glass and shale ornaments, bone implements, industrial waste, pottery, heavy stone and chipped stone tools, pumice and steatite objects, fish bones and marine shells, animal and bird bones, carbonised plant remains, soil samples and human remains. The findings make it possible to tease out the daily and seasonal rhythms of people's lives, from craft work to food production and waste management, and how these changed over time.

The settlement's scale and complexity remain unknown. It may have extended much further towards the sea and there are 19th-century accounts of a broch at the site, but no traces of one were found. The architectural and artefactual evidence suggests connections and affinities with other communities along the eastern seaboard of Shetland, for example at Bayanne on the neighbouring island of Yell.

Around the 2nd century AD, Milla Skerra began to contract. Some people may have moved farther inland for shelter from increasingly windy conditions, and finally winds smothered the settlement in sand. Perhaps within living memory, a man's body was buried next to the abandoned buildings. This burial in the mid-2nd–late 4th century AD was followed by at least one other nearby in the 4th–5th century and the construction of square cairns of white quartzite pebbles, excavated in the 1980s by Dr Gerry Bigelow. These broadly coincided with activity on the dune that by this time covered the old settlement. In the mid-1st millennium AD, Milla Skerra may have been a place where people came specifically for burial and related acts – the former home of an ancestral community, a spot suitable for rites that would connect the living community with its roots and traditions.

The project was set up and managed by the SCAPE (Scottish Coastal Archaeology and the Problem of Erosion) Trust and funded by Historic Environment Scotland, the Heritage Lottery Fund, Unst Community Council, the Shetland Amenity Trust, the Hunter Archaeological Trust and the Russell Trust.

Chapter 1

Uncovering Milla Skerra

Olivia Lelong

At 60°74'16" north, Unst is the most northerly of the Shetland Isles. The island's coast has its own rhythms, ones set by the tides, seasons and weather. In summer, the sea gently washes the beach; in winter, easterly gales ram waves into the foreshore. Sometimes winds pile the sand into dunes or cast sudden sandy blankets over the turf, while other times they scour the foreshore bare.

Over thousands of years, people have found ways to live here at the interface of land and sea. Archaeological excavation at Milla Skerra on Easting beach, beside the bay of Sandwick, revealed the rhythms of a community's life over several hundred years. From around the late 6th century BC, generations of people were building and rebuilding a settlement on this spot. They were fishing, farming, hunting and cooking; making the things they needed and breaking them; sorting and piling up their rubbish and sometimes ploughing it back into the land to grow more food. Buildings tumbled or were pulled apart to make new ones; hearths were swept out and renewed; floors were buried under heaps of midden and fresh ones laid. Layers of detritus and superimposed structures built up like a tiny tell until, around the 2nd century AD, winds covered the settlement with sand and life became untenable. Settlement carried on nearby, however, and people appear to have expressed some memory of the place through particular acts for generations afterward.

Traces of the settlement first came to light in 2003, when members of the Unst Archaeology Group, who regularly walk the island and record its abundant archaeological remains, noticed that winter storms had torn into the sandy foreshore at Easting (NGR: HP 6195 0217) (Fig. 1.1). In the cliff face they observed newly exposed walls and upright stones in a mound made up of thick layers of midden and artefacts, including pottery and bone (Fig. 1.4). They alerted Val Turner, Shetland Council Archaeologist, to the presence of a potentially important prehistoric site. Tom Dawson of the SCAPE (Scottish Coastal Archaeology and the Problem of Erosion) Trust initiated the site's investigation as part of its Shorewatch Project, which encourages and assists local communities to locate, record and monitor coastal archaeological sites around Scotland's coasts (Dawson *et al.* 2011).

Over 14 weeks spanning four summers (2004–2007), teams of volunteer and professional archaeologists recorded and excavated the eroding mound under the direction of the principal author. Each season of work had explicit training objectives as well as specific research aims, which evolved as the work progressed. The volunteers – many from Unst Archaeology Group but also farther afield, including university students – received training in a wide range of archaeological field techniques under the guidance of professional staff, with Ingrid Shearer serving as Training Director. Material from the excavations along with the project archive are held at Shetland Museum and Archives.

The lie of the land

Sandwick is a wide-mouthed bay on the eastern shore of Unst. The name, given by settlers from Norway who began farming the island from the 8th century AD, means 'sandy bay'. Milla Skerra (from the Old Norse *skerra* or rock) is the name of a slight promontory above shingle and outcropping bedrock dykes which are exposed at low tide, and which have put up some resistance to storm erosion over the millennia (Fig. 1.2). At the time of excavation, the base of the eroding archaeology was 2–3 m above the Mean High Water Mark and the Mean High Water Springs washed against it.

Today, undulating fixed dune grasslands extend inland from the coast for up to 80 m, with rabbit burrows and sheep scrapes exposing windblown sand beneath the turf. The fixed dunes give way to boggy ground, and beyond the land climbs in a series of terraces to a ridge and the

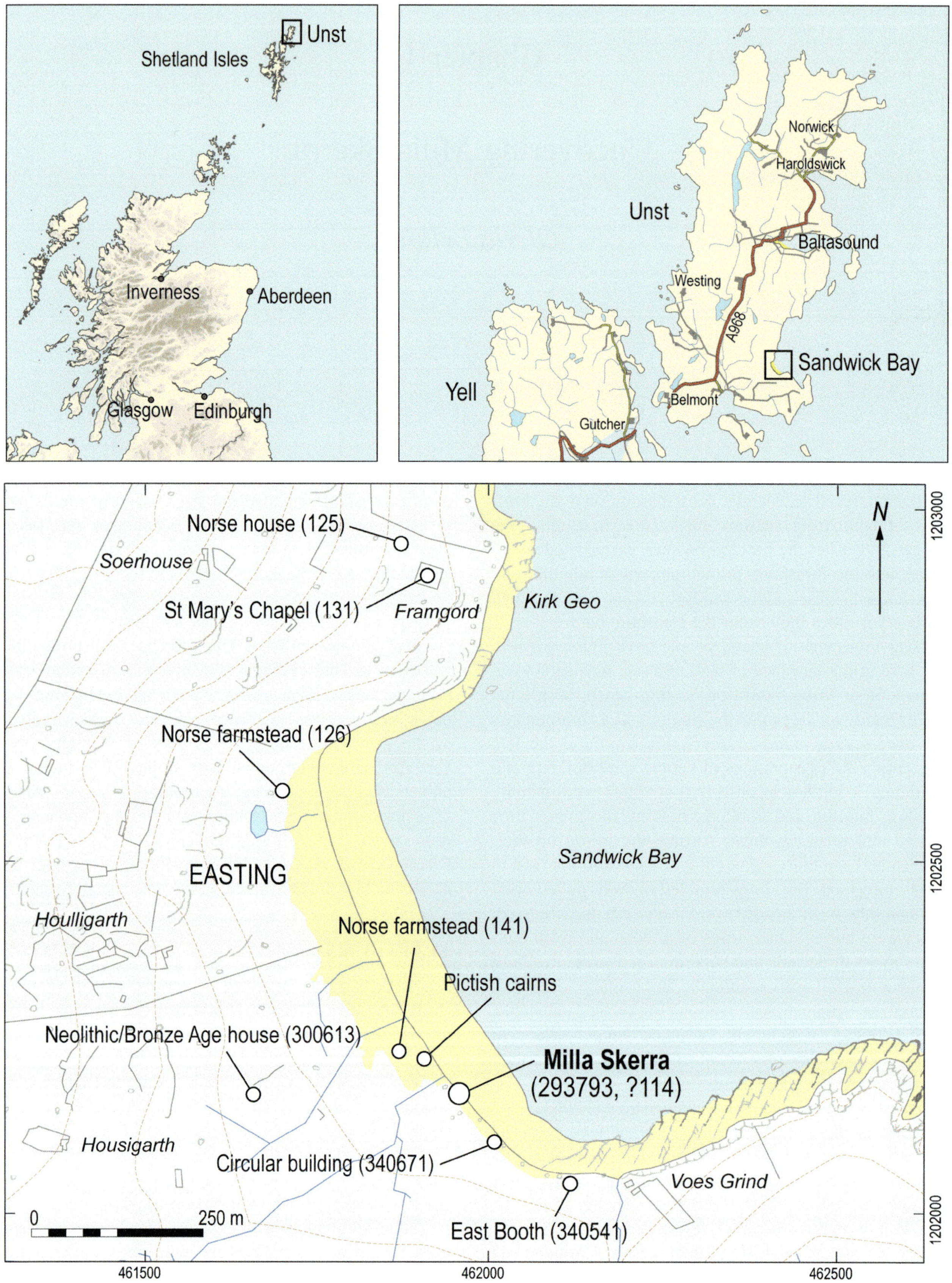

Figure 1.1 Location of Milla Skerra and its immediate context

Figure 1.2 Sandwick from the air in 2009. Milla Skerra is the concentration of stone and shingle on the beach to the left of the burn; the excavated Norse longhouse is under turf and sand to the right of the burn; East Booth is to the far left, and Hannigarth is at the top of the frame (©HES, DP 197289)

old croft house of Hannigarth (at *c.* 50 m above OD). A burn runs an incised course down the slope, flowing into the sea to the north-west of Milla Skerra.

The geology at Sandwick is of three different types. Across most of the foreshore and hinterland it consists of Upper Metagabbro (Shetland Ophialite) and Metagabbro, metamorphic bedrock formed about 444–488 million years ago in the Ordovician period. A wedge of metalava and metatuff of the Gruting Greenschist Formation, which formed 416–488 million years ago in the Silurian and Ordovician periods, runs down to the shore immediately south-east of Milla Skerra. These were originally igneous rocks formed by intrusions of silica-poor magma and later altered by low-grade metamorphism. Across the uplands and coast to the south and east is semipelite, metamorphic bedrock of the Muness Phyllites formations that formed in shallow seas 416–488 million years ago. The drift geology behind the foreshore consists of undifferentiated till and morainic deposits, formed up to three million years ago through the actions of glaciers and meltwater in the Quaternary period, and windblown sand of post-glacial age (http://mapapps.bgs.ac.uk/geologyofbritain/).

The landscape bordering the bay is a dynamic, fragile environment that has been shaped significantly by Aeolian (wind-driven) processes. These generate cycles of deflation, accretion and erosion that scour and redistribute the sediments. High-energy waves batter the sandy beach during winter, and strong winds lift and remove turf cover that has been weakened by burrowing and grazing, exposing the underlying sand to deflation. Historical documents and photographs, as well as archaeological evidence from Milla Skerra, demonstrate how quickly this can happen: thick layers of sand sometimes accumulate almost overnight, while at other times the changes are more gradual. Aerial photographs show that in the 1940s the foreshore around the settlement was mostly bare of vegetation, with only the settlement mound itself and another small area to the SSW retaining turf cover, but later aerial photos document the turf steadily creeping back to its current extent.

Like many other areas with dune systems around the coasts of northern Britain (Ashmore and Griffiths 2011), Sandwick attracted settlement at many points in the past and it has a rich and complex archaeological heritage which is extremely vulnerable, presenting challenges for management and conservation.

Layers in the landscape

Abundant upstanding archaeological remains, spread along the slopes around Sandwick, show how people occupied this relatively sheltered and fertile pocket of Unst at least intermittently from early prehistory to the 19th century – a period of about 5,000 years.

In 2009, field survey by the former Royal Commission on the Ancient and Historical Monuments of Scotland (RCAHMS, now Historic Environment Scotland) identified a sub-rectangular building with thick stone walls (Canmore ID 300613 on Fig. 1.1). It is comparable to early prehistoric buildings recorded elsewhere in Shetland, such as the Benie Hoose on Whalsay (Calder 1963; see Fig. 8.10). Although it is described as Neolithic, research is showing that these houses can also date to the Bronze Age (mid-3rd to early 1st millennium BC) (Downes and Lamb 2000, 121).

Evidence of occupation around the bay from the 1st millennium BC onward crops up in various antiquarian and modern accounts. Traditions of a substantial structure which was washed away in the early to mid-20th century have persisted into living memory (Margaret Hunter, pers comm). In his list of brochs on Unst, the antiquarian J. T. Irvine (nd) noted the presence of one at 'Sandiveck', two-thirds of the way along the shore towards the bay's eastern end, a location that corresponds approximately to Milla Skerra. It was first observed by the schoolmaster of Uyeasound after north-easterly gales blew away some of the sand that covered it, but only a small part was visible in 1863 (Canmore ID 114). Whether or not it was a broch, this apparently substantial building may have been part of the excavated settlement.

The RCAHMS also found a roughly circular building, defined by spaced orthostats (upright stones), eroding out of the foreshore about 20 m south-east of Milla Skerra (Canmore ID 340671 on Fig. 1.1). It appeared very similar to house 1 in the excavated settlement (Canmore ID 293793; see Fig. 1.1 and Chapter 2). A possible broch was also recorded in the 19th century at Brough Taing, 2 km along the coast to the north, where erosion has since scoured the land surface to bedrock (MacKie 2002, 58; Canmore ID 116), and late prehistoric walls and midden are also eroding from above the shore nearby at Blue Geos (David Leask, pers comm; Canmore ID 121) (see Fig. 8.11).

Sandwick is especially rich in the archaeology of people from the periods of Pictish (late 3rd–8th centuries AD) and Norse (8th–12th centuries AD) occupation. The foreshore was a focus for human burial in the mid-1st millennium AD. Two square cairns about 80 m to the north-west of Milla Skerra were investigated in the 1980s (Bigelow 1984). One contained the extended burial of a female about 50 years of age, radiocarbon dated to 1530±55 BP (GU-1291), or cal AD 420–640 (95.4% probability, calibrated using OxCal 4.3). There are other, vague records of human remains in short cists having been found along the shore (Canmore ID 135), and in 1953, a skeleton in a short cist was found on the beach and reported to Shetland Museum (see Chapter 8 and Fig. 8.13).

From the late 8th century, Unst was the first landfall for Vikings who sailed west from Norway intent on raiding, trading and land-taking. The island has the highest density of rural Viking settlement remains known anywhere, including in Scandinavia, with about 60 early longhouses so far recorded (Turner *et al.* 2013). With its long sweep of white beach, Sandwick would have been highly visible and attractive to ships seeking places to land and eventually settle (Fig. 1.3). Early Viking artefacts have been found in middens eroding further north-west along the beach from Milla Skerra (Canmore ID 112). There are also the excavated remains of a Norse farmstead dating from the 11th century (Canmore ID 126; Hansen 1995) and another that was occupied from the mid-12th to the late 15th centuries (Bigelow 1978; 1979; 1980; Canmore ID 141 on Fig. 1.1). Other probable Norse houses have been recorded around the bay, such as the Priest's Hoose at Framgord (Canmore ID 125 on Fig. 1.1; Bigelow 1980, 26).

These farmsteads eventually developed into the larger crofting townships of Soerhouse, Framgord, Hannigarth, Housigarth, Houlligarth and Voes Grind. Their remains – the footings of houses, outbuildings, planticrubs, kale yards, animal pens, head dykes and clearance cairns – sprawl across the slopes that surround the bay. Tenant farmers traded surplus dried fish and wool for goods like salt, tar, tobacco, shoes, pottery and soap at East Booth, a trading post built by German merchants of the Hanseatic League in the 1600s (Canmore ID 340541 on Fig. 1.1); its ruins stand at the south-east end of the beach. On the north side of the bay is the ruined chapel of St Mary's, which served local communities for perhaps 700 years. Its burial ground was still in use in 1878 (RCAHMS 1946, 141, No. 158; Canmore ID 131 on Fig. 1.1) but, like the crofting settlements, it fell out of use as the local population declined in the late 19th century.

Fieldwork methods

The approach to assessing and excavating Milla Skerra was designed to achieve a balance between safely recovering as much archaeological information as possible and delivering high-quality training to the volunteers. Ultimately, the decision was taken not to excavate the structural remains fully, although excavation did proceed to the base of the stratigraphic sequence in some areas.

Fieldwork began in 2004 with a two-week assessment of the eroding site, which was then visible as the turf-covered mound and eroded cliff section described above (Fig. 1.4). The assessment involved topographic, geophysical and auger surveys of the mound (Figs 1.5 and 1.6); cleaning and recording of the eroded section, along with limited excavation of part of it, and walkover survey of the surrounding area.

The fieldwork methodology worked around certain challenges, including the depth of windblown deposits covering the site and the instability of the oldest and tallest structure (the yard 5 wall, context 83). In 2005,

Figure 1.3 Sandwick from the south; Milla Skerra is under excavation at the centre of the photo

Figure 1.4 Panoramic view from the north-east of the eroding coastal section before excavation

excavation of the mound began from the top down in a trench measuring (at its base) *c.* 17 m north-west/south-east by 9 m, with wheelbarrow ramps extending into it on the west and south-east. The same area was re-opened in 2006 and 2007 minus a 2 m-wide strip on the south-west, an area of Iron Age infield that was excavated in a series of test pits to sterile subsoil in 2005. The blown sand over the site was over 1.5 m thick in places and very loose, so the sides of the trench were cut with a batter of 30° and covered with debris netting and sandbags to prevent their collapse. Excavated sand was dumped on the beach against the eroded coastal edge to create a working platform and stabilise the cliff face; each following winter it was swept away by storms.

Excavation in 2005–07 (Fig. 1.7) worked through the upper structures (2, 3 and 4) and exposed the earliest one (5). The paved floor of structure 5 was partly removed, but its eastern half was left *in situ* along with a high wall (context 83) that stood along its south-east edge. A baulk was also left through part of the massive wall that had defined the south-west part of a later yard (3), above and along the south side of the earlier yard (5). A house (structure 1) was left largely intact, although part of its paved floor was removed and the underlying deposits excavated, and a slot trench was cut through the upstanding stone wall.

The decision not to excavate the site entirely was taken by the Unst Archaeology Group. They chose instead to reinstate the remains of the settlement, in order to leave it open to view for as long as it could withstand the elements. This was done at the end of the 2007 fieldwork season, under the Adopt-a-Monument programme run by the former Council for Scottish Archaeology (now Archaeology Scotland).

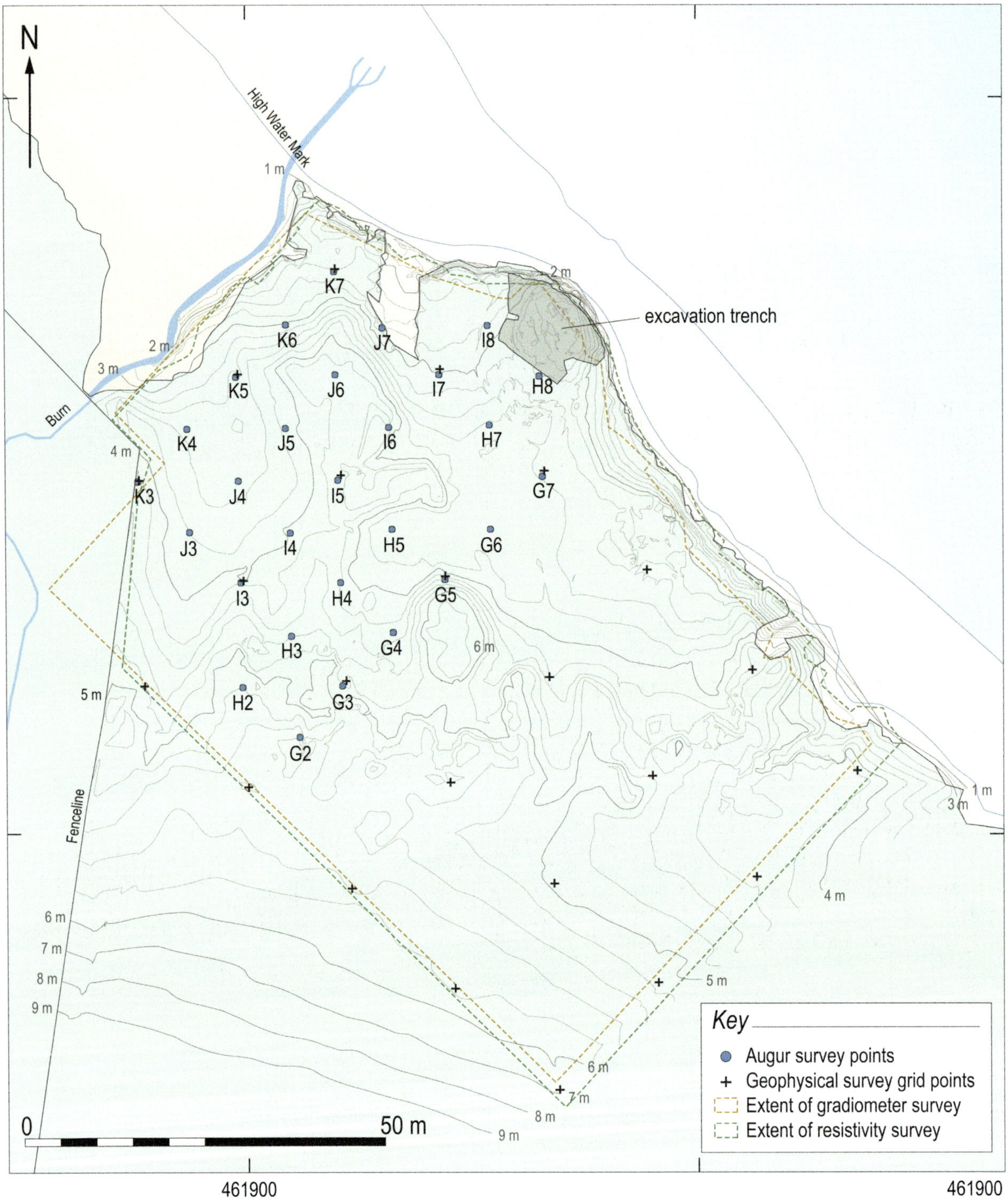

Figure 1.5 Contour survey of the settlement mound, showing auger point locations

The reinstatement was led by stonemasons experienced in stabilising the extensive prehistoric settlement at Old Scatness on mainland Shetland (Dockrill *et al.* 2015). They worked with the excavation team to rebuild the walls and replace the paved floor of the later yards (structures 3 and 4) and sections of walling and flooring in the house (1). Sandbags covered with fishing nets were placed against the seaward section as additional protection.

As cycles of weather continue to chip away at the remains of Milla Skerra, more evidence for how the settlement was built, occupied and abandoned may emerge as time goes on, creating scope to expand and refine the narrative presented in this volume. The discovery and excavation of the settlement have enriched our understanding of how people were living in the very north of Shetland two millennia ago and more.

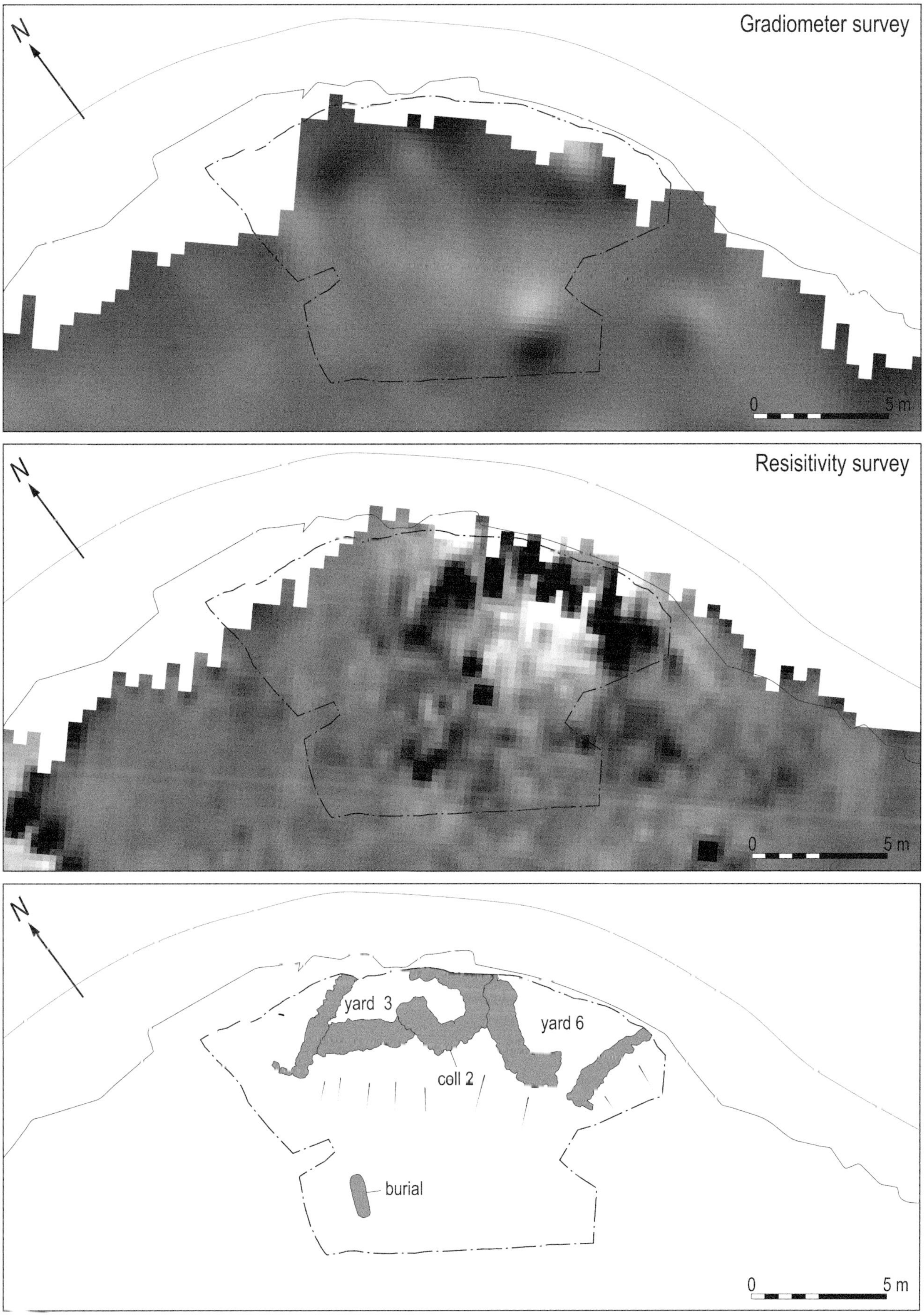

Figure 1.6 Results of resistivity and gradiometer survey of the mound, with a schematic plan of the latest structures

Figure 1.7. Volunteers excavating in 2007

The project also demonstrates how valuable and important is the work of local volunteers in monitoring and recording eroding archaeological remains - especially in the dynamic and often fragile environments of Scotland's 18,000 km of coastline. The abundant, diverse heritage sites in these areas, as in other littoral zones around the world, are under increasing pressure from rising sea levels and extreme weather events due to climate change (Hambly 2017; Orkivu *et al.* 2003; Rennie and Hansom 2011). As repositories of the stories and material culture of past lives, they hold enormous potential to help us construct narratives about the past and understand what they mean to us. Partly reconstructed beside the beach at Sandwick, Milla Skerra is once again a feature of Unst's coastal landscape, contributing to the island's historical texture and its sense of place in the present.

Chapter 2

The life and death of Milla Skerra

Olivia Lelong

Excavation at Milla Skerra established that the settlement developed over the course of six main phases from the 6th century BC to the 2nd century AD, with both earlier and later sporadic activity in the immediate vicinity. This chapter presents the archaeological evidence for the stratigraphic sequence from the earliest events to the latest, interwoven with key findings from the specialist analyses of artefacts and environmental evidence; these are presented in detail in Chapters 4–7.

Six structures were identified during excavation: a dwelling and four yards, one with a small cellular annexe. These are numbered 1–6 with the numbers pre-fixed by a descriptor thus: house 1, cell 2, yard 3, yard 4, yard 5 and yard 6. Context numbers are shown in parentheses as (234) and artefact numbers are pre-fixed with 'SF'.

Chronology

Milla Skerra presented a fairly clear stratigraphic sequence, well-preserved except where it had been truncated by coastal erosion on the seaward side. Phasing of the site is based on the observed sequence with refinements provided by the results of artefactual, geochemical and micromorphological analysis (Chapters 4–7).

Absolute dating of the sequence is provided by radiocarbon determinations for 19 samples from across the phases (Table 2.1); they were calibrated using Oxcal v 4.3, which works with the IntCal 13 estimate of the radiocarbon calibration curve. These have been interpreted in light of the taphonomic processes, waste management practices and foraging strategies that contributed to the formation of this compact, intensively used, long-lived site. Since much of the carbonised plant material probably derived from driftwood, only one of the dates was obtained from willow charcoal (*Salix*), three were from carbonised grain and one from human bone; the rest were obtained from animal bone.

Throughout the settlement's history, the inhabitants managed the waste from domestic life and craft processes in deliberate ways. Much of it was stored in and beside yards, with some evidence for sorting and deposition of different kinds of material in different places. Food and hearth waste were piled up in the house and periodically cleared out, and some of it was spread and ploughed into infield beside the structures to enhance crop yields (see Ellis, Chapter 3). At certain times, midden was also used strategically to achieve other things, both tangible and intangible - for example, to raise the ground level in preparation for new structures (phase 4) and to close a house that had ceased to be occupied (phases 6 and 7). Sometimes (as demonstrated by a radiocarbon date for cereal grain in context 49 (SUERC-26145)), this involved using older material that had been quarried from an ancient midden heap. Contexts of deposition at the site were thus not only primary and secondary, but sometimes tertiary. In other words, artefacts (made objects) and ecofacts (such as burnt grain, charcoal, animal bone and fish bone) were sometimes found where they first fell or were discarded (primary context), more often where they were subsequently placed (for example, on a midden heap, their secondary context) and sometimes where they were later moved as part of quarried midden (tertiary context).

The intensity with which space was used and re-used sometimes resulted in the downward stratigraphic movement of material, for example as stones were moved around and re-used and soft, sandy sediments were disturbed. Animal burrowing may also have been a factor in anomalous dates returned from cattle bone that was younger than the use of yard 5 but found in the old ground surface (234) that pre-dated it (SUERC-26144) and

Table 2.1 Radiocarbon dates from Milla Skerra

Lab Code	*Material*	*Context*	*Description*	*Years BP*	∂C^{13}	*1 sigma (68.2%)*	*2 sigma (95.4%)*
SUERC-26136	Bone	205	Cattle tooth	2415±30	-21.3‰	530–400 BC	750–390 BC
SUERC-26148	Carbonised grain	238	*Hordeum vulgare* var *vulgare*	2410±30	-23.1‰	520–400 BC	740–390 BC
SUERC-26144	Bone	234	Cattle distal humerus	2310±30	-21.9‰	405–370 BC	410–230 BC
SUERC-26135	Bone	171	Cattle tooth	2245±30	-20.6‰	390–230 BC	400–200 BC
SUERC-26142	Bone	130	Cattle tibia	2215±30	-21.8‰	360–200 BC	380–200 BC
SUERC-26138	Bone	102	Sheep/goat scapula	2110±30	-21.5‰	180–60 BC	210–40 BC
SUERC-26147	Charcoal	90	*Salix*	2105±30	-25.4‰	180–50 BC	200–40 BC
SUERC-26145	Carbonised grain	49	*Hordeum vulgare* sl	2025±30	-25.2‰	55 BC–25 AD	160 BC–60 AD
SUERC-26143	Bone	184	Sheep/goat mandible	2020±30	-20.8‰	50 BC–25 AD	110 BC–60 AD
SUERC-26126	Cremated bone	122	Cattle bone / ?tooth	1950±30	-12.1‰	15–85 AD	40 BC–130 AD
SUERC-26127	Cremated bone	127	Horse bone / ?tooth	1930±30	-15.4‰	25–125 AD	0–140 AD
SUERC-26146	Carbonised grain	57	*Hordeum vulgare* sl	1970±30	-23.7‰	0–70 AD	50 BC–90 AD
SUERC-26132	Bone	7	Cattle tooth	1845±30	-20.7‰	125–215 AD	80–240 AD
SUERC-26133	Bone	33	Cattle tooth	1860±30	-20.9‰	80–220 AD	80–240 AD
SUERC-26134	Bone	36	Cattle tooth	1860±30	-20.0‰	80–220 AD	80–240 AD
SUERC-26137	Bone	215	Cattle tooth fragment	1810±30	-25.5‰	130–250 AD	120–330 AD
SUERC-26125	Cremated bone	59	Cattle bone / ?tooth	1780±30	-13.6‰	210–330 AD	130–340 AD
SUERC-10745	Bone	23, Sk 1	Human rib	1755±35	-20.0‰	235–335 AD	130–390 AD
SUERC-26128	Bone	5	Cattle tooth	1595±30	-20.9‰	420–540 AD	400–550 AD

from younger cattle bone found in phase 3 hearth waste (SUERC-26137).

In order to construct a tighter chronological model for the settlement's duration and phases of occupation, Bayesian analysis was conducted using OxCal 4.3. This analysis combined the observed stratigraphic relationships between samples with absolute radiocarbon determinations to produce realistic estimates for the dates of different phases of activity, or posterior density estimates (Buck *et al.* 1996). It should be noted that they are interpretive estimates only, and may change in light of new data and different approaches to modelling (Bronk Ramsey 2009).

Table 2.2 summarises the sequence of phasing and presents the posterior density estimates for the phases alongside calibrated radiocarbon dates. Fig. 2.1 shows the main features of each phase in schematic form.

Phase 1: Intermittent activity – 3rd to early 1st millennia BC

Intermittent activity took place along this part of the foreshore as early as the 4th millennium BC. The base or tip of a leaf-shaped quartz arrowhead (CAT 1003, Fig. 6.14) was found in a test pit excavated through a later prehistoric cultivation soil (40) beside the settlement. Two scale-flaked knives (CAT 3481, 3537), both found in deposits that formed in the early phases of the settlement, date to the Neolithic or early Bronze Age (see Ballin, Chapter 6). Communities based in houses like the one identified in 2009 to the west (see Fig. 1.1, Canmore ID 300613) may have lost or discarded these tools while they were hunting, fishing or processing food along the foreshore. Analysis of the heavy stone tool assemblage identified several objects of probable Bronze Age date (see Clarke, Chapter 6), which could indicate the excavated settlement was preceded by another in close proximity.

Phase 2: The early settlement – 6th to 4th century BC

Phase 2A: First buildings

The earliest traces of occupation consisted of pottery, stone tools, worked quartz and pumice, bones from cetaceans and domestic cattle, sheep/goat and pigs, and the broken handle of a bone spatulate object (SF 2221, Fig. 6.16). These had been trampled into a settled, sandy ground surface (234, 244) that formed over clay weathered off the glacial till. Phosphate levels in the ground surface show that activity intensified just before the first structure (5) was built (see McKenzie, Chapter 3).

The earliest structure identified was a yard (5), built on this surface (Fig. 2.2). On excavation it measured 6 m north-west to south-east and was truncated by erosion on the north, so that only about 2 m of its width survived. Across the east it had a floor of large, closely set paving slabs (220) and it was partly defined by a drystone wall

Table 2.2 Summary of the phases of activity identified at Milla Skerra, showing calibrated radiocarbon dates and posterior density estimates calculated using OxCal v4.3 at 95% probability

Phase		*Events*		
1	Intermittent activity takes place along the foreshore.			3rd – early 1st millennia BC
	1.1	A quartz arrowhead is broken and discarded in the early Neolithic (early 4th millennium BC). Early Neolithic		
	1.2	Two scale-flaked knives are broken and discarded in the Neolithic or early Bronze Age (later 4th or 3rd millennium BC).		
2	A settlement is established at Milla Skerra, including a paved yard (5). Ashy waste from adjacent occupation accumulates in and around it.			6th–4th century BC
2A	2.1	The ground becomes trampled with occupation debris.		
	2.2	Yard 5 is constructed with a curving wall and paved floor.		
2B	2.3	Hearth waste is repeatedly swept/dumped into E part of yard, with a hiatus during stormy weather.		
	2.4	Food waste and other domestic rubbish are trampled into W part of yard.		
	2.5	Midden builds up outside the yard on W and SW.	SUERC-26148: 710–400 cal BC (2 sigma) Posterior density estimate: 540–410 cal BC	Context 238 - Burnt grain from midden outside yard
2C	2.6	A substantial wall is built across SE end of the yard.		
	2.7	More hearth waste (including burnt manure) is dumped in the yard.		
	2.8	A rough hearth is built in the yard and used to roast shellfish.	SUERC-26136: 750–400 cal BC (2 sigma) Posterior density estimate: 495–400 cal BC	Context 205 - Cattle tooth from mixed, mottled hearth waste
3	The wall that defines yard 5 is robbed and tumbles and the yard becomes covered with thick layers of midden.			4th–3rd century BC
3A	3.1	Midden (possibly urine-percolated) builds up over W part of the yard.	SUERC-26135: 390–210 cal BC (2 sigma) Posterior density estimate: 390–230 cal BC	Context 171 - Cattle tooth from waxy, ashy midden
	3.2	Layers of midden build up over and against the tumbled wall on W.	SUERC-26142: 370–200 cal BC (2 sigma) Posterior density estimate: 360–195 cal BC	Context 130 - Cattle bone from packed layer of animal/ fish/ seabird bones, marine shells, pottery, tools (earliest in midden sequence)
3B	3.3	A rubble partition is built across the yard, dividing the thickly midden-covered W part from the E part, which appears to continue in use.		
4	The ground above yard 5 is raised with stony midden and two new yards (3 and 4) are built, along with a house (1) immediately to the south.			2nd–early 1st century BC
4A	4.1	Stones and midden are deposited over yard 5, raising the ground level.	SUERC-26138: 200–50 cal BC (2 sigma) Posterior density estimate: 205–90 cal BC	Context 102 Sheep/goat scapula from stony midden
4B	4.2	A paved yard (3) and clay-floored yard (4) are built on the raised ground.		
	4.3	A house (1) is built to the SE, with a clay/stone hearth and paved floor.		
	4.4	Ash-midden builds up around the first hearth in the house.		

Table 2.2 Summary of the phases of activity identified at Milla Skerra, showing calibrated radiocarbon dates and posterior density estimates calculated using OxCal v4.3 at 95% probability (Continued)

Phase			*Events*	
4C	4.5	A clay floor is laid over the paving in the SE yard (3) and an informal hearth burns on it.	SUERC-26147: 200–50 cal BC (2sigma) Posterior density estimate: 170–50 cal BC	Context 90 - Salix from scorched clay.
4D	4.6	Yard 4 becomes obsolete as yard 3 is redefined with a new clay floor.		
5 The house (1) continues to be occupied and a small cell (2) is built at the SE end of yard 3.				1st century BC– 1st century AD
5A	5.1	A new hearth is built in house 1 and the partition wall is modified.	SUERC-26143: 110 cal BC–cal AD 60 (2 sigma) Posterior density estimate: 100 cal BC–cal AD 10	Context 184 - Sheep/goat mandible in matrix of paving
	5.2	Ash-midden builds up around the second hearth.		
	5.3	A third hearth is built above the second.		
	5.4	Waste builds up around the third hearth.	SUERC-26127: cal AD 0–130 (2 sigma) Posterior density estimate: cal AD 40–130	Context 127 - Horse bone/?tooth in orange/black ash in mound of waste that built up behind hearth.
5B	5.5	The SE end of yard 3 is dismantled and a tiny cell (2) is built, re-using the phase 2 wall (83) and truncating the clay floor.		
	5.6	A trampled surface builds up in both yard 3 and cell 2, with constituents pointing to their use as workshops.	SUERC-26146: 50 cal BC–cal AD 90 (2 sigma) Posterior density estimate: 25 cal BC–65 cal AD	Context 57 - Burnt grain from trampled surface associated with construction of cell 2
6 The house (1) ceases to be lived in, its floor is rapidly covered with midden and its walls collapse or are pulled down.				1st century AD
	6.1	The floor of house 1 is covered in loose midden as food, metalworking and hearth waste and broken objects (including a tuyère) are spread over it.	SUERC-26126: 20 cal BC–cal AD 130 (2 sigma) Posterior density estimate: cal AD 5–90	Context 122 - Cattle bone/?tooth in loose midden
	6.2	The walls of house 1 collapse inward and more midden, including some older material, is deposited over the ruins.	SUERC-26145: 150 cal BC–cal AD 60 (2 sigma) Posterior density estimate: 55 cal BC–cal AD 45	Context 49 - Burnt barley from spread of peat ash, charcoal, large pot sherds over tumble
7 Midden builds up in an informal yard (6) created from the ruins of the house, while yard 3 and cell 2 see final use before midden-rich sand accumulates over the tumbling structures.				late 1st–2nd century AD
7A	7.1	A heap of bog iron ore is left in the cell.		

Table 2.2

Phase			*Events*	
7B	7.2	The yard (3) and cell (2) begin to tumble as sticky trampled midden and hearth waste build up in them.	SUERC-26134: cal AD 80–230 (2 sigma) Posterior density estimate: cal AD 75–190	Context 36 - Cattle tooth from trampled midden
	7.3	A rough wall is built to define a yard (6) over the ruins of the house.		
	7.4	Midden accumulates in yard 6.	SUERC-26133: cal AD 80–230 (2 sigma) Posterior density estimate: cal AD 100–220	Context 33 - Cattle tooth from greasy midden
7C	7.5	Midden mixed with wind-blown sand accumulate over the tumbling structures.	SUERC-26132: cal AD 90–240 (2 sigma) Posterior density estimate: cal AD 135–245	Context 7 - Cattle tooth from midden-rich sand over structures
8	The settlement is inundated with sand and abandoned.			2nd–3rd century AD
9	A man's body is buried next to the sand-covered ruins.			3rd–4th century AD
	9.1	A grave is dug through windblown sand and the body of an adult male is laid in it.	SUERC-10715: cal AD 150–390 (2 sigma) Posterior density estimate: cal AD 225–380	Context 23 - Rib from Sk 1
	9.2	A miniature cairn is built on the dune that seals the settlement and some carved antler rings are left beside it.		
10	The surface of the settlement mound sees temporary or seasonal use and cairns are built on the foreshore, one of which contains a burial.			5th–6th century AD
	10.1	A temporary camp on the dune leaves residues of fires and cooking and ephemeral structural remains.	SUERC-26128: cal AD 400–540 (2 sigma) Posterior density estimate: cal AD 390–530	Context 5 - Cattle tooth from greasy occupation spread
	10.2	Two square cairns are built on the foreshore nearby. One contains the body of an adult female under a covering of beach boulders and quartzite pebbles (Bigelow 1980).	GU-1291: cal AD 420–640 (2 sigma)	Human bone from burial under square cairn

(203). The wall was later robbed and became dishevelled, but two courses remained and tumbled stones indicated it had had at least one additional course. This wall curved around the unpaved part of the yard on the west and south. On the east it ran beneath the wall of a later structure (yard 3) which was not completely excavated, so its full extent could not be established.

Phase 2B: The yard (5) in use

During the course of adjacent occupation, perhaps in houses and outbuildings that had formerly stood between the yard and the sea, deposits built up that contained the residues of cooking, eating and craftwork. Ashes from cleared-out hearths accumulated in the eastern part of the yard: clay silt flecked with bright orange peat ash (235) built up between the paving slabs, followed by a thin lens of peat ash (222) and finally a thick layer of fine, salmon-pink sandy silt, banded with pale grey ash (215), which covered the paving (Fig. 2.3).

Micromorphological analysis of the sediments clarified the sequence of events (see Ellis, Chapter 3). On at least two occasions, people dumped the remains of cooking fires

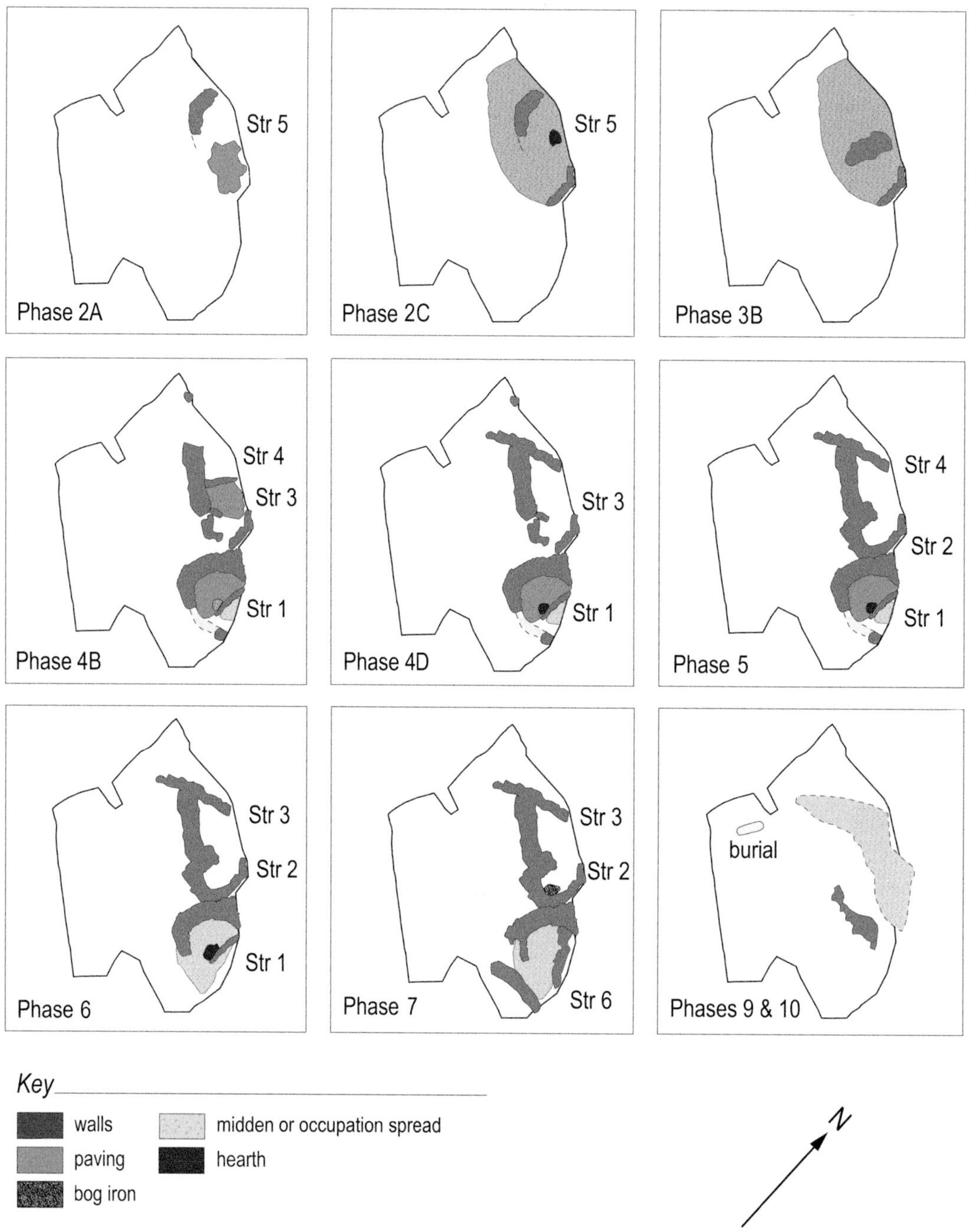

Figure 2.1 Schematic plans of each main phase

(well-combusted peat ash with fragments of burnt bone and pottery) into the yard. During a subsequent period of stormy weather, hearth waste ceased to accumulate and the wind blew sand and ash onto a thin layer of brown clay that formed in a puddle. After the weather settled, more layers of mixed peat ash, midden and windblown sand built up. All of these were exposed to the elements, confirming that the yard was unroofed. Over the western, unpaved part of the yard, people trampled peat ash, marine shells, degraded animal bone, decomposing organic material and windblown sand into a series of thin layers (212, 213, 226, 227, 229) that built up over time. Small stones (230) were scattered over the surface at times, perhaps to consolidate it. Broken pottery, a stone polisher, a quartz scraper and a cetacean vertebra rough-out were found in these layers.

In the meantime, people were also depositing domestic rubbish outside the yard on the south-west, creating a midden heap more than 4 m across and up to 0.3 m thick that sloped down from the wall's outer face (Fig. 2.4). It consisted of layers of dark orange-brown sandy silt, mottled with bright orange peat ash and other burnt material (224, 238, 197, 206) including charcoal from heather, spruce, conifer, hazel, oak and willow; six-row barley, wheat and wheat chaff, and cabbage-type seeds (Miller and Ramsay,

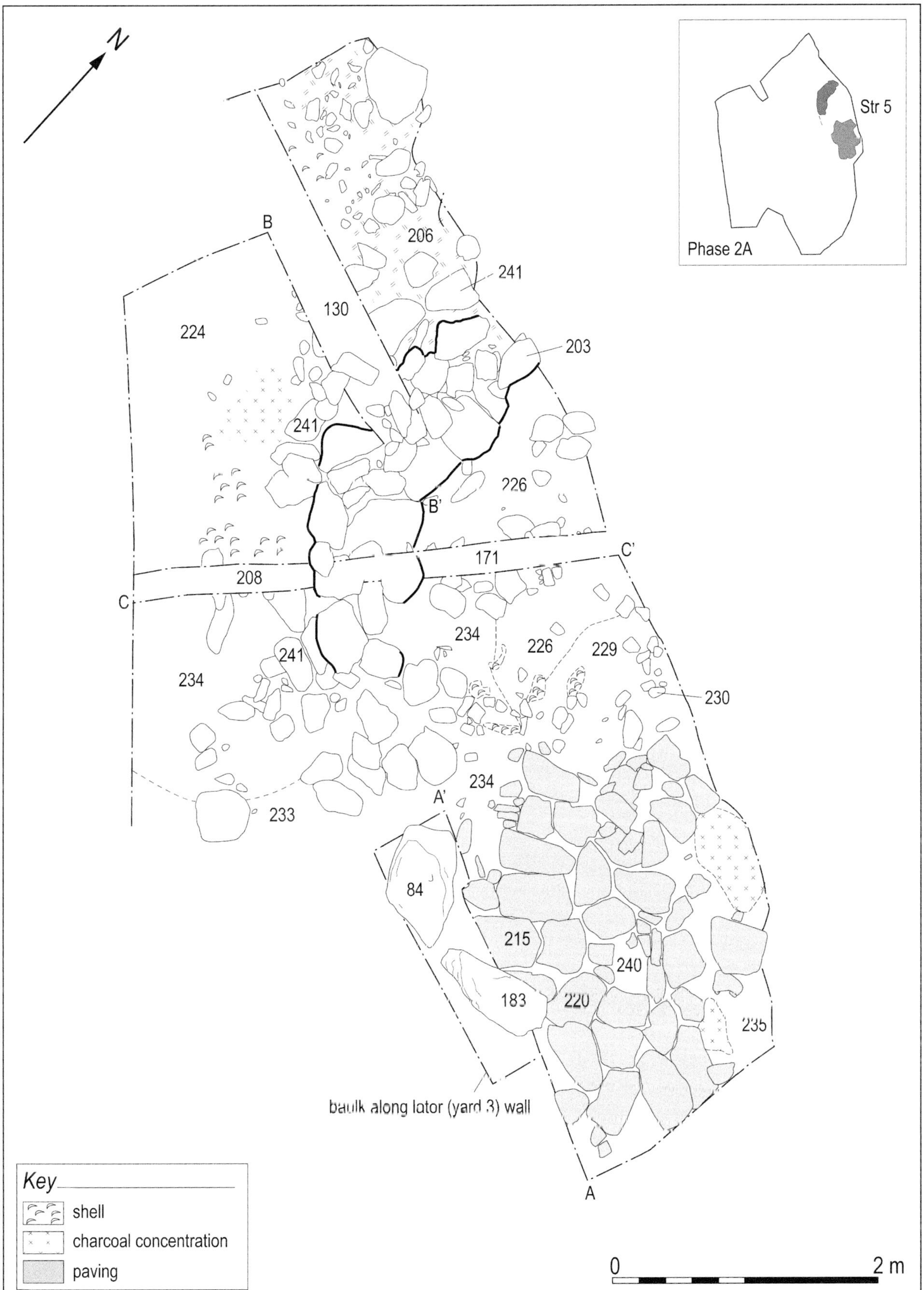

Figure 2.2 Plan of yard 5 in phase 2B, with paved floor and occupation deposits

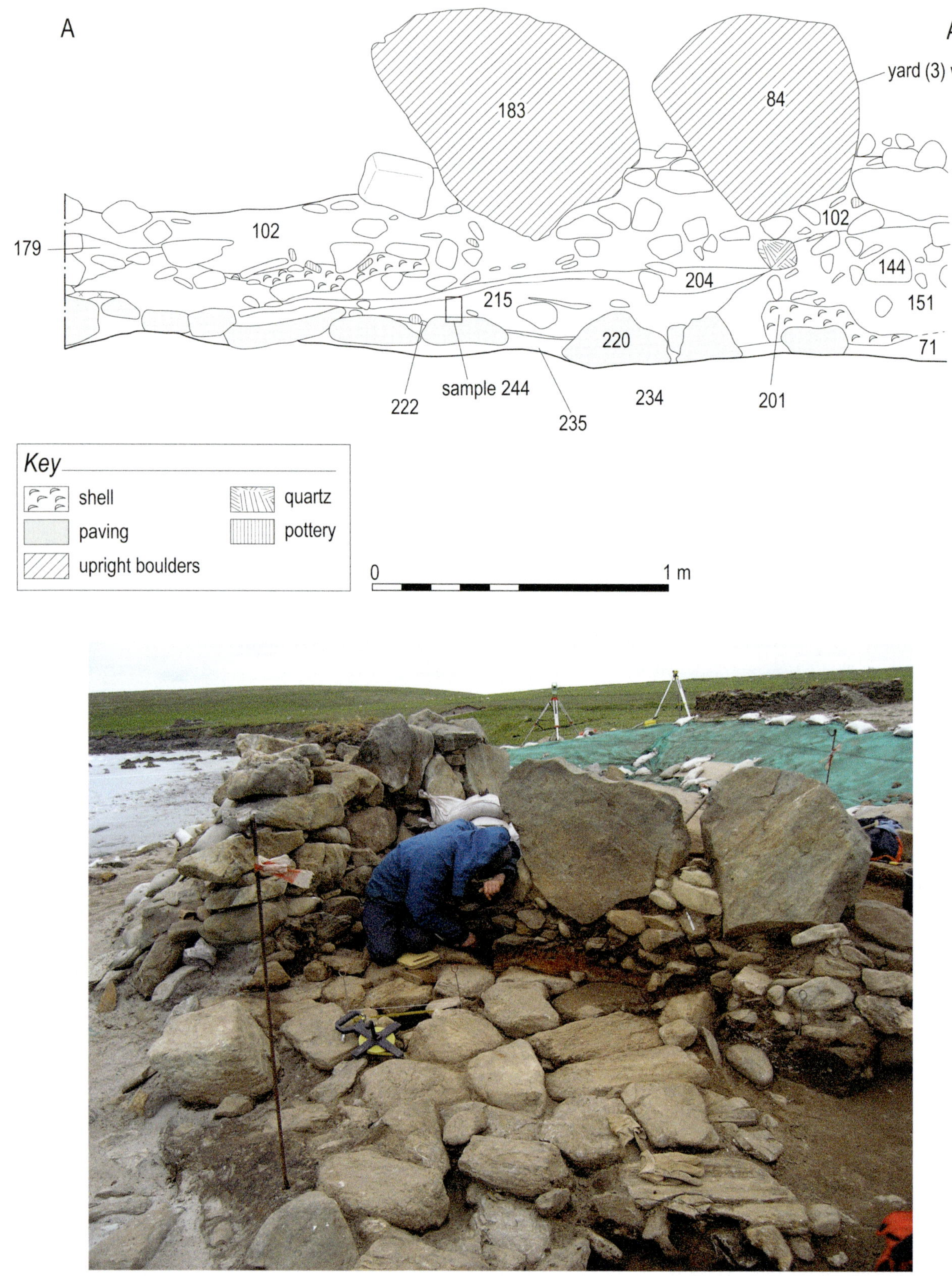

Figure 2.3 Above: section (A–A' on Fig. 2.2) through the peat ash deposits that lay over the paved floor in yard 5 (phase 2B–C). Below: looking south-east across the paved floor, with peat ash preserved in section beneath the boulders of later wall 84/183, and the inserted wall (83) behind the excavator

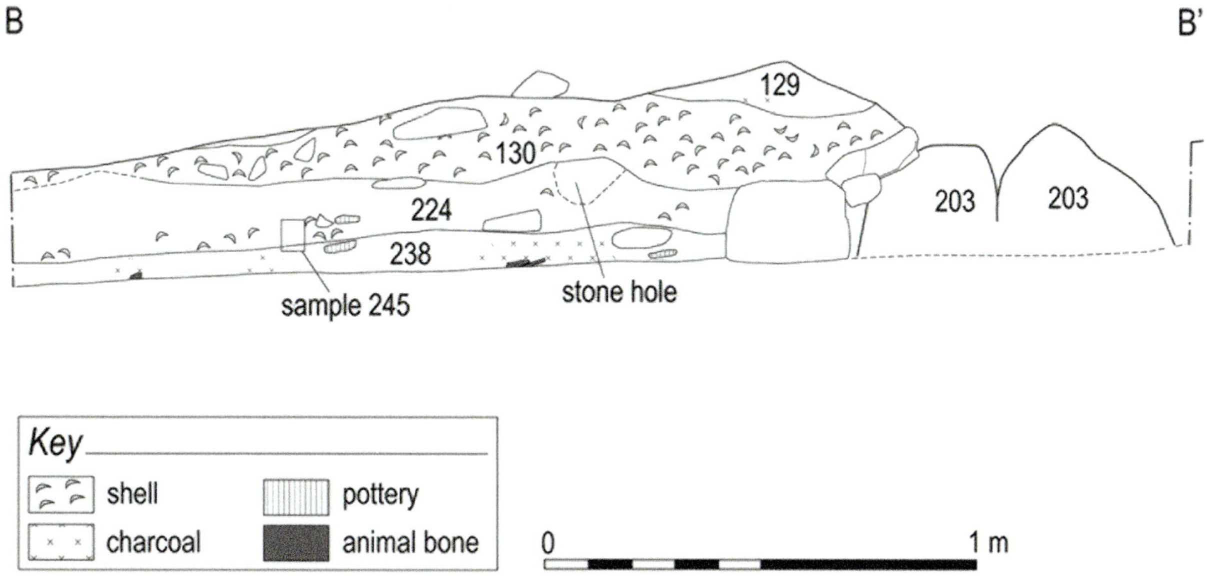

Figure 2.4 Above: section (B–B' on Fig. 2.2) through the midden outside yard 5. Below: the midden heap that built up against tumbled wall 203 outside the yard, excavated to the surface of context 224, from the south

Chapter 4). The midden was also packed with marine shells and the bones of fish, cattle, sheep/goat, pig and cetaceans. It produced the first evidence for the hunting of seabirds, in the form of bones from great auk, gannet, guillemot, sea eagle, duck species and little auk (Smith, Chapter 4).

Some of the artefacts evoke particular actions and crafts. Four perforated cattle phalanges, found close together, may have been toggles that fastened a net or a leather bag which was thrown onto the midden (Goldberg and Hunter, Chapter 6; Fig. 6.17). Pieces of pumice and stone had been used to sharpen tools or smoothe pots. Hammerstones and chipped quartz tools may have been used to prepare food and work bone, metal and leather. High levels of manganese, copper and zinc in the sediments suggest that metal was being worked at the settlement during this phase (see Derham, Chapter 3).

While someone was roughing out the shape of a long-handled comb from a cetacean bone and cutting grooves for teeth, it broke. The comb rough-out was tossed first onto a fire and then onto the midden (SF 2140, Fig. 6.16). Among the other objects discarded there were a bubbly blue glass bead (SF 2002, Fig. 7.2), many large, unabraded sherds of pottery and an ard point that may have broken during ploughing.

Phase 2C: Outdoor cooking in a re-shaped yard

At some point during this phase, a substantial wall (83) was built over the paved floor, closing off the yard on the east. Built of roughly coursed drystone masonry, it stood on excavation over 1m high and more than 2.6 m long and rested on the thick layer of salmon-pink hearth waste (215) (Figs 2.3 and 2.5). It had been truncated on the north by coastal erosion. The wall was not dismantled for safety reasons, but it appeared to stand almost back to back with the upstanding wall of the later house (structure 1). After its construction, black to light brown mottled hearth waste (205) accumulated over the eastern part of the yard, lapping against its base (Fig. 2.5). Ash and midden continued to build up in the western part; some of it derived from peat that was damp when it burnt and some from what may have been a single deposit of manure that was burnt as fuel (see Ellis, Chapter 3).

Someone also built a hearth in the yard by creating an oval setting of stones (218) around a slab base and packing green-yellow clay (219) inside it (Fig. 2.5). Numerous fires scorched the clay red, orange and pink and left interleaving bands of black and orange-pink silt and small burnt pebbles. The pebbles may have been heated in the hearth as a matrix for roasting shellfish: abundant burnt marine shells were found scattered around it.

Phase 3: A midden heap covers the yard (5) – 4th to 3rd century BC

Phase 3A: The yard's wall tumbles, midden piles up

The use of this part of the settlement changed over the course of later periods of occupation. The character of extensive midden deposits and an informal wall suggest that Milla Skerra's inhabitants were no longer using this area for activities such as craftwork and cooking.

First, the wall (203) that enclosed the yard (5) was robbed for stone and allowed to tumble. Then large quantities of domestic rubbish were left over the area, covering the tumbled wall and spilling onto the ground outside. It accumulated as silty midden (217), the constituents of which included a cetacean bone rough-out for a blade tool (SF 1859, Fig. 6.16) along with broken pottery, pieces of struck quartz, industrial waste and butchered animal bone. Next, a thick layer of mixed, yellow-purple-brown clay silt (171) with waxy and ashy lenses built up (Figs 2.6 and 2.7). Micromorphological analysis indicated it was made up of mixed peat and sandy turf ash-midden containing charred peat and bone, and its dense, silty matrix may have been due to the percolation of urine through it (see Ellis, Chapter 3). This suggests that the western part of the yard was now being used as a latrine or for penning animals, or both. Objects in this midden layer included a small, delicate disc bead carved from marine ivory (SF 1898, Fig. 7.2), hammerstones, a lump of bog ore, animal bone, worked quartz and sherds from up to 37 pots.

More layers of food and hearth waste built up to a depth of *c.* 0.35 m to the west, partly overlying the tumbled wall and the phase 2 midden heap (see Fig. 2.4). The earliest layer (130) was packed with bones from cod and ling, marine shells and animal and seabird bones, as well as abundant pottery and stone tools, including a grinding slab and smoother that were found together (SF 1814). Radiocarbon dating of a cattle tibia from this layer returned a date range of 370-200 cal BC (SUERC-26142), virtually identical to that from a cattle tooth in midden 171 of 390-210 cal BC (SUERC-26135) (both at two sigma). Successive deposits (186, 129) of fine orange silty peat ash followed, containing worked pumice and rather less food waste and pottery. Animal and fish bone, ground steatite, a pounder/grinder (SF 1887, Fig. 6.7) and sherds from up to 28 vessels were deposited to the south of the yard. They lay in diffuse spreads of orange-pink ashy silt (208, 232), the character of which suggests they formed as ash-midden was spread over infield and ploughed - a practice in evidence at other Iron Age settlements in the Northern Isles (Guttman *et al.* 2004).

Yet another distinctive spread of midden accumulated across the centre of the former yard, sealing the outdoor cooking hearth (219) and overlapping the waxy, possibly urine-soaked midden (171). This consisted of greasy, plastic dark brown silty clay with high organic content (151). Lying on it was most of a broken, thick-walled cooking pot (V 573) that had burnt on a fire (see Fig. 2.7).

Phase 3B: The area is partitioned

A rough rubble wall (144) was built directly over the greasy midden (151) and the burnt cooking pot, using rounded boulders and cobbles gathered from the beach (Fig. 2.6 and Fig. 8.2). It eventually tumbled to form a linear spread.

Phase 4: New yards and a house – 2nd to early 1st century BC

In what radiocarbon dates suggest was a fairly rapid sequence, this part of the settlement was redeveloped with new structures that saw intensive use and then remodelling.

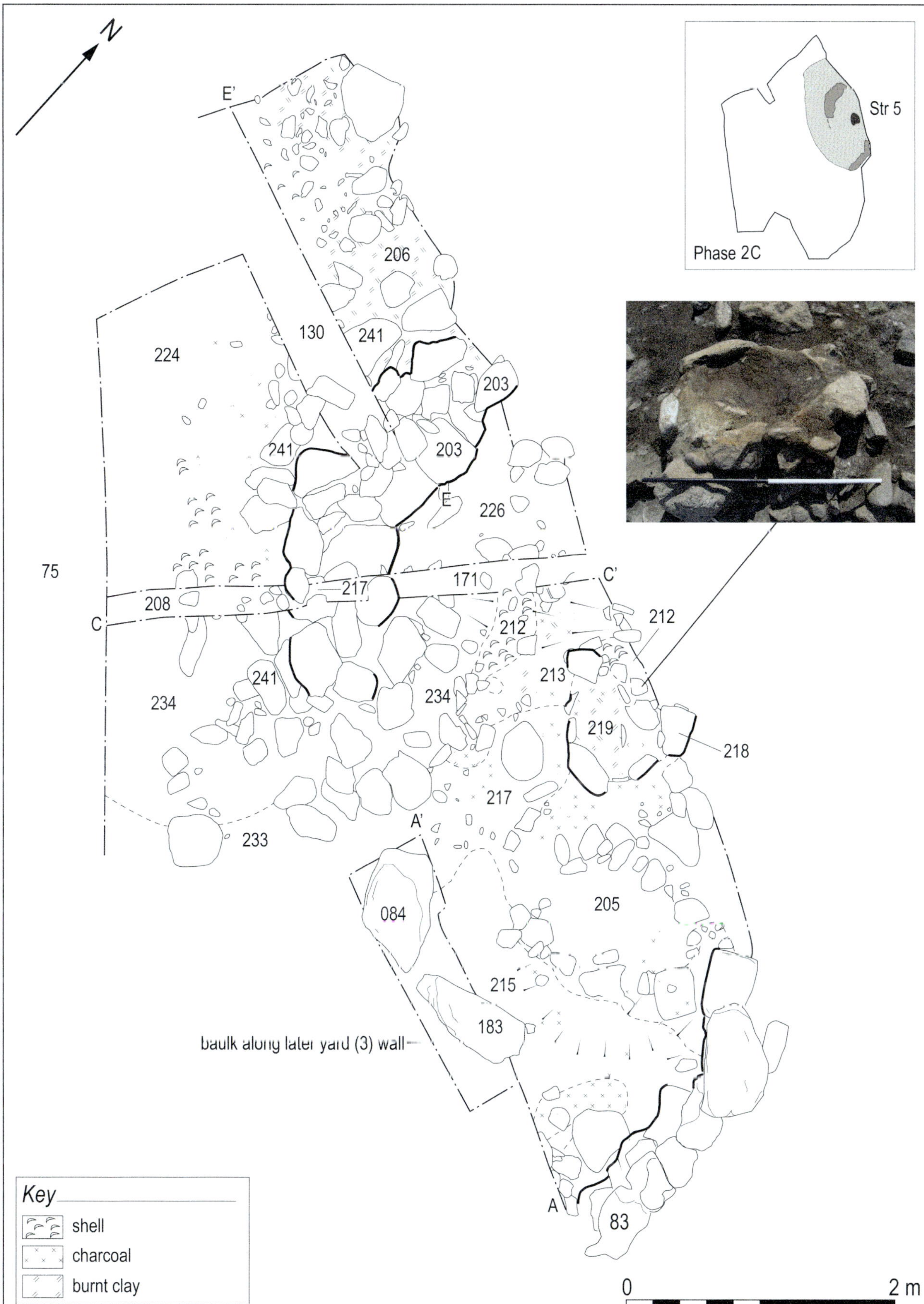

Figure 2.5 Plan of the hearth (219) and occupation deposits that built up in yard 5 later in phase 2C, with the inserted wall (83) at its east end; the inset photo shows the hearth (219)

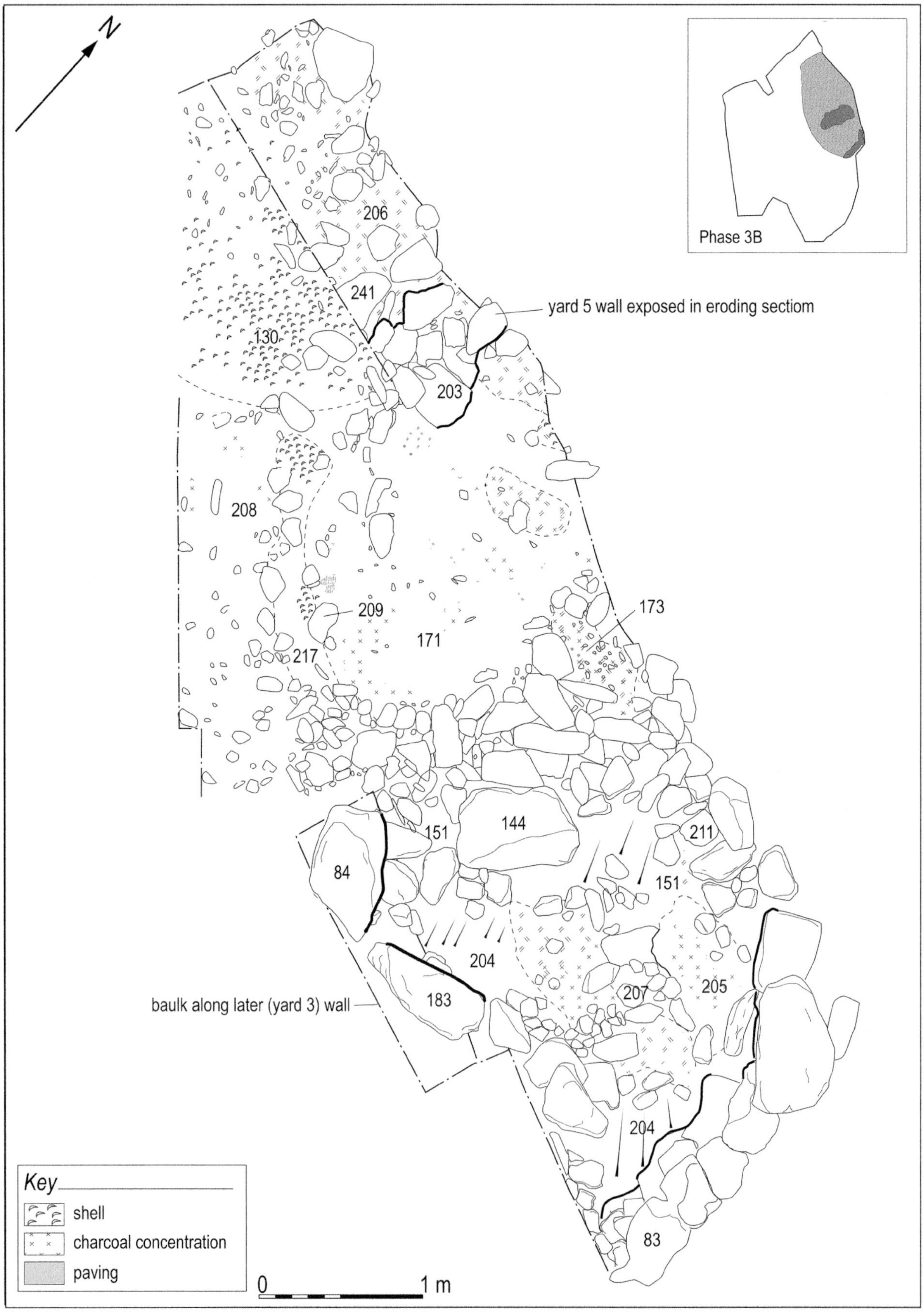

Figure 2.6 Plan of the phase 3 midden spreads that covered yard 5 as it fell out of use, with 207/204 to the east

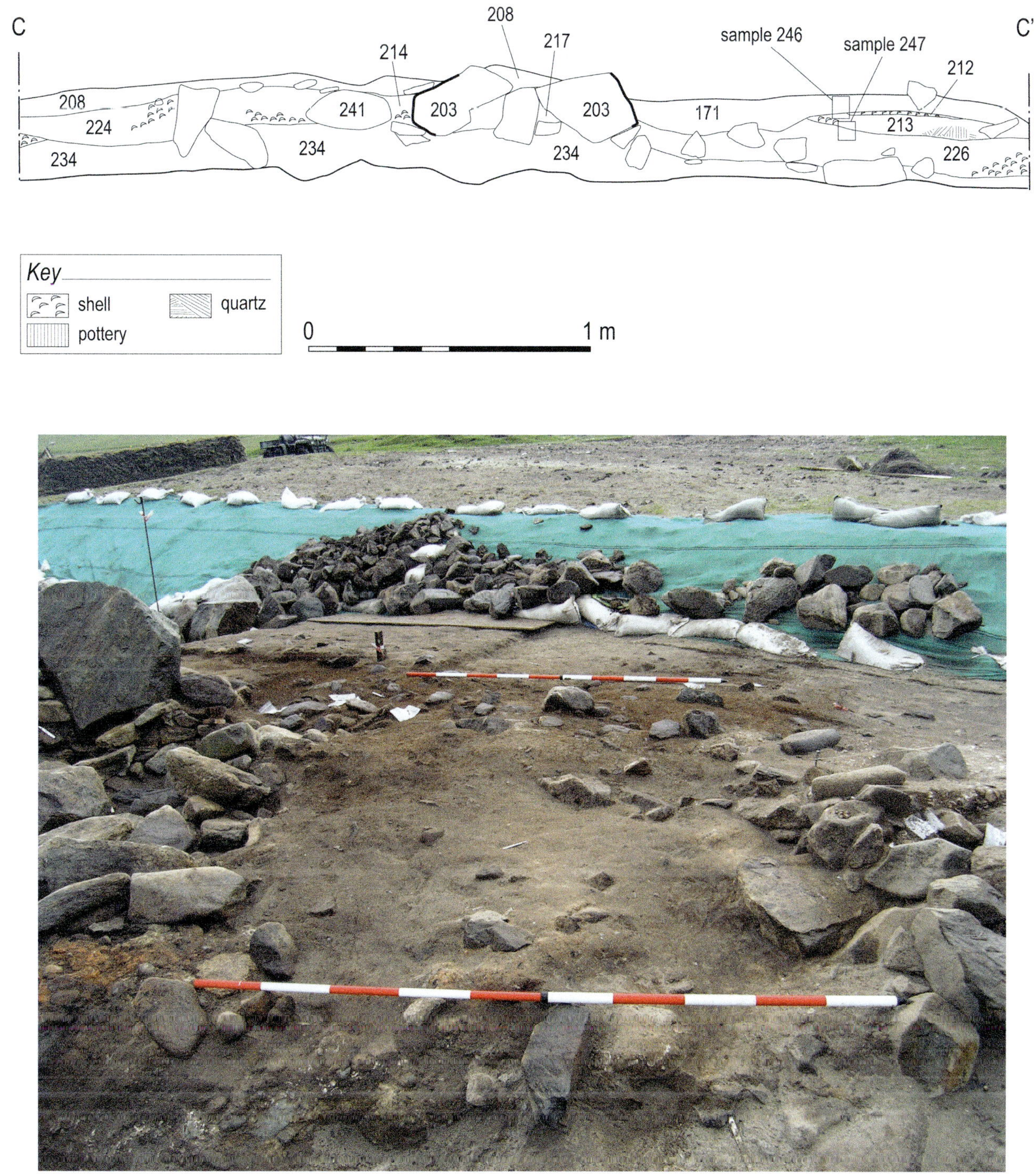

Figure 2.7 Above: section (C–C' on Fig. 2.2) through the occupation and midden deposits sealing yard 5 on the north in phase 3. Below: the midden (162) covering the west part of the yard, with rubble wall 144 to the left and a burnt, squashed cooking pot (V 573) in the foreground, from the north

Phase 4A: Raising the ground level over the first yard (5)

Large amounts of midden continued to pile up over the former yard (5) during the 2nd to mid 1st century BC. To the west of the rubble wall (144), a thick layer of firm, waxy, purple-brown clay silt (162) accumulated that was heavily flecked with hearth waste (Fig. 2.7). It sealed the possibly urine-soaked midden (171) of the previous phase and was very similar to it, suggesting that people may have continued to use this area as a latrine or stable as well as for storing domestic waste.

Meanwhile, a different kind of midden was piling up over the east part of the former yard, between the by-now tumbled rubble wall (144) and the upstanding phase 2C wall

Figure 2.8 The fallen orthostat 179 (beside near end of ranging rod) lying on the phase 4A midden 102 and beside earlier wall 83, from the north

(83), in what may have been a deliberate effort to raise the ground level. This was looser and thicker (0.35 m) brown clay silt, heavily flecked with orange peat ash and lenses of blue-grey clay (102) (see Fig. 2.3). It contained abundant food waste, including limpet shells and bones from fish, seabirds and domestic animals, hammerstones, worked pumice, and sherds from up to 44 pottery vessels. A large (1 m long) schist slab (179) lay on the surface of the midden (Fig. 2.8), with green clay adhering to its tapered end. It may have originally stood upright with the clay packed around its base, like the orthostatic slabs that formed a partition wall in the house (1) (see below), either on this spot or as part of dismantled building. The midden also contained many rounded cobbles. These and the context's loose compaction suggest that it accumulated rapidly, with stones gathered from the beach and midden brought from elsewhere in the settlement to raise and consolidate the ground before the construction of new yards. A sheep/goat scapula from the stony midden (102) returned a date of 200-50 cal BC (SUERC-26138) (95.4% probability).

Outside to the south, a topsoil (75) developed during this phase; it appeared on excavation as orange-brown clay silt flecked with charcoal and burnt peat (see section H - H', Fig. 2.23). Its southern edge was overlapped by slightly sandier, sticky, homogenous red-brown clay silt (40) that was heavily flecked with tiny quartz fragments and charcoal/burnt peat. Micromorphological analysis indicates that both were middens which had been ploughed (see Ellis, Chapter 3).

Phase 4B: New yards (3 and 4) and a house (1) are built

Two adjoining yards were built on the thick, stony midden (102): structure 3 to the south-east and structure 4 to the north-west. Before construction commenced, someone set a painted pebble on the surface – a broken quartzite stone which had been painted on three different occasions with wavy lines and dots (SF 119, Fig. 7.1; see Goldberg and Hunter, Chapter 7). It sat just beneath the edge of a new wall (84) that defined both yards on the south.

Five massive, angular boulders were manoeuvred into place to create the wall's inner face (84) (Fig. 2.9). They sat upright, end to end, revetted on the south with a low bank of quarried topsoil and small stones (200) and with an outer face of stone blocks (20) that incorporated two flaked hammerstones and an anvil. The boulders graduated in size, increasing in height to 0.7 m at the east end where the wall curved slightly to meet another upright, flat-faced boulder (183), set at an angle to it; this would later serve as a fireback for an informal hearth. Several further boulders (167) continued the wall line south-east towards the old upstanding wall of the first yard (83). The builders wedged

Figure 2.9 Plan of yards 3 and 4 in phase 4, including the south-eastern part of yard 3 with fallen orthostat 179

Figure 2.10 Above: looking north-west across yard 3 in phase 4B, with its paved floor extending to partition wall 97 (beside far end of ranging rod). Below: the clay surface and scorched deposits in yard 4 with wall 97 to the left, from the north

slabs beneath the boulders to level them and packed small slabs and yellow clay into the gaps between them. Most of a small, globular, finely burnished cooking pot (V 745) was set into the clay bonding in the south-eastern section of the wall (167).

The area thus defined by wall 84 was divided in two by a low cross wall of stone blocks (97), which was truncated by erosion on the north-east. A large upright boulder (128) to the west may have defined an entrance into yard 4. This yard had a floor of green-yellow clay scattered with small stones (152); the clay was worn thin except in the corner formed by the walls (84 and 97) (Fig. 2.10). Charcoal, windblown sand, a few sherds of abraded pottery and some worked quartz and burnt animal bone had been trampled into it and peat ash (159) lay banked against the corner, but it was otherwise fairly clean.

The south-eastern yard (3) was given a more robust floor which was renewed several times, suggesting this area saw more intensive use. The first, paved floor was made of closely set schist slabs and sub-round stones (118) (Figs 2.9 and 2.10).

At around the same time, a house (1) was constructed to the south of the adjoining yards (3 and 4). The builders first levelled its footprint to a depth of up to 0.2 m, cutting into the glacial till and trampling the surface. To create the inner wall face they set large, upright stones like evenly spaced teeth (orthostats) against the edge of the cut (155): three tall, triangular slabs on the north flanked by short, squat boulders. Above they built masonry using large stone blocks, massive slabs and pinning stones, uncoursed and bonded with yellow clay (113) (Fig. 2.11). On excavation the wall stood to over a metre high on the north and curved inwards slightly as it rose, indicating it was probably of part-corbelled construction (Fig. 2.12). Rubble and topsoil (239) were packed behind it and retained by an outer wall face of stone blocks, which survived to two courses high on excavation. A hammerstone (SF 631), a perforated steatite disc or spindle whorl (SF 629, Fig. 6.5) and some small sherds of pottery were found in the wall core.

On the south-west, the wall as excavated ended in a ragged, rubbly slope that gave way to a shallow trench 0.6 m wide (155), which continued the line of its curve and defined the southern arc and a probable entrance. The ragged end of the upstanding section was probably disturbed when the wall collapsed in phase 6 and then robbed in phase 7. At the east end of the wall trench, two large stones (111) pitched against its side above the eroded coastal edge (see Figs. 2.16 and 8.3). These were remnants of the south-eastern wall arc, which was robbed in phase 7 to create a rough wall defining an informal yard (6) (see below). The intervening arc of wall trench (155) was packed with small stones (156) under patchy green clay (154). Ashy deposits raked out from the first hearth filled the top of the trench and had been trampled over it, their extent mirroring its outer edge as if they had spread only as far as a barrier (see phase 5A below). The evidence was somewhat difficult to interpret, but it may be that this arc contained a doorway that was set into a lighter section of walling, which could be removed to allow more sunlight and ventilation into the room during the summer.

The part of the house that survived coastal erosion consisted of a semi-circular room, defined by a partition wall that extended along the eroded section from the north wall to a hearth (Fig. 2.13 and see Fig. 2.16). The partition wall (78) was made of large, thin slabs set upright, with light green clay packed around their bases for support, along with some horizontal coursed blocks. The southernmost orthostat in the partition, a sturdy, triangular stone, formed a fireback for the hearth; its western face was reddened and finely cracked from long proximity to heat (see Fig. 2.17).

Paving (124) lay around the hearth, the slabs resting on bedding stones that included a cobble dug out of bog iron ore. The builders began by laying the largest slabs along the wall and continued in concentric arcs towards the hearth, wedging smaller stones and a hammerstone (SF 2261) into the gaps. Around the hearth, the slabs were smaller and less regularly set (Fig. 2.16). The eastern part of the house, on the other side of the partition wall (78), had also had a paved floor; a few slabs remained along the top of the eroded section, including a re-used saddle quern (SF 1304, Fig. 6.13) (see Clarke, Chapter 6).

The first hearth was carefully constructed, with one large slab and several smaller ones (199) placed at the base of the fireback and packed with green-yellow clay (189, 193, 196). Sherds from at least two large, steatite-tempered pots (V 25 and V 30, Fig. 5.3) were set into the clay, forming a level surface about 0.35 across (Fig. 2.13). The sherds had been placed with their silvery, highly burnished surfaces facing up. The remains of a house mouse were found in the clay (see Smith, Chapter 4), where it must have found a warm, protected matrix for a burrow.

Phase 4C: A new floor, an informal hearth and a workshop in the southern yard (3)

In the raised yard (3) that abutted the house on the north-west, compression and use fractured the paved floor; the slabs sank into the stony midden (102) beneath and the surface became uneven. A new floor of yellow-grey sandy clay (96), up to 0.2 m thick, was laid over the paving and beyond into the unpaved south-east end. It was laid in a single event and, like the clay used elsewhere to bond walls and make hearths, it had been quarried from the glacial till (see Ellis, Chapter 3). A flat-based slot cut through the clay floor may have held a light partition between the main part of the yard and the south-east end. A concentration of rubble (42/92) at the north-west end of the yard may have been an informal drain. As the clay floor became worn and compressed over the uneven paved surface, more slabs (86) were set here and there to consolidate and level it.

The south-east end may have been used as a workshop. A large stone block (142) with a flat top, about 0.5 m across and 0.35 m high, was set inside it, perhaps to provide an

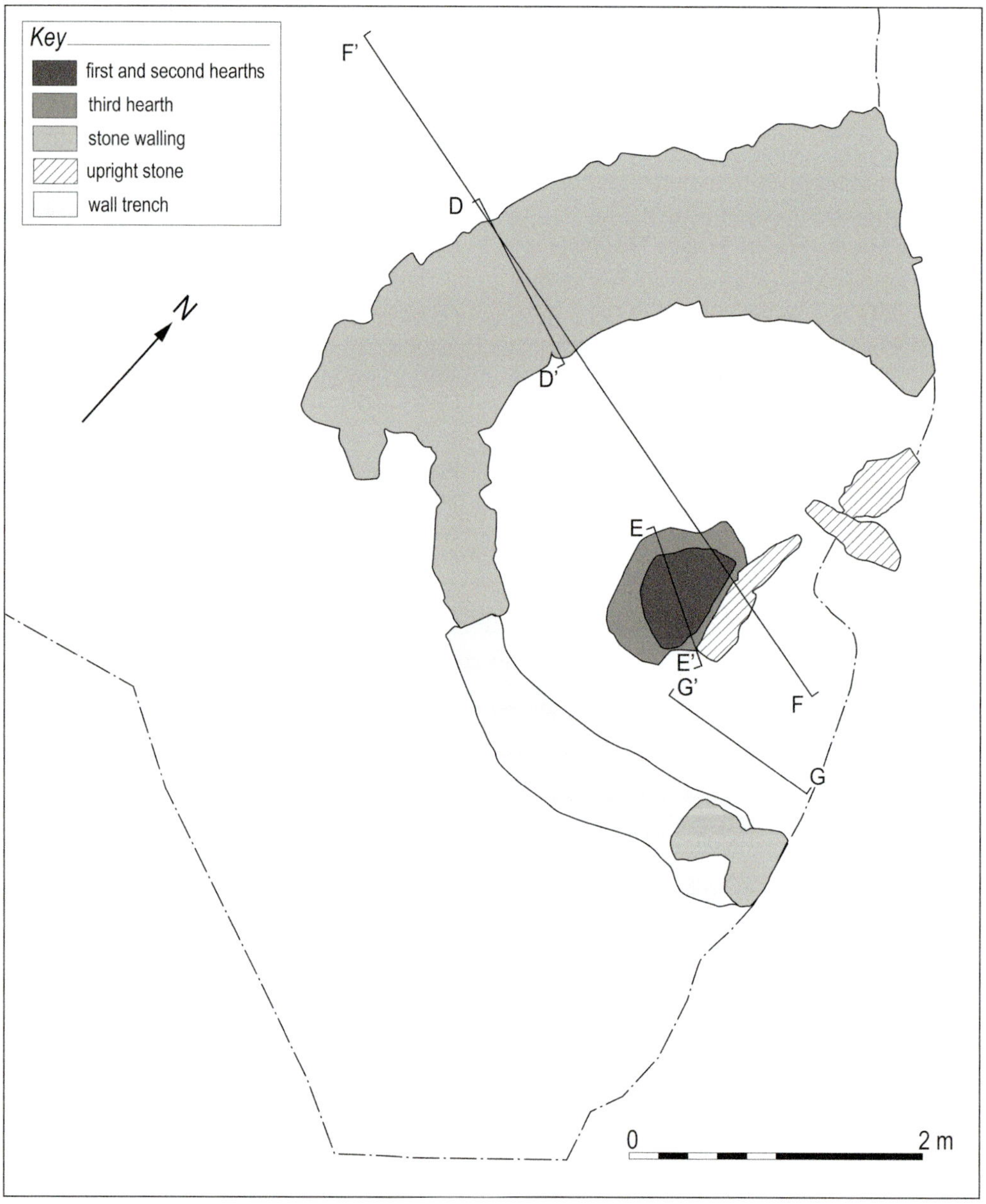

Figure 2.11 Above: house 1. Below: schematic plan of the house, showing section lines

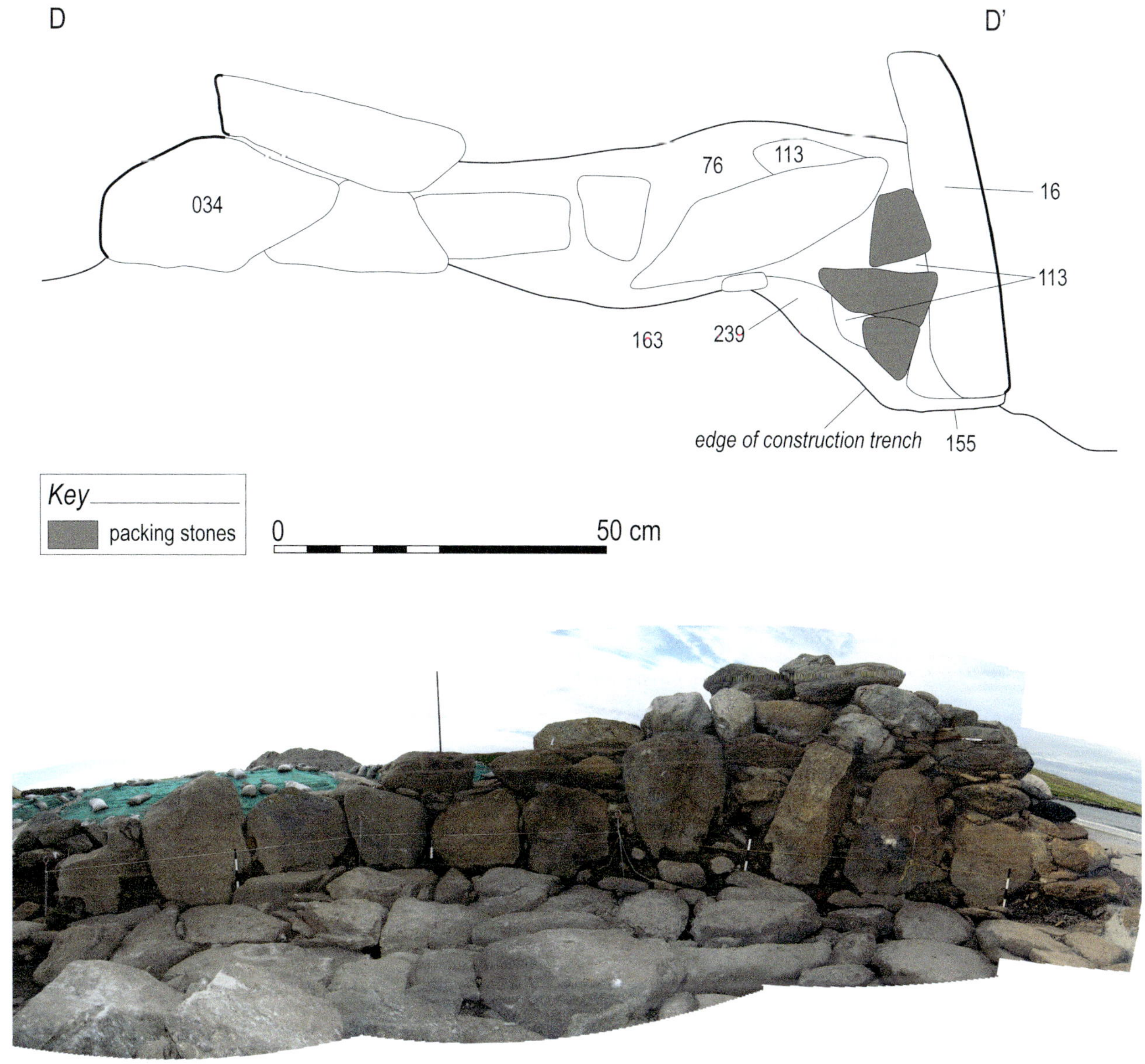

Figure 2.12 Above: south-facing section (D–D' on Fig. 2.11) through the wall of house 1. Below: the paved floor and surviving western arc of the wall

anvil or working platform (see Fig. 2.20). A quartz core and a large smoother (SF 1073), which had also been used as a hammerstone, were found nearby. A painted pebble (SF 1048, Fig. 7.1) found in the clay floor beneath the edge of the putative anvil was marked with irregular lines and loops and had been damaged at one end.

While the clay floor (96) was in use, an informal hearth burned in the yard (3) against the largest upright boulder (Fig. 2.14). A thick spread of hearth waste – consisting of dark red clay silt (90) flecked with bright orange and black clay and fragments of burnt bone – built up against the base of the boulder. While Ellis (see Chapter 3) interpreted the spread as redeposited midden, the reddish scorching visible on the boulder's face (183) and the underlying paving (118) suggest burning took place in situ.

Phase 4D: The southern yard (3) is extended, subsuming the northern yard (4)

Later, the south-eastern yard (3) was modified and the north-western one (4) became obsolete. The inhabitants built a new wall (19) to form the north-west end of a larger version of yard 3. It was constructed of large stones, two to three courses of which survived, and it sat directly over the earlier cross-wall (97) but on a different alignment (Fig. 2.15). This new wall extended over the yards' original south wall (84) and continued beyond it. The now-larger yard (3) received a fresh floor of yellow-grey sandy clay (58) which, like the previous floor (96), was laid in a single event (see Ellis, Chapter 3). A small pot sherd and about 20 fragments of thin sheet iron, which had probably formed a thin, straight-edged plate (SF 767), were found

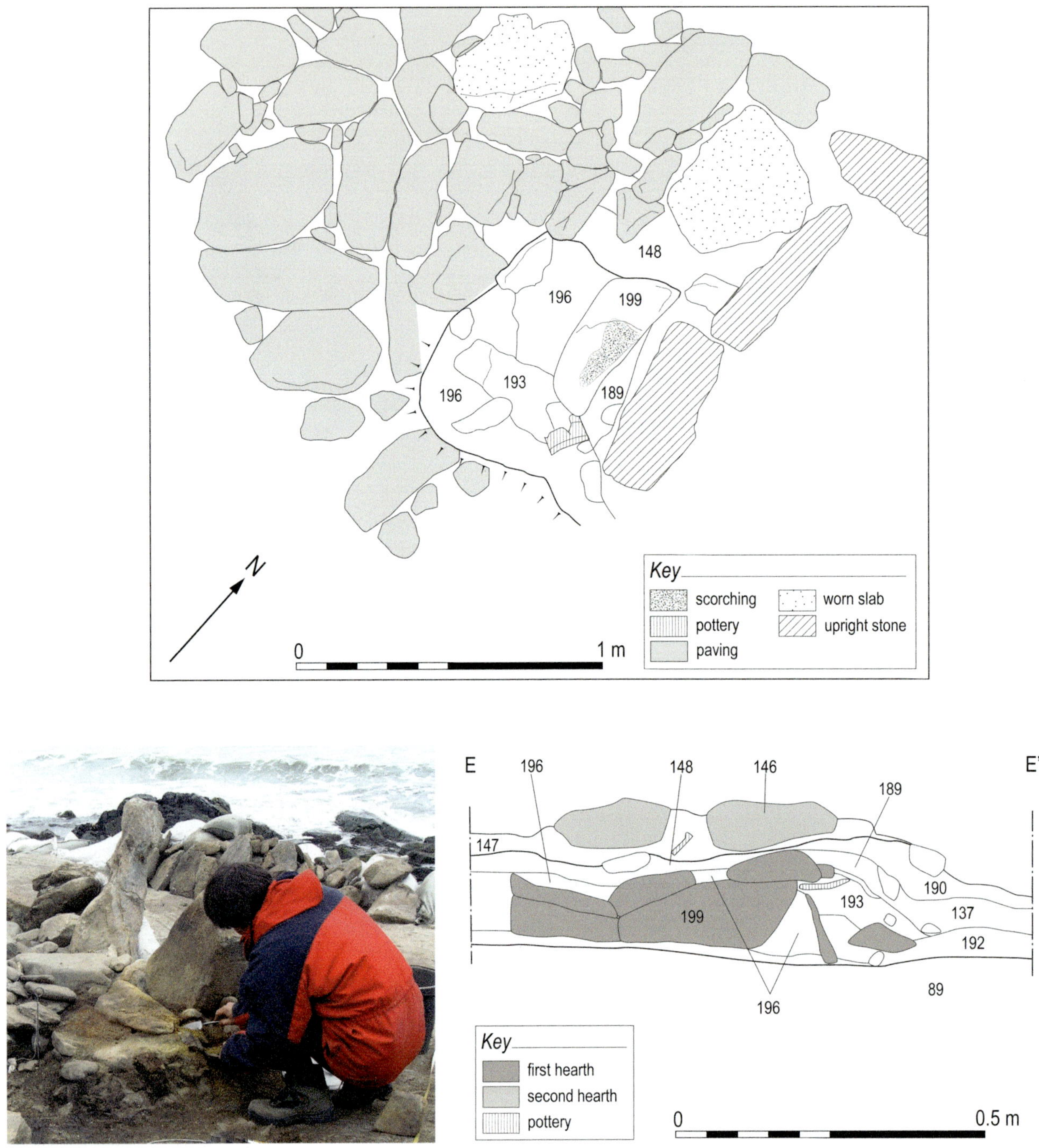

Figure 2.13 Above: plan of the earliest hearth (199) in house 1. Below: hearth 199 from the south during excavation (left), and section through the hearths (E–E' on Fig. 2.11)

pressed into the clay, but otherwise there were few residues of domestic life.

Phase 5: Continued occupation of the house (1) and remodelling of the yard (3) – 1st century BC to 1st century AD

People living in the house (1) during this phase renewed the hearth at least twice. During the same time span, the south-east end of the yard (3) was dismantled to create a tiny cell (structure 2).

Phase 5A: Using and renewing the hearth

The occupants of the house (1) left abundant evidence for what they were eating, the fuel they were burning and the objects they were making and using. A little of the debris from their occupation trickled between the stones, forming a sticky, dark brown clay silt (184) that contained animal bone, limpet shells, steatite chips and pot sherds, but much more domestic rubbish was piled near the hearth. A sheep/goat mandible from this context returned a date range of 110 cal BC - cal AD 60 (SUERC-26143) (95.4% probability).

Figure 2.14 The secondary clay floor and patchy paving in yard 3 (phase 4C), with scorched clay in the foreground against upright stone 184, looking north-west

The paved floor was probably covered, as only two of the slabs exhibited wear. It may have been covered with an organic material such as straw that was regularly refreshed, as in contemporary buildings at Old Scatness (Dockrill *et al.* 2015, 470) (Fig. 2.16). One well-worn paving slab (see Fig. 2.19), with a smooth surface and definite patina, sat immediately north of the hearth in a shallow alcove in the partition wall (78); the alcove was formed by a thin, upright stone that stood perpendicular to the line of the wall. This may have been a favourite warm seat. Given its position, with back support and the fire blocking draughts from the doorway, it may have been reserved for an important member of the household. Another slightly worn slab sat slightly proud of the paving beside the hearth on the west.

The clay surface of the first hearth became scorched salmon-pink and black through repeated use, with hearth waste spread and trampled around it. Greasy clay silt flecked with charcoal, burnt peat, orange peat ash and lenses of light green clay (108) formed over the floor to the south, with a clear curving edge that mirrored the curve of the wall trench (155), as if it had built up against the doorway and a putative light structure bedded in the trench. A smoother (SF 1094), pot sherds, seal bone and a quartz ?scraper were found in it. As people repeatedly swept the hearth, layers of soft orange peat ash (137, 190, 191) with burnt bone and stones, pumice, pot sherds and a serpentine smoother/polisher accumulated against its southern edge and spilled north-eastward (seaward) through the gap in the partition wall.

At some point, the inhabitants built a new hearth above the first one. It consisted of an oval stone setting packed with light yellow clay (146/147) and a large pot sherd (V 51); the surface of the hearth was oxidised dark pink through exposure to heat (Fig. 2.17). At the same time, they set a stone block (174) on top of the accumulated ash-midden, thus extending the line of the internal partition southward but leaving a gap next to the hearth through which ash and cooking waste continued to be swept. A thick, well-stratified mound of ash-midden built up against the partition's eastern face. It was made up of layers of greasy black-brown silty clay with burnt stones (138, 145), orange and black silt (157), greasy black silty clay (158) and bright orange peat ash (150). Similar deposits continued to accumulate on this spot throughout the life of the house, creating a well-defined mound (Fig. 2.18). Its discrete extent suggests it was contained by some barrier, such as a little wickerwork fence.

Later still the hearth was renewed again, this time with green-yellow clay (132) that was retained by several large stones on the south, and the gap in the partition was filled with two stone blocks (250). This latest hearth extended only as far as the putative seat (the worn slab in the alcove in the partition wall 78) (Fig. 2.19). On several occasions its surface was refreshed by spreading more clay quarried from glacial till, sealing thin layers of peat ash and eventually creating a mound over 0.3 m thick and 0.4 m in diameter. The final firings scorched the surface dark red-brown and left fragments of charcoal, carbonised peat, pottery and burnt bone (see Ellis, Chapter 3).

As people used and renewed this third hearth, they continued to clear ash, food remains and other domestic debris away from it and heap it on the other side of the partition wall (78). More interleaving layers of different character built up: soft, greasy, waxy or loose silts and clays, ranging from bright orange to black to dark brown and orange-black (121, 131, 127, 115, 107, 106, 105). Many of them contained large and sometimes conjoining sherds of pottery (from up to 64 vessels altogether) which probably broke during cooking. Chemical analysis of sherds from two layers (106, 127) shows that some pots were used to cook a seed-based food such as grain or nuts, for example oatmeal (see Derham, Chapter 3). Animal bone, stone tools and a small iron fitting or clamp (SF 1004, Fig. 6.15) were also tossed onto the ash-midden heap as it accumulated.

Micromorphological analysis of three kubiena samples taken through six layers (105, 137, 150, 138, 136, 131) found that they derived from numerous fires. The uppermost (105) actually comprised three stratigraphic units derived from peat ash with abundant bone fragments, including burnt fish bone, in one. The thickest stratigraphic unit represented several firings at a slightly higher temperature than the others, and four stratigraphic units were identified in layers 136 and 131, one of them derived from peat that was still damp when it burned (Ellis, Chapter 3).

Phase 5B: A small cell (2) is added to the yard (3)

Sometime during the last century BC to the 1st century AD, the enlarged yard (3) was altered again with the addition of a tiny oval cell (structure 2) at its south-east end. This was created by connecting two sections of old wall (167 and 83) with a newly built one (15) (Fig. 2.20). The inner face was oddly constructed, with large, upright sub-angular stones and horizontal slabs set on top of uncoursed smaller stones and bonded with yellow clay. An outer face up to three courses high retained a core of brown silty sand. The

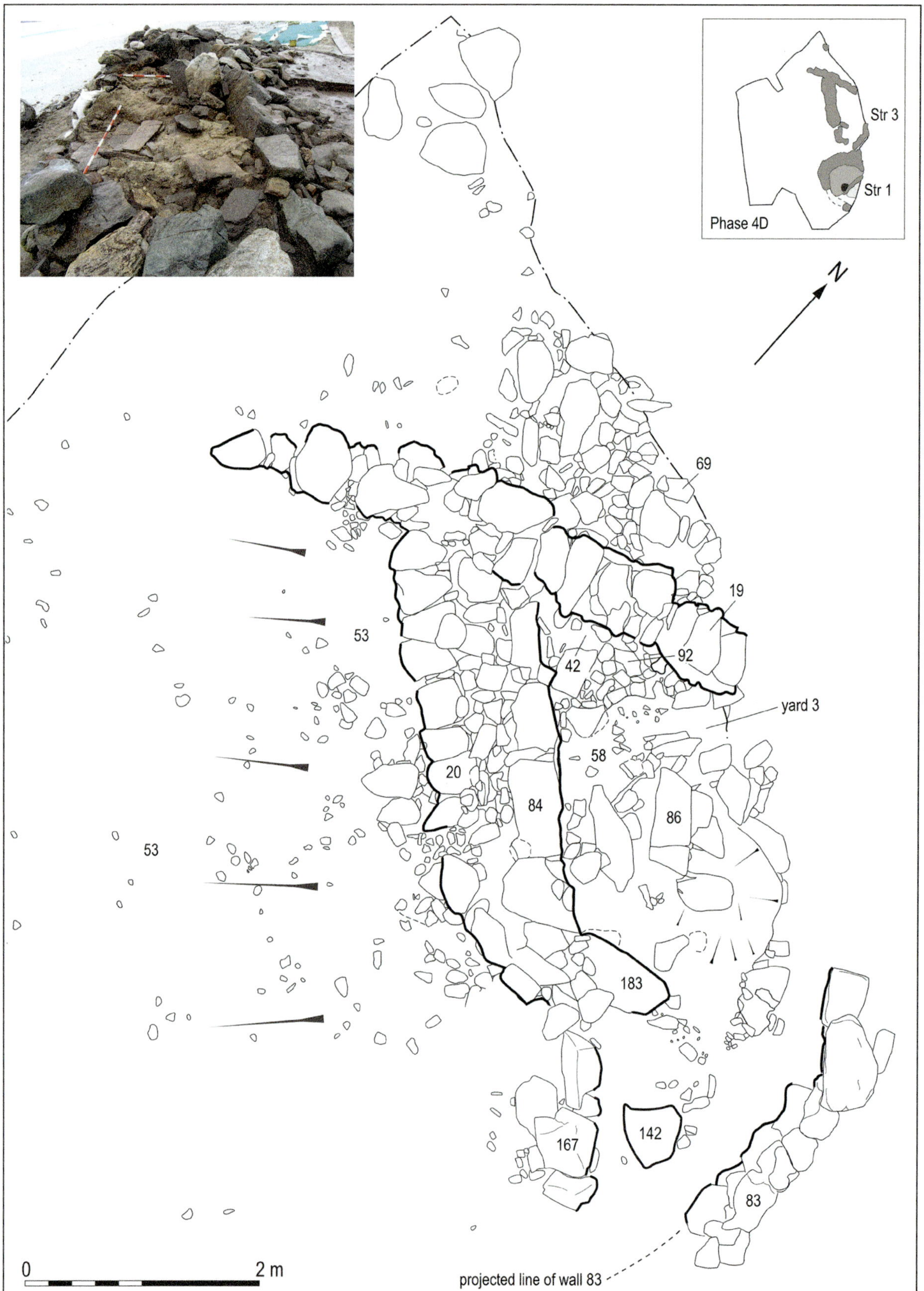

Figure 2.15 Plan of the modified yard 3 in phase 4D, with yard 4 now obsolete. Inset: the yard at this phase from the north-west, with wall 92 in the foreground

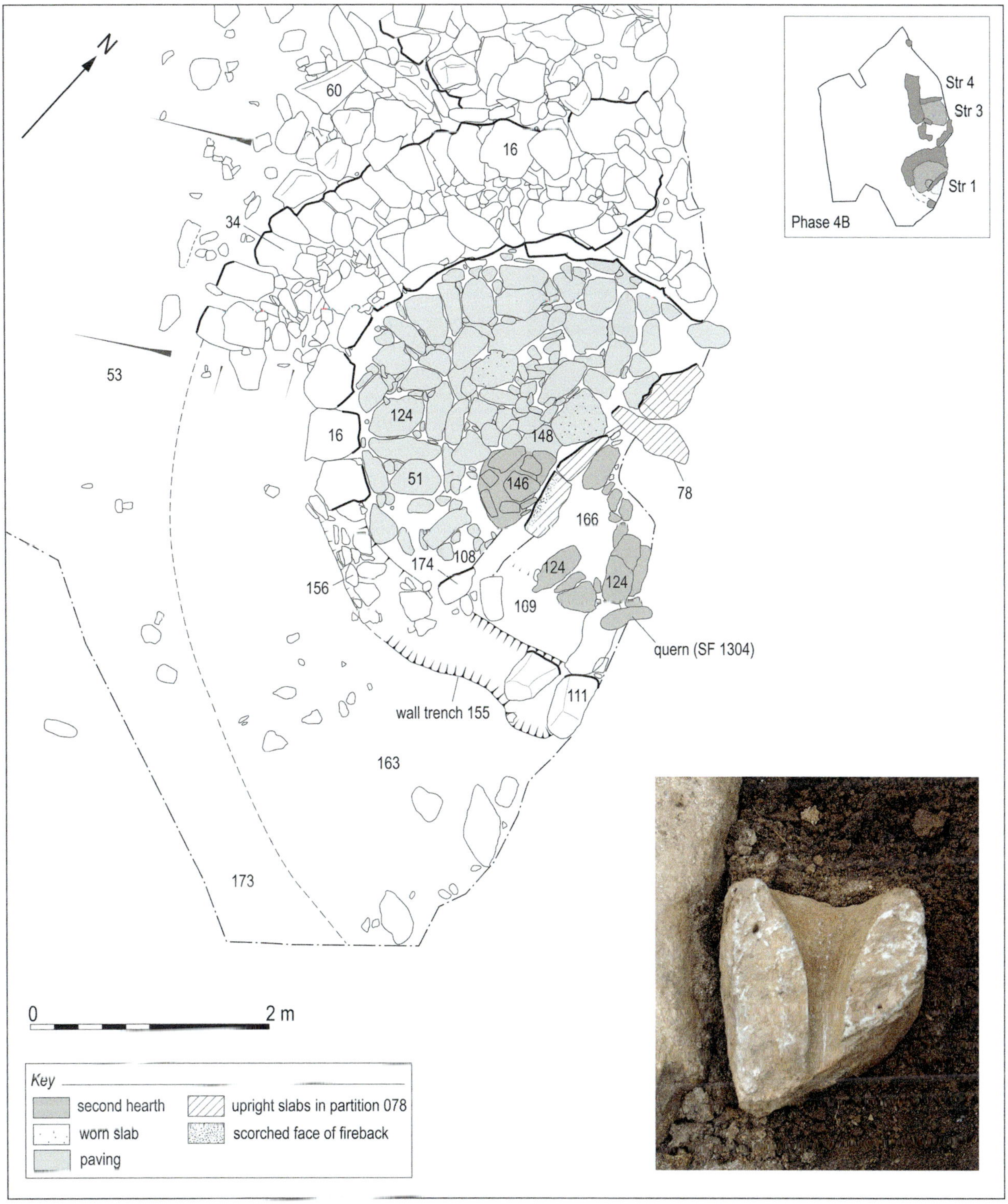

Figure 2.16 Plan of house 1 in use during phase 5A; the inset photo shows the broken tuyère (SF 942) that was left on the floor in phase 6A

outer face rested on an external ground surface, flecked with burnt peat, degraded pottery and crushed shell (53), which had built up during the use of yards 3 and 4 over the older ploughed midden (40) (see Fig. 2.23). A greasy, trampled deposit (72) formed over it during construction of the cell.

The builders also placed a triangular wedge of masonry in the angle between the south-east section of yard 3's wall (167) and the rear of the massive fireback (183) in the yard. Finally – although this may have happened slightly later – they built a new skin of walling (73) against the south wall (83) of the first yard (5), which by

Figure 2.17 The second hearth in house 1, where fires burned against the scorched upright hearth back (78), from the south-west

now was several hundred years old with only its upper courses visible; perhaps they doubted its stability. The new wall skin (73) consisted of upright boulders topped with drystone, coursed and random rubble masonry. Three orthostats that continued its line north-eastward along the coastal edge may have been remnants of it. Again a partition divided the yard from the cell, this time seated in a linear, rubble-packed slot (81). The second yellow clay floor (58) was chopped away on the south-east when the cell was built, but the massive stone block (142) remained in place.

Greasy, red-brown silty clay (57) built up in both the yard (3) and the cell (2). It was heavily flecked with hearth waste and contained worked pumice, pottery and worked quartz.

Phase 6: The house (1) is abandoned while the yard (3) and cell (2) continue in use – 1st century AD

Quite suddenly, people stopped living in the house and instead left abundant rubbish inside the semi-circular room with its successive hearths. The paved floor became covered in what appeared on excavation as thick, loose, friable, sticky clay silt (122), generally dark brown but with distinct variations in colour and content. It was full of hearth waste, food remains – especially from saithe and other fish and the burnt shells of limpet, prickly cockle and oyster – and discarded objects. These included a loom weight (SF 954) and hammerstone (SF 995) (see Fig. 6.8) and mostly large sherds from up to 64 pots.

Someone placed a broken block tuyère, carved from steatite, on the floor of the abandoned house (SF 942, Fig. 6.1 and see inset, Fig. 2.16). This, only the fourth block tuyère so far found in the Northern Isles, would have been used during metalworking to protect the bellows from the heat of the fire. It probably broke during use (see Forster and McLaren, Chapter 6). Organic and inorganic chemical analysis of the midden (122) found high levels of manganese, copper and zinc, which indicate it also included waste from metal-working (see Derham, Chapter 3).

Several thick lenses of fine, pale grey silt, burnt marine shells and burnt animal bone (123, 126) lay against the wall, as if people had dumped basketfuls of ash from cooking fires there. The midden's loose compaction indicates that it was not trampled by everyday traffic, and its general spread contrasted with the well-contained ash-midden that built up behind the hearth during use. A burnt cattle bone from the loose midden (122) yielded a radiocarbon date range of 20 cal BC–cal AD 130 (SUERC-26126, 95.4% probability), which is virtually identical to one from a horse bone/tooth from near the top of the ash-midden heap (127). This suggests that occupation of the house ceased and the midden accumulated in fairly rapid succession.

After the loose midden built up, the upper wall of the house collapsed or was pulled down and rubble (64) covered the floor (see Fig. 2.21). The nature of the stones – long, thin slabs and massive blocks (up to a metre long) with some smaller stones – indicates something of the wall's construction. Some lay horizontally and others at steep angles against the wall face; there were voids between them and patches of yellow clay adhered to many. The rubble lay mainly across the north-western part of the interior, as if it was the northern wall arc that had collapsed. The fact that so much good building stone was left here, rather than re-used in another structure, could suggest that the settlement was already in decline by this time. The abundant rich midden and building material may also have been closing deposits, the result of acts to deliberately end the life of this particular house.

Afterwards, people continued to leave hearth waste and midden over the collapsed house and it eventually covered much of the rubble. The different deposits evoke many episodes of dumping and trampling. Hearth waste, consisting of bright orange and white ash (103) and black, charcoal-rich silt (104), covered the southern part. Sticky brown clay silt (87) lay to the north under bright orange-pink peat ash (49) that was packed with charcoal and burnt grain, large sherds from up to 32 pots and a hammerstone (SF 784).

Figure 2.18 Above: north-facing section through the mound of ash-midden to the east of partition wall 78 in house 1 (G–G' on Fig. 2.11). Below: the south-facing (middle image) and north-facing sections through the mound, with large pot sherds visible in the south-facing section

Figure 2.19 Above: north-facing section through the last hearth and across house 1 (F–F' on Fig. 2.11). Below: the eastern part of the section through the hearths and hearth waste deposits to either side of the hearth back (78)

Lying on one of the slabs was a thin deposit of very fine, silky, creamy-white sediment with tiny, light orange mottles throughout (63), about 0.3 in diameter (63). This was interpreted in the field as heat-affected talc (degraded steatite) on the basis of its texture and appearance, but analysis by X-ray diffraction of a sample did not indicate the presence of talc (see Jones, Chapter 6).

Phase 7: Final use of the yard (3) and cell (2) and an informal yard (6) in the ruins of the house (1) – late 1st to 2nd century AD

Phase 7A: Last acts in the yard (3) and cell (2)

Late in the life of the settlement, more residues of craft activity and metalworking were left in the yard (3) and cell

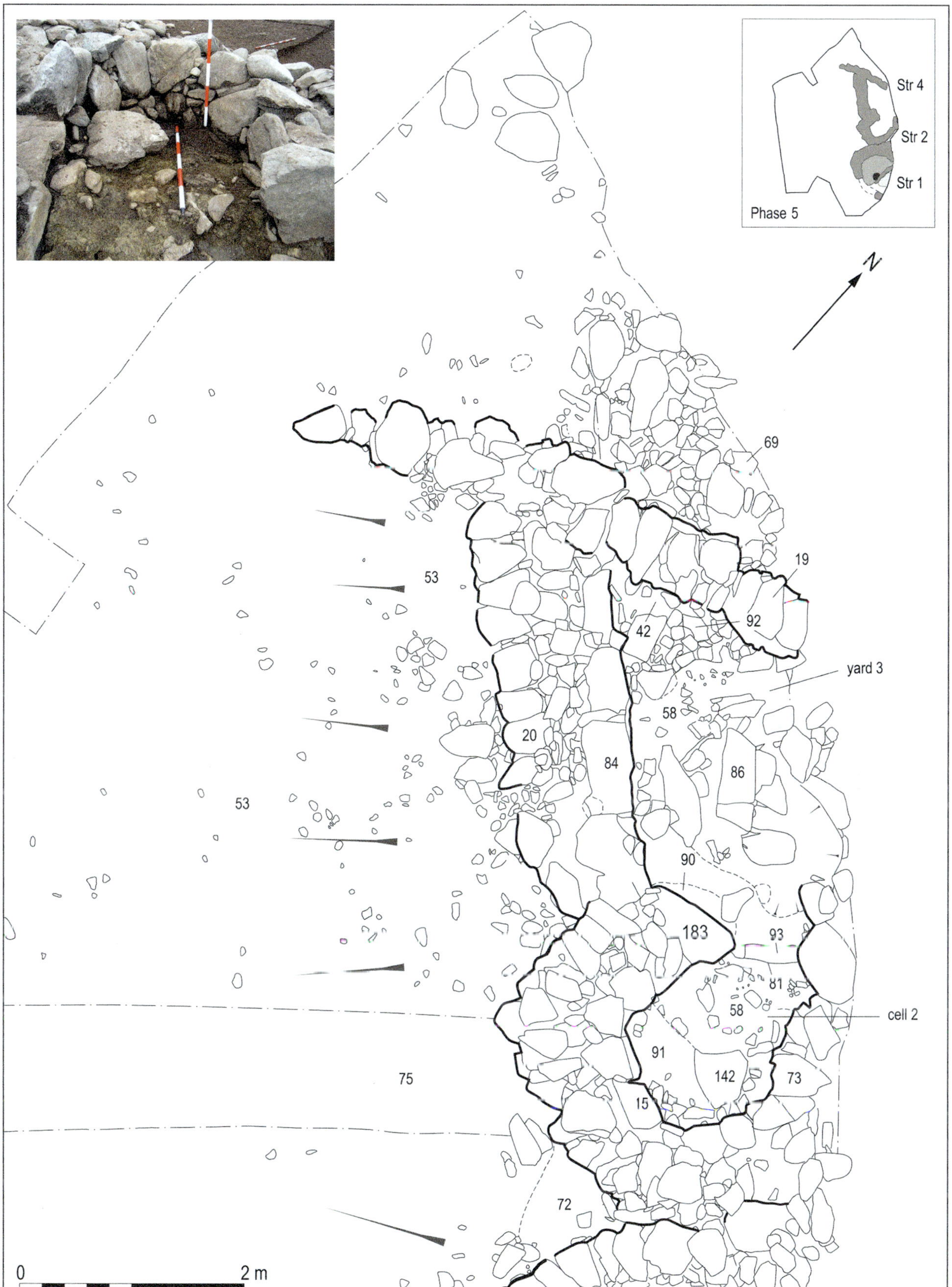

Figure 2.20 Plan of cell 2 and yard 3, phase 5B. Inset: cell 2 from the north with the large stone block or anvil (142) in situ

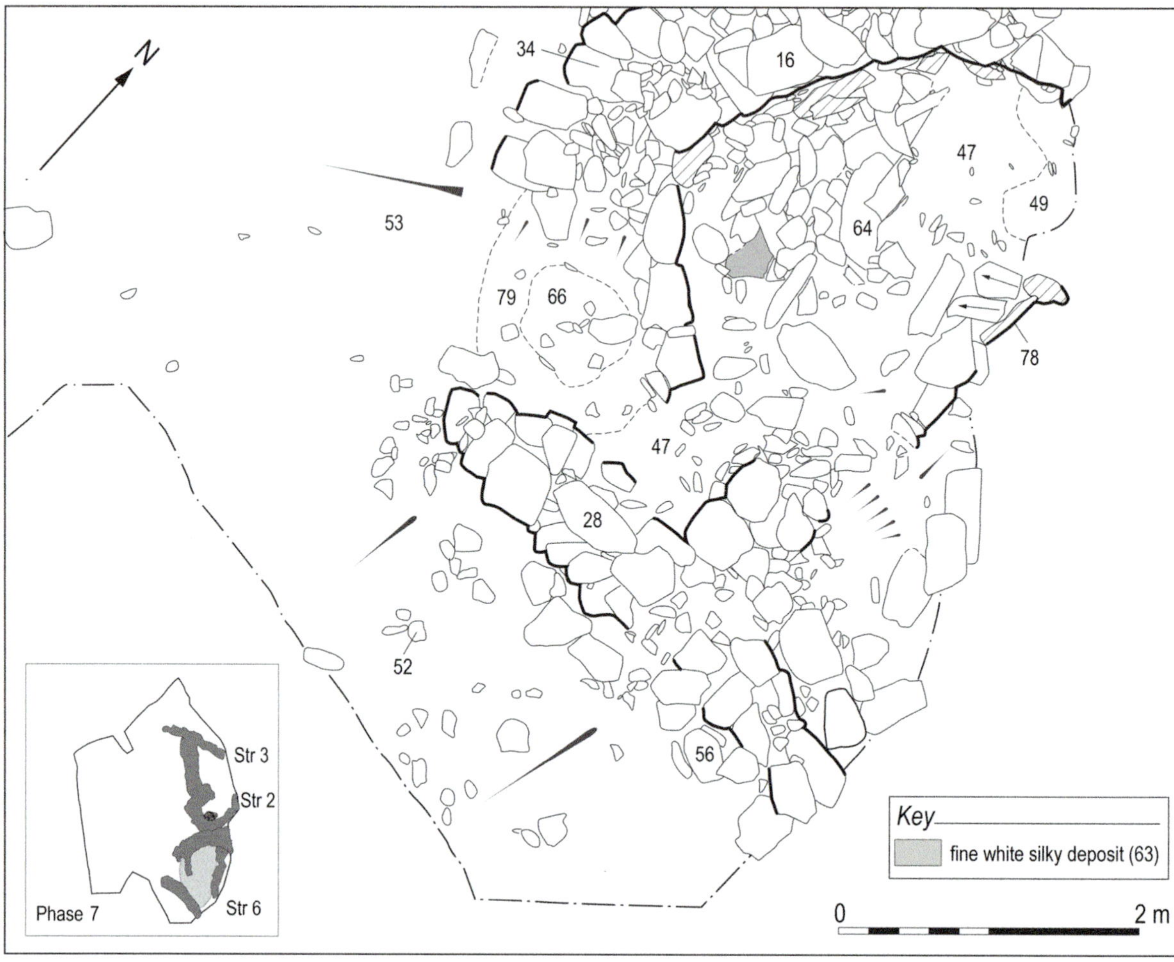

Figure 2.21 Rubble collapse (64) in house 1, partly sealed by midden and showing the rough wall (28) that defined yard 6 in phase 7

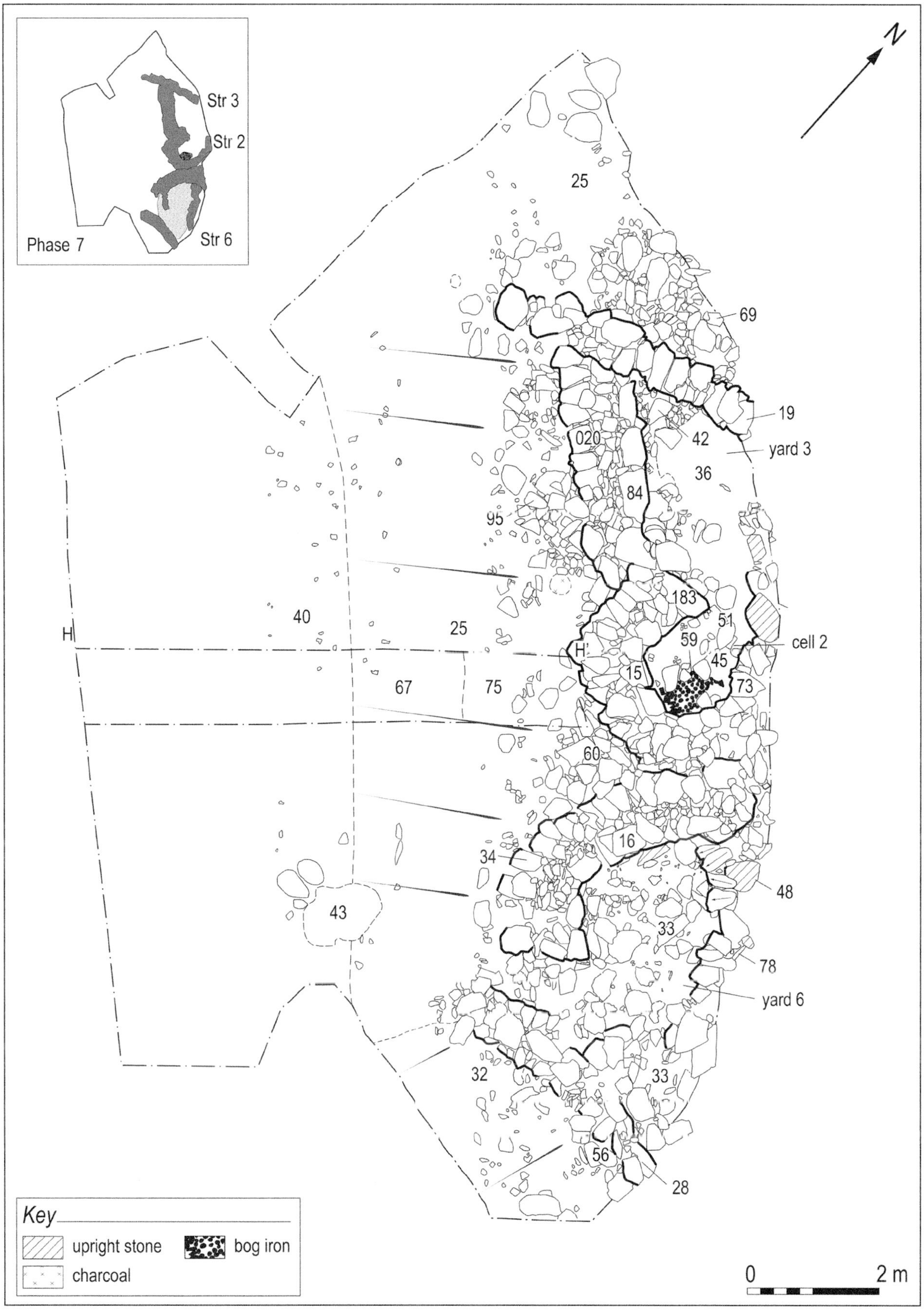

Figure 2.22 Plan of the settlement in phase 7B, showing the remains of yards 3 and 6 and the heap of bog iron ore in cell 2

(2). A large heap of unprocessed bog iron ore (59) – 27.5 kg of it – was placed in the cell, on and around the stone block (142) (Fig. 2.22 and see Fig. 8.6). The ore had been broken into many lumps up to 0.18 m across, probably as it was dug out of the ground (see McLaren, Chapter 6); the lumps lay in a sparse, dark brown clay silt matrix. None had been roasted, vitrified or otherwise prepared for smithing. This could suggest that while metalworking was underway in the vicinity, perhaps even in the part of yard (3) that was lost to erosion, the cell (2) was being used for storage. Alternatively, it could have been a kind of closing deposit, like those in the house.

A schist slab with a pointed end, bearing two pecked, oval hollows like eyes (SF 597, Fig. 6.12), was found close to the ore. It may have been an anvil (see Clarke, Chapter 6). Orange-red peat ash and charcoal (45) were dumped against the east side of the ore heap and rubble and domestic midden (51) accumulated on the floor, leaving a spread of sticky, dark brown sandy clay and burnt animal bone, limpet shells, a smoother/polisher used as a hammerstone (SF 438), grooved pumice pieces, iron slag and pottery. Another, more trampled sticky dark midden layer (35, 36), with a similar range of constituents and some industrial waste, formed across both the cell and yard.

Phase 7B: Midden builds up in an informal yard (6) as the older yard (3) and cell (2) fall into disrepair

The tumbled house (1) was converted to an informal yard (6) with the construction of a rough but substantial wall (28) along the south (Figs. 2.21 and 2.22). This wall was at least three courses high and, along with the robbed-out terminal of the house's stone wall (16), it defined an entrance to the yard on the south-west; erosion had truncated it on the east. The stones used to build it were probably taken from the south-eastern arc of the house's wall, leaving just a couple of large stones (111) pitched against the side of the wall trench (see Fig. 8.3).

People continued to deposit midden over the rubble of the house and an extensive spread of brown greasy silt (47), flecked with hearth waste and a little industrial waste, built up across it (see Fig. 2.21). Sandy silt (79) that accumulated in the entrance contained a serpentine polisher (SF 2282; see Clarke, Chapter 6). On one occasion, someone emptied a container of burnt limpet and periwinkle shells, saithe vertebrae, charcoal and burnt peat (66) in the entrance. Outside, a ground surface formed of greasy red-brown clay silt (25, 32) with abundant crushed shell, degraded pottery and charcoal or burnt peat trampled into its surface.

As midden accumulated in the yard (6), it formed a fairly consistent layer of greasy, dark brown clay silt (33) that lay banked against the north wall of the old house and sloped down over the rubble. It contained bones from cattle, sheep/goat, pigs and abundant cetaceans; oyster shells; steatite chips, and large sherds from up to 46 pots, including one that was squashed where it lay. Cattle teeth from this midden layer (33) and the sticky dark midden (36) in yard 3 returned identical calibrated radiocarbon date ranges of cal AD 80-230 (SUERC-26133 and SUERC-26134 respectively) (both at 95.4% probability).

Later still, people modified the yard again by constructing a rough wall (48) north to south across it; this extended the line of the original partition wall (78), which still protruded through the post-abandonment midden deposits (Fig. 2.22). First they levelled the midden surface with small stones (50) and then set some large, sub-angular blocks upright, along with courses of smaller blocks. Several of the large blocks slipped out of line and tipped into the yard before windblown sand covered the area. While this midden (66) lay exposed, more stones tumbled onto it from the wall of the house.

Phase 7C: Midden mixed with windblown sand builds up as all the buildings tumble

People continued leaving midden in these areas during the final phase of the settlement, when there is evidence that environmental changes were underway. The structures were no longer maintained and, as stones began to slip from walls, an extensive layer of sticky, red-brown silty sand (6, 7, 14, 18) built up to a depth of about 0.10 m over and around them. It contained abundant animal bone from cattle, sheep/goat, pig and especially cetaceans, some of which had been chopped to extract oil (see Smith, Chapter 4). There were also many marine shells and seabird remains, especially gannet and shag, and the bones of two great auk. Discarded and broken objects and waste from craft work littered the area: smoothers and smoother/polishers, steatite chips, worked pumice, a few pieces of iron slag and vitrified spheres from smithing hearths, and sherds from up to 104 pots. Concentrations of marine shells and hearth waste in the general spread evoke many discrete acts of deposition as the buildings continued to fall down. Although the more substantial wall lines would still have been visible, this part of the settlement would have now looked like a ruin that was gradually being obscured by midden and sand (Fig. 2.23). A calibrated date range of AD 90-240, from a cattle tooth found in the sandy midden (7) (SUERC-26132, 95.4% probability), is statistically identical to those from phase 7A/B midden deposits (see above).

The accumulating deposits were much sandier than any of the underlying ones. This could indicate that vegetation had been cleared from the fixed dunes in the vicinity and they were deflating (collapsing as sand was blown out of them). Alternatively, wind strength was increasing or the prevailing wind direction changing, blowing more sand over the foreshore.

Phase 8: Inundation – 2nd to 3rd century AD

In a dramatic shift, the settlement was covered in windblown sand (8). A layer of clean shell sand, up to half a metre thick, built up over the structures. Occasional bones of

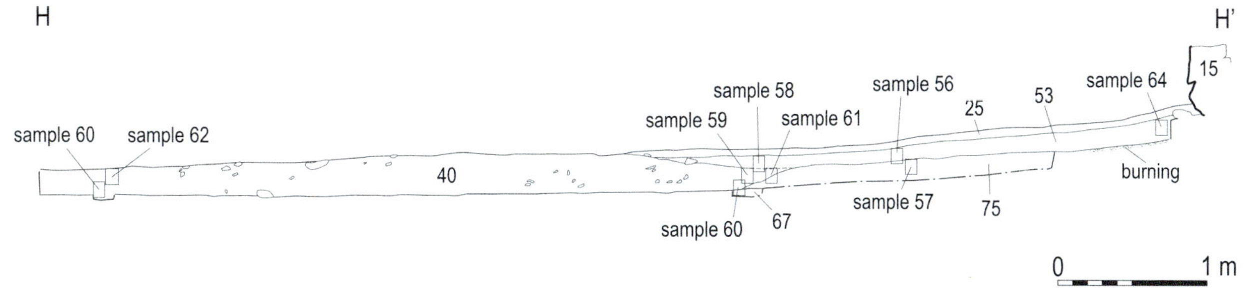

Figure 2.23 Above: south-east-facing section through exterior ground surfaces to the west of structures 2, 3 and 4, extending from the wall (15) of cell 2 to the south-west edge of the excavation trench. Below: the tumbled structures partly sealed by midden-rich sand in phase 7C, from the south-west

domesticated animals and seabirds, with knife cuts on the latter, show that people were still using the area at times. However, the initial inundation must have been considerable – enough to make settlement on the foreshore untenable – and it was followed by a longer period when sand continued to accumulate at least intermittently. Patchy bands of darker sand within the thick shell sand layer indicated some periods of stability when turf was able to develop.

Phase 9: The burial – 3rd to 4th century AD

Probably during the 3rd or 4th century AD, the body of a person was buried close to the former settlement (Fig. 2.24). A grave was dug through the windblown sand, its base clipping an older cultivated soil (40), and the body of a probable man, 50–60 years old, was laid in it (Duffy, Chapter 7). He was placed on his back with his head to the SSW, facing north-west. His left arm was folded across his torso, his right arm extended with hand above groin and his legs drawn together at the knees. Radiocarbon dating of a rib bone indicated he died between cal AD 150-390 (95.4% probability) or probably cal AD 240-330 (68.2% probability) (SUERC-10745).

A few stones were placed around his feet and lower legs. A small ornament made of two opaque yellow glass beads on a copper alloy spiral ring (SF 221, Fig. 7.4) was

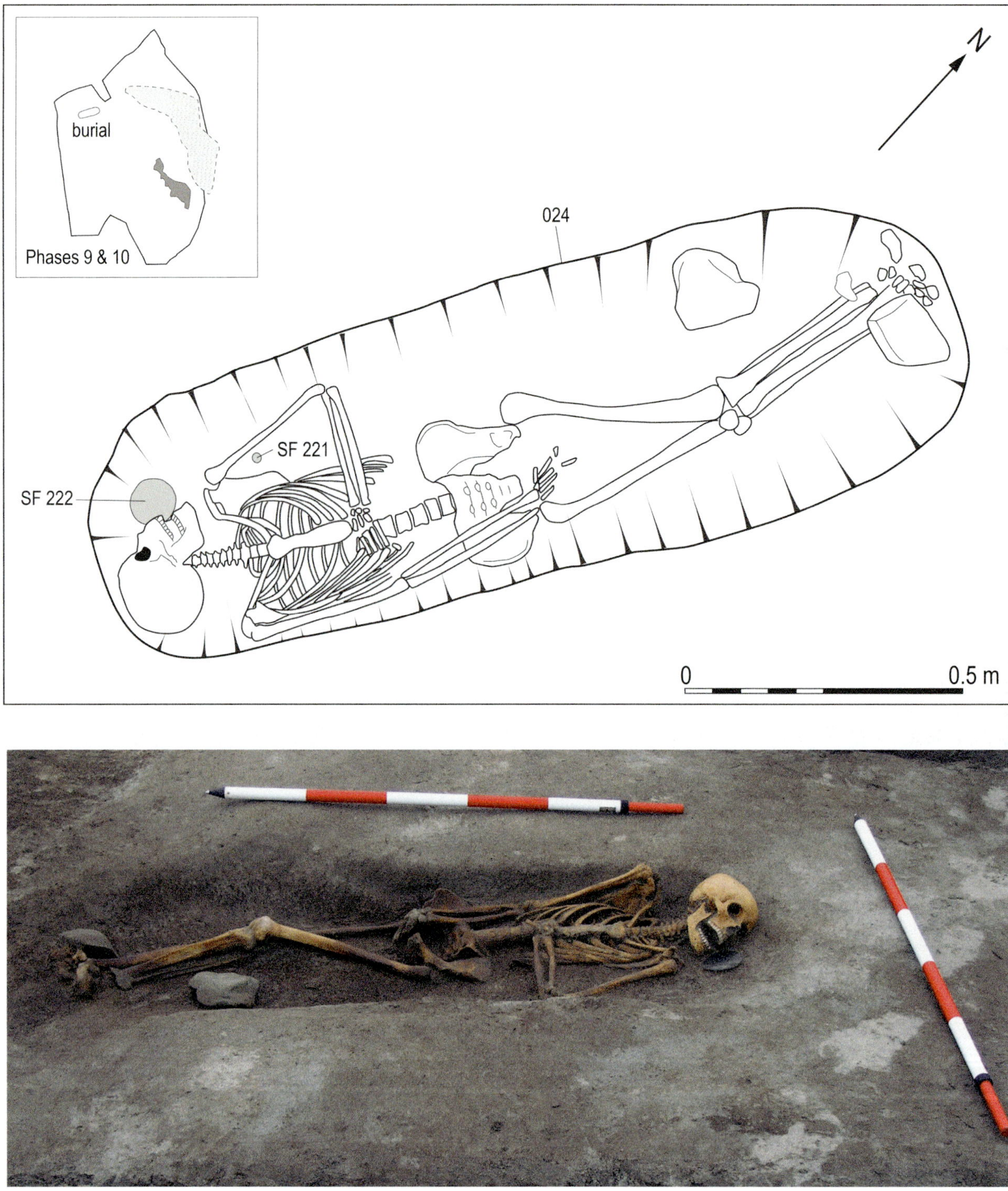

Figure 2.24 The burial in plan (above) and from the north-west

found beside his left arm; it may have been worn on his clothing or body, perhaps piercing the skin (Goldberg and Hunter, Chapter 7). A perfectly circular, polished stone disc (SF 222, Fig. 7.4) was set beside his mouth. Sticky, soapy white sediment was found adhering to its underside. This might have been some cosmetic, narcotic or edible substance, but analysis has not so far been able to establish its origins (Jones, Chapter 6).

The grave was first filled with clean windblown sand that also contained a large steatite bead (SF 87, Fig. 7.4) (Forster, Chapter 7) and then with sand mixed with topsoil. A cluster of large stones (17, not illustrated) was found lying approximately over the south-west end of the grave's fill; they may have been placed to mark its location.

At some point during this phase, a tiny cairn (9) was built on the dune which by now covered the former

Figure 2.25 The settlement mound excavated to phase 10 deposits (5th–6th century AD), with the ephemeral remains of temporary occupation on the dune

settlement. It was made of quartz pebbles and angular schist stones and measured half a metre across (Fig. 8.13). Next to it were a complete, partly polished ring sawn from a deer antler and fragments of two unfinished rings (SF 17, Fig. 6.18).

Phase 10: A temporary camp and further burial – 5th to 6th century AD

A stable ground surface formed over the sloping dune that sealed the settlement, the grave and the surrounding area. It was represented by a thick layer of firm, orange-brown sand (4). This was flecked with charcoal and burnt peat, occasional pot sherds and animal bone, which together indicated contemporary activity in the vicinity.

On the surface of the dune, someone constructed a slight boundary about 4 m long, made of intermittent stones (3) that might have supported a light structure such as a fence or windbreak (Fig. 2.25). The stones sat on a thin skin of pale sand that had blown onto the surface (4). A short phase of occupation here left a spread about 10 m across of firm, greasy dark brown clay silt mottled with peat ash and charcoal (5). It contained sherds of distinctive, thin-walled pottery, very different to that produced in the settlement (Lelong and Ballin Smith, Chapter 5); bones of cattle, sheep/goat, pig and seabirds; the remains of large cod, limpet and mussel shells; and a small bead carved of schist (SF 2380). A small fragment from an angular stone block, which appeared to have been dressed to shape, was found nearby in the old ground surface (4).

This may have been a temporary camp which was occupied during a fishing or hunting season - or during the rites surrounding burial and monument-building on the foreshore. A radiocarbon measurement from a cattle tooth recovered from the occupation spread (5) is broadly contemporary with the death of a woman whose body was placed in one of two square cairns, built less than 50 m to the north-west (Bigelow 1980) (see Table 2.1). The cattle tooth returned a date of cal AD 400–540 (SUERC-26128) and human bone from the burial a date of cal AD 420–620 (both at 95.4% probability, Oxcal v 4.3).

Afterwards, windblown sand continued to accumulate over the area to a depth of between 0.4 and 0.6 m, with periods of stability indicated by humic layers within the sand cover. There were also periods of deflation, indicated by the patchy nature of some of the old turf lines.

The fairly compact area excavated, which had been so intensively used and reworked over the course of hundreds of years, was part of a larger settlement. Although its extent and full character are unknown because of its truncation by coastal erosion, the analyses of artefacts, sediments, food remains, burnt fuel and human remains have produced abundant information about how people lived at Milla Skerra and the person who was later buried there. The chapters that follow present the findings.

Chapter 3

Refining interpretations of the archaeological deposits

Brendan Derham, Clare Ellis and Jo McKenzie

At Milla Skerra, a combination of factors – an alkaline burial environment, the occupants' habit of piling up midden and building on top of it, and the sand dune that eventually sealed the abandoned settlement – together encouraged the formation of thick, well-stratified occupation deposits that were highly informative. Samples taken of sediments across the sequence were analysed to better understand their formation processes, levels of phosphate (organic inputs) and geochemical composition. The findings of these analyses shed light on how the various midden, occupation, hearth and cultivation layers formed and some of the practices behind their formation.

Soil micromorphology analysis

Clare Ellis

Micromorphological analysis was conducted for 13 kubiena samples taken from a variety of representative features, including old ground surfaces, hearths and hearth waste deposits, clay flooring, midden and occupation deposits. The locations of most of the samples are shown on the relevant section drawings: Fig. 2.3 (sample 244), Fig. 2.4 (sample 245), Fig. 2.7 (samples 246 and 247), Fig. 2.18 (samples 151 and 152), Fig. 2.19 (sample 132) and Fig. 2.23 (samples 56, 58 and 61). The samples were prepared for thin-section analysis at the Geological Institute of the University of Ghent and were assessed using a MEIJI ML9200 polarizing microscope following the principles of Bullock *et al.* (1985), Fitzpatrick (1993) and Stoops (2003). A range of magnifications (×40–×400) and constant light sources (plane polarised light – PPL, cross-polars – XPL, circular polarised light and oblique incident light – OIL) was used in the analysis.

The sampled contexts comprise silts and sandy silts that are poorly to well sorted; the majority of the contexts have a high amorphous organic content. The silt- and sand-sized mineral component comprises sub-rounded to rounded plagioclase feldspar, weathered proxene, olivine and serpentine with gabbro, phyillite, talc, serpentinite and schist rock fragments. The sand-sized mineral component is thought very likely to be Aeolian in origin. All the contexts have been affected by bioturbation and this has imparted compact, vughy and/or channel microstructures to many of the contexts. Consequently, the fine material of the majority of the units is in the form of dense microaggregates which comprise coalesced excrement pellets.

The utilised fuel resource

The presence of rubified fine material (red, orange and bright yellow colours in OIL), fragments of charred peat, burnt silty peat/turf and peat charcoal, combined with the domination of silt-sized mineral grains, indicates that the main fuel constituents used for heating, lighting and cooking were peat, silty peat and possibly turf (Simpson *et al.* 2003; Simpson *et al.* 2006).

Many of the deposits are well mixed, and it is evident that many of the fuel residues observed are in secondary depositional contexts and have been extensively reworked by soil fauna, including earthworms, fungi and bacteria. The predominance of charred amorphous organic matter, silt-sized charcoal and larger charcoal fragments within the fuel residues is indicative of low-temperature fires (around 400°C) typical of domestic hearths, as opposed to higher temperatures typical of fires used for industrial purposes, in which all organic matter is combusted at temperatures of around 800°C (Courty *et al.* 1989; Simpson *et al.* 2003).

Those ashes with dominant charred amorphous organic matter mixed with very few to few coarse charcoal fragments and few to frequent disseminated silt-sized charcoal are interpreted as partially combusted peat ashes produced in a low-temperature fire, for example that used to smoke or grill food. Charred peat also occurs as dark yellowish brown to black clasts in which the fibrous tissue residues are visible. These clasts exhibit an undifferentiated b-fabric in XPL and are black to dark brown when observed under OIL. The charred peat is occasionally associated with phosphate staining. This type of ash is present in the hearth waste layers in house 1 (sample 105 and two units from samples 151 and 152).

Well-combusted peat ash is generally dark greyish brown in PPL and bright orange (reddened or rubified) in OIL; the orange colour of the fine material in OIL indicates a fire temperature of not more than 400ºC (Simpson *et al.* 2003). The ash generally exhibits an undifferentiated b-fabric in XPL. Charcoal fragments in this ash are generally absent. This ash also exhibits very few to few biogenic silica, mainly phytoliths and rare to occasional diatoms frustles. This type of ash occurs in many of the deposits but is dominant in sample 244 (context 215 in yard 5).

Clasts of fully combusted and/or weathered ash are found in the hearth waste of samples 105 (context 103, overlying house 1 collapse), 151 (hearth waste in house 1) and 244 (hearth waste in yard 5), with minor amounts in samples 246 (midden 171/213 overlying yard 5) and 152 (hearth waste in house 1). These clasts are characterised by a pale greyish cream colour in PPL, greyish in XPL and dull to bright yellow in OIL. They comprise silt-sized mineral grains and few to frequent phytoliths; the clasts exhibit a finely stippled, speckled b-fabric in XPL. Possible remnants of peat combusted under a higher than normal temperature occur in sample 152 (Unit B); this material is dark red to bright yellow in OIL due to the segregation of iron oxides.

Yard 5 hearth waste, external midden and overlying midden (phases 2–3)

Sample 244 comprises context 215, which includes four units: A and B, moderately sorted silt, and C and D, moderately sorted coarse sandy silt. Units A and B comprise a dump of well-combusted, mixed peat ash with very few burnt bone fragments and very few fragments of pottery. Significantly, there is no silt-sized charcoal in these deposits. In unit A, silica ash remnants have also been washed down from layers above into very few voids. The mixed clay silt peat ash of unit B is well compacted, and fine silt ash around some of the vughs and channels attests to its compaction through bioturbation and possibly trampling. Accumulation of this ashy waste ceased and soil fauna reworked this horizon. Then, within a relatively short period of time, localised erosion resulted in the accumulation of thin brown clay in a shallow puddle. While the silty clay was still damp, there followed an episode in which windblown sand mixed with windblown ash-midden material (unit C) accumulated. Further mixed peat ash-midden with high silt content was then dumped on top of unit C with some windblown sand and midden material being incorporated. The evidence indicates that these units accumulated while exposed to the elements. This material was subsequently partially reworked by soil biota.

Sample 245 was derived from two successive middens that lay outside yard 5 on the west (224 and 238). Only a single unit was discernable in thin section and this closely resembles samples 58, 56 and 61, taken through a series of external ground surfaces. However, excavation recovered numerous large artefacts and pieces of animal bone from the middens, while the old ground surfaces contained much smaller fragments of bone and artefacts, suggesting that complex and varying formation processes were at work. Additional inclusions visible microscopically in the midden deposits include pottery fragments, a few larger burnt bone fragments (up to 5 mm) and very few fragments of shell.

Samples 247 and 246 were taken through a series of successive occupation deposits (226, 213) that built up inside the yard (5) in phase 2 and through a thick midden (171) that accumulated over it in phase 3. A single unit was discernable in sample 247 (226/213). It comprises a bioturbated sandy silt ash-midden. Most of the sand-sized mineral grains are distributed randomly, but there are a few zones of nearly pure coarse sand, indicating that much of the sand was incorporated into the midden by Aeolian processes and subsequently redistributed through the activities of soil biota. The ash-midden has been subject to chemical weathering, resulting in few phosphatic coatings and degradation of much of the frequent bone. Frequent iron oxide hypocoatings are associated with decomposing amorphous organic matter. A layer of shell fragments marks the transition from (226) to (213), although there is no significant micromorphological difference between these two contexts.

Five units are discernable in sample 246 (213/171); all the units have been subject to bioturbation, resulting in vughy, spongy and channel microstructures. The lowermost (unit A) comprises a moderately sorted sandy silt peat ash-midden with significant windblown coarse sand content. Many of the iron oxide hypocoatings are rounded and broken; this is likely to have been caused by the activities of Enchytraeidae (Dawod and FitzPatrick 1992) as well as Aeolian transportation. The sharp boundary into unit B indicates a sudden change in the mode of deposition; unit B is a dump of very mixed peat/silty peat ash-midden. Over this was dumped a thin (4 mm) layer of ash-midden (unit C), dominated by burnt organic matter which has been mostly replaced by iron oxide. The presence of frequent fragmentary phytoliths and diatoms indicates that the dominant source was a damp peat. There is a very sharp boundary into the overlying unit (D – 4 mm thick), which contains common phosphate coatings and infillings, some mixed with charcoal and charred peat clasts and small, often rounded fragments of bone. This horizon is tentatively interpreted as a single dump of coprolitic stable material that has been partially burnt (utilised as fuel?) prior to dumping. The final unit (171) comprises a mixed peat and sandy turf ash-midden which contains clasts of material very similar to units C and D. There are frequent phosphatic coatings associated with charred peat clasts and fragments of bone. The silty infilling of some of the voids and the dense silty fabric may have been caused by the percolation of organic-rich solutions derived from urine.

House 1 clay hearth and hearth waste deposits (phases 4 and 5)

Sample 132 was taken through what was interpreted as a clay hearth (132, 135) in the house (1). A single unit comprising poorly sorted silt with common rock fragments is discernable. This material is very similar to the poorly sorted silt of the floor deposits in yard 3 and is believed to be of similar origin. In addition, there are two thin horizontal bands of peat ash; the ash bands have sharp boundaries with the silt. There is no indication that the silt has been affected by heat, although given the relatively low temperature required to burn peat, coupled with the dearth of organic matter within the silt, this lack of evidence is not surprising. It seems likely that the ash bands represent the barest remnants of *in situ* peat fires, lit directly upon the hardened non-combustible silt, the ashes of which were deliberately removed prior to hearth renovation. The surface of the hearth was renewed with up to 15 mm of poorly sorted silt; the weak horizontal orientation of the larger rock fragments indicate it was roughly spread and compressed onto the underlying surface. The sharp boundaries have been slightly disrupted in places by post-depositional bioturbation. Slight weathering of the lowermost ash band is evident in the form of a few goethite hypocoatings within the silt beneath.

Three distinct units were identified in sample 105, which was taken through re-deposited hearth waste (105) in house 1; this deposit comprised the uppermost layer of the thick mound of hearth waste that accumulated against the east side of the internal partition. Peat ash is the basis of all three units and comprises poorly sorted silt with very few mineral grains and few rock fragments, bright orange fine material/organics in OIL (dark brown to black in PPL), few to fragmentary biogenic silica, very few fragments of charred peat and frequent to common clasts of biogenic silica mixed with silt-sized mineral grains. Some of these clasts are yellow due to the presence of phosphate. In addition, in unit C there are frequent degraded fragments of bone that survive as dusty phosphate. Some of the less-degraded bone is clearly burnt, and much of it appears to be derived from fish – perhaps incorporated into the ash during grilling or thrown back into the fire as it was consumed. All three units have been disturbed by post-depositional bioturbation and compaction. Unit B is approximately 30 mm thick and as such is very unlikely to represent a single firing. It contains more silica-rich ash clasts than the other two units, indicating that the ash was produced under slightly higher temperatures than that in units A and C.

Two samples were taken through successive deposits farther down in the same mound of hearth waste. The lowermost, sample 151, comprises three units: A and B, equating to context 137, and C to contexts 150 and 138. All three units comprise poorly sorted silt with frequent small stones; coarse sand-sized mineral grains are frequent in unit A but few in units B and C. All three units are compact and exhibit microstructures that are the result of extensive bioturbation. Peat ash is again the basis of all three units, although the organics of unit B appear more combusted than those of units A and C, as there is no charcoal in those zones dominated by orange fines (observed in OIL). The ash content of all three units appears to be derived from numerous different fires. There are different clasts of peat ash; some are indicative of incomplete combustion, others of moderate combustion and others of complete combustion. Additional waste material that was probably mixed with hearth ashes during cleaning includes small fragments of bone (some burnt and some clearly derived from fish), small clasts of peat, one piece of pottery (unit C), and two clasts of re-worked till-like fragments, the latter probably derived from the hearth base.

The upper deposits of the peat ash mound are represented in sample 152, in which four units were identified: A, B and C probably representing context 136 and D context 131. Units A, C and D comprise moderately sorted silts, while unit B is poorly sorted. The sharp and distinct boundaries between the units indicate temporary hiatuses in accumulation, possibly representing those intervening days or weeks between the removal of excessive ash from the hearth. The lowermost unit A comprises mixed peat ash, much of which is only partially combusted. There is frequent peat charcoal and a layer of this defines the sharp boundary into unit B. Unit B is dominated by very coarse sand-sized to grit-sized, sub-rounded fragments of black to bright orange/red material. The material is isotropic in XPL and dark red in OIL. One explanation of this material is that the peat being utilised as a fuel was not fully dried and so had a relatively high ferrous iron content (Fe^{2+}), which oxidized (Fe^{3+}) during heating on the fire, forming stable crystalline and amorphous components of the iron oxides. This is overlain by a thin layer of mainly silt-sized charcoal, frequent charred fragments of peat, some with phosphate coatings, very few fragments of bone, and a few fragments of iron oxide plant pseudomorphs. In turn, unit C is capped by a mixed peat ash created in a low-temperature fire. It is dominated by charred peat fragments and with clasts of peat charcoal, silica peat ash and very few bone fragments. There are very few rounded clasts of till-like material derived from a hearth base. All the units have been subject to post-depositional bioturbation, although there is minimal mixing between the units.

Yard 3 floor deposits (phase 4C)

Two samples (133 and 129) were taken through successive yellow sandy clay deposits within yard 3, which are interpreted as deliberately laid clay floors. One unit was visible in sample 133 (taken through context 96) and three units were distinguishable in sample 129 (taken through contexts 96, 90 and 58). The sediment in sample 133 and the equivalent, unit A in sample 129, comprises compact, poorly sorted silt with few coarse sand-sized mineral grains and frequent grit-sized rock fragments. Organic matter, derived from ash, is confined to very few clasts that have been incorporated through the activities of soil biota. The fabric, although generally massive, in places comprises welded clasts, the internal fabric of which is perhaps a relic of the original till deposit from which the material appears to have been sourced. The floor material was deposited in a single event.

Charred amorphous organic matter dominates the overlying moderately sorted, compact silt (unit B, sample 129), although there are very few coarse and silt-sized charcoal fragments. Other derivatives typical of the domestic hearth include very few clasts of burnt peat, frequent biogenic silica including diatoms, and few minute bone fragments. The occasional bone fragments are rounded and of a similar size to the excrement pellets that make up the dense microaggregates of the fabric.

The sharpness and clarity of the wavy boundary between the re-deposited till and the overlying silt loam (contexts 96 and 90, sample 129) is indicative of a hiatus in sedimentation/accumulation. The implication is that the underlying floor material (unit A) was sufficiently impervious so as not to become mixed (through bioturbation/trampling etc) with the overlying silt loam and it was either laid in a very uneven manner or it subsequently contorted under compaction. It seems unlikely that during the utilisation of the yard the mixed hearth and domestic waste (unit B) was allowed to accumulate, especially in view that this deposit was clearly biologically active. An alternative explanation to account for the lack of mixing between the two horizons, despite the significant re-working of unit B and the uneven nature of the surface of unit A, is that unit B represents a deliberate deposit that had been biologically blended prior to deposition. Therefore, this material may represent a dump of midden in a conveniently located disused structure. Alternatively, if the yard was being utilised to contain stock, the midden material may have been deliberately spread over the existing floor of the structure to supplement the bedding and to help soak up urine and faeces (Fenton 1978; Adderley *et al.* 2006). It is worth noting, however, that these interpretations appear to be at odds with the archaeological evidence for *in situ* scorching of the adjacent wall face and underlying paving (see Chapter 2).

The upper boundary between units B and C is also sharp, and represents a renewal of the mineral-based floor (context 58). The mineral grains and some of the rock fragments of the upper deposit show a weak horizontal preferred orientation as if smeared and compacted into place; again it appears to have been deposited as a single event. The presence of few goethite hypocoatings towards the top of the slide indicate that this unit has also been subject to limited illuviation which occurred after its physical disturbance and bioturbation. One explanation is that these hypocoatings were produced by the puddling and trampling effect of stall stock (Courty *et al.* 1989, 130), although alternatively these could have been the product of the post-depositional weathering of ash rich in potassium, as the latter encourages local clay movement (ibid, 113).

Exterior ground surfaces

Samples 58, 56 and 61 were taken through sedimentary horizons (53, 75 and 40) which were interpreted during excavation as successive ground surfaces to the south of the structures. Only one unit is identifiable in each thin section and there is no significant sedimentary difference between the sampled units. Samples 58 and 61 comprise moderately sorted silt loam and sample 56 poorly sorted silt loam. All the contexts contain few coarse sand-sized mineral grains; the latter are likely to be windblown in origin. Silt-sized mineral grains are typical of many ash middens (Guttmann *et al.* 2004). Coupled with the organic content of the unit (dominant charred and burnt amorphous organic matter, very few burnt silty peat/turf clasts, very few peat clasts, few coarse sand-sized peat and wood charcoal, few silt-sized charcoal fragments, very few minute fragments of bone and very few sclerotia (produced by the soil fungus *Cenococcum geophilum* (FitzPatrick 1993)), these deposits exhibit the characteristics of what is essentially a mixed source, well-established domestic midden.

Is it possible that these linear midden deposits at Milla Skerra were once cultivated? Guttmann (Guttmann *et al.* 2004; Guttmann 2005) has demonstrated at Tofts Ness (Orkney) and Old Scatness (Shetland) that Neolithic, Bronze Age and early Iron Age midden heaps were cultivated; this cultivation was in addition to that of off-site soils to which midden was added to improve fertility. Since deposition, the deposits have been blended by the activities of earthworms and other soil fauna. The result is a compact channel microstructure in which the fine material is in the form of microaggregates, comprising coalesced excrement pellets. Compaction is greatest in sample 58, the highest in the sequence; this could be a consequence of surface trampling.

Phosphate analysis

Jo McKenzie

Samples for phosphate analysis were taken from 78 of the archaeological deposits identified at Milla Skerra, with a total of 80 samples in all. These encompassed a wide range of contexts: occupation deposits from all six structures, surfaces identified by trampling or anthropogenic inclusions, episodes from specific activity such as burnt deposits, hearth waste and shell dumps, and middens associated with occupation and post-abandonment phases both inside and outside the house and yards. Outside the structures, old ground surfaces associated with specific occupation and pre-occupation phases and even a possible agricultural soil are identified. Samples from less-typically intensive contexts – wall core material, construction deposits and post-abandonment surfaces from late in the sequence – complete the sample set, helping to provide an overall idea of phosphate accumulation and background phosphate values within the Milla Skerra sequence as a whole.

Phosphate values for the sample set range from 13 to 49.75 µm P per kg of soil, with five samples (contexts 234, 223, 201 and 102 in, under and over yard 5 (phases 2A, 2B and 4A) and context 157 in house 1 (phase 5A)) showing a value of > 50 µm P, a high set of readings outside the parameters of measurement. These amounts are similar to those obtained for P through investigations using XRF analysis (see Derham, below).

Detailed information on the background phosphate content of the area is not directly available. The sample taken from a pre-occupation deposit (old ground surface 67, pre-dating yard 5) appears physically related to the depositional sequence. However, it would appear that overall phosphate content is not likely to have been greatly affected by downward movement of modern phosphate into the archaeological sequence (that is, through vegetation cover or current human activity). Total P levels in the uppermost, post-abandonment deposits (6, 7 and 5) show some of the lowest readings of the sequence (between 20 and 29.5 mgP/kg soil, compared to a sequence maximum of > 50 mgP/kg soil). Downward movement of modern phosphate would be likely to preferentially enhance these uppermost deposits (McKenzie 2006), and it can therefore be assumed that modern input has not seriously affected these measurements.

Six separate structures were identified during excavation. Table 3.1 presents the results of the P-analysis of all sampled deposits stratigraphically by structure (with the stratigraphically separate house 1 sequence, which includes deposits from the later yard 6, given first). Although the total P content fluctuates repeatedly between and within all structures, house 1 and yard 5 show generally higher P content than later yards 3 and 4 and cell 2, and a slight, though marked tailing-off in total P content can be seen moving up the stratigraphic sequence and into the upper deposits. This may indicate a less-intensive overall occupation in these upper structures; however, the shift is gradual and the majority of sampled contexts in the phase 4 yards (4 and 3) show a P content of over 30 mg/kg soil, comparable to that observed in house 1.

P content by structure only shows real significance in the midden material that covered yard 5. This shows consistently higher P than the majority of other sampled contexts, particularly in the post-occupation sequence of deposits beginning at context 171. The exception to this is context 215, a thick spread of hearth waste over the yard's paved floor. As an ash-rich deposit should show elevated phosphate levels (as seen, for example, in contexts 157 and 205), this reading is unexpected.

The fluctuations in this P content appear to show a relationship with the observed archaeological sequence. A point of change is evident after the insertion of the wall (83) at the east end of yard 5, with hearth waste deposit (205) showing a P peak of 49 mgP/kg, and occupation deposit (223) showing a > 50 mgP/kg 'non-measurable' peak. After this point, almost all deposits within and overlying yard 5 show P measurements of more than 40 mgP/kg. Variation between deposit types is discussed below, but it is possible that these consistently high readings could indicate use of the building in the latter period of occupation and certainly post-occupation for animal stabling as well as midden deposition. The interpretation of the phase 3 midden deposits as connected with an outdoor activity area or yard therefore fits well with the evidence from the phosphate analysis. It is notable that the two sampled deposits located further away from the structure (165, 162) show slightly lower P. Also notable are the two successive readings of > 50 mgP/kg seen from overlying stony midden (102) and shell midden (201) – the highest peak in the sequence. Archaeological interpretation suggests that these deposits represent the spreading of waste generated through domestic activity nearby; the P readings support that view and point to nearby occupation/stabling activity.

Moving on to consider measurements of P within individual deposits, it is difficult to obtain a more detailed understanding of the mode of P-input at Milla Skerra, and therefore the makeup of different deposit types in the sequence. Table 3.2 again shows the results of the analysis in stratigraphic order, here highlighted into simple deposit types: hearth-related, occupation-related, middens, old ground surfaces, and miscellaneous (including spreads, construction-related deposits, and features such as wall core material and a bog iron deposit). It can be seen that there is no correlation between specific types of deposit and higher or lower P content. Some of this is unexpected: for example, consistently high P values might be expected for the ash-rich hearth deposits, but this is not the case. Midden and occupation deposits also vary widely, prohibiting speculation as to the overall nature of activity and/or waste materials on site. Individual observations, such as the far higher reading noted for the partition slot fill (93) between yard 3 and its annexe (48 mgP/kg) compared to trampled surface (71) (35.75 mgP/kg) further indicate the unpredictability of the sample set. Once again, the only real archaeologically meaningful enhancement within the

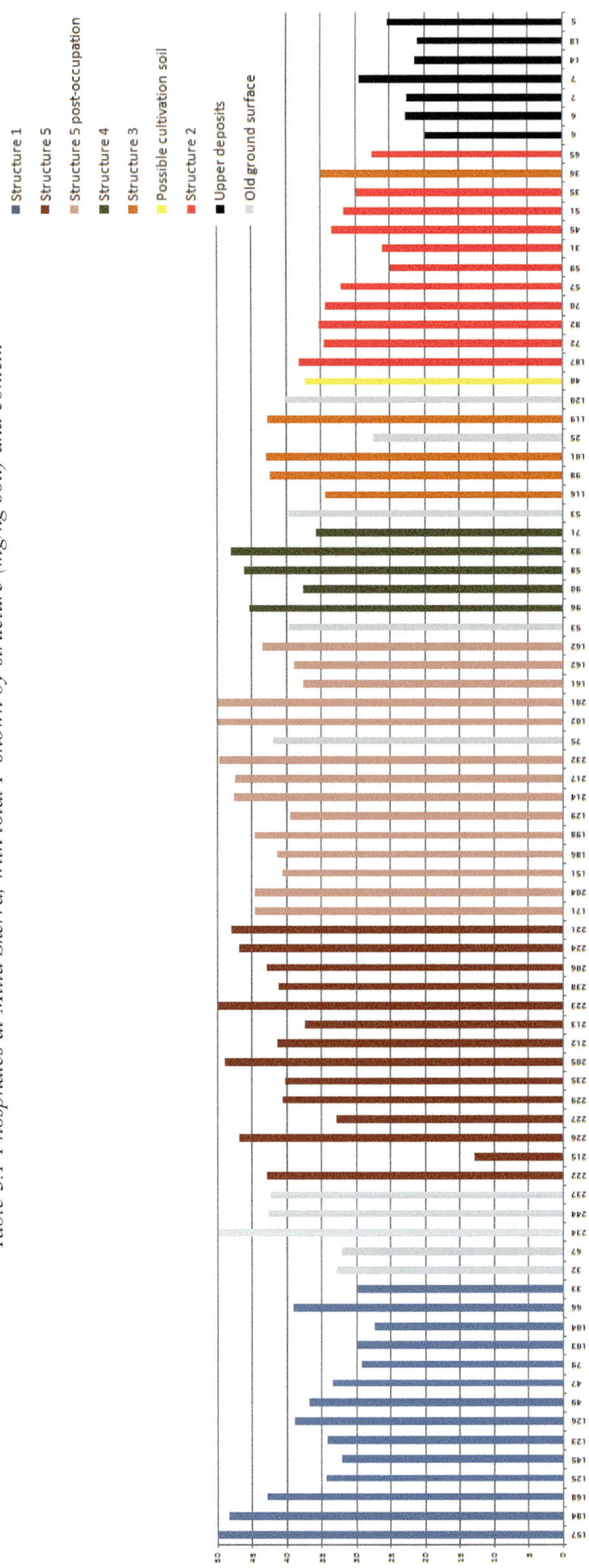

Table 3.1 Phosphates at Milla Skerra, with total P shown by structure (mg/kg soil) and context

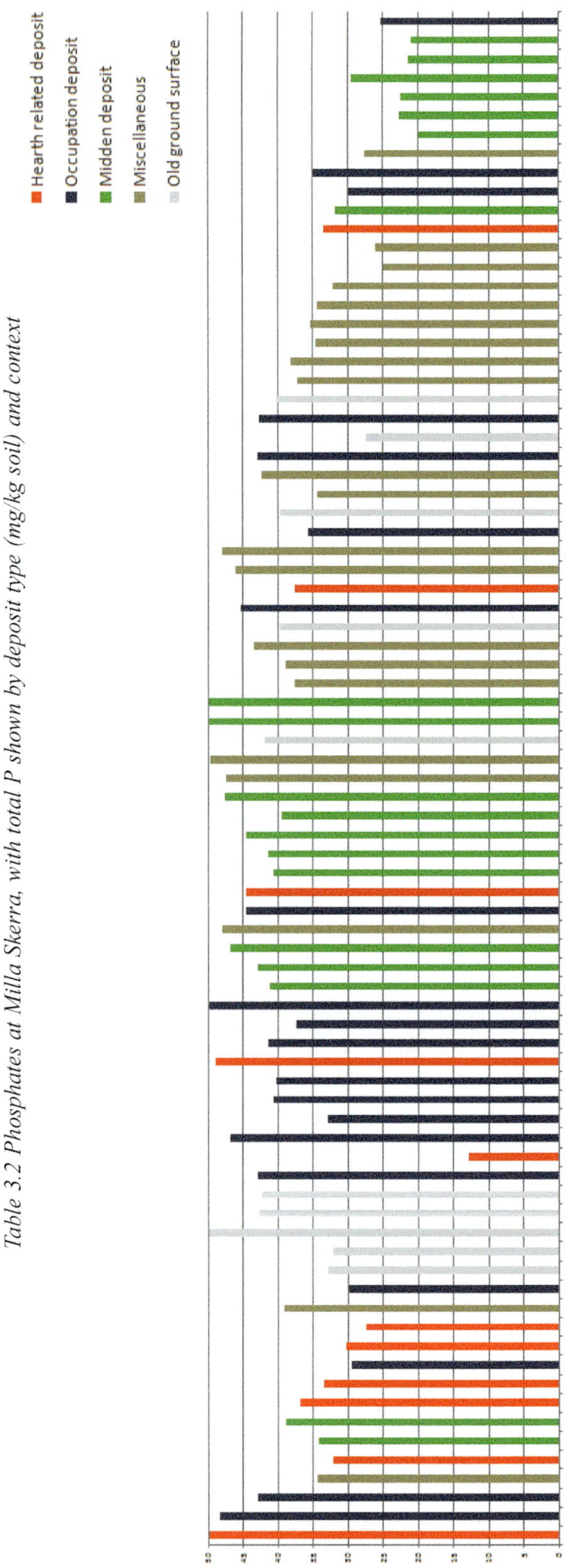

Table 3.2 Phosphates at Milla Skerra, with total P shown by deposit type (mg/kg soil) and context

sequence is that seen throughout the majority of the yard 5 sequence.

However, additional individual points can be made. It is interesting to see the sudden jump in P content between old ground surfaces (67) (32.25 mgP/kg) and (234) (> 50 mgP/kg). Although both surfaces were formed before the construction of yard 5, it would appear that there was an intensification of activity in this area immediately prior to settlement activity at the start of phase 2. Although this could be interpreted as linked to construction activity, this leap in P is significant: all other ground surfaces associated with the structures show lower P values. Context 40, interpreted as a possible cultivation soil, can also be assessed. The measurement of 37.25 mgP/kg is within the range for the sequence, and is low for a cultivated (and thus presumably fertilised) soil – far higher P concentrations would typically be expected here (McKenzie 2006). It is interesting that there appears to be a range of differentially enhanced deposits outside of the structures at this point in the sequence – the two old ground surfaces to the south of the structures show very different P values (27.5 – 40.25 mgP/kg), with the earliest possible cultivated soil (40) in this area. This could indicate preferential organic waste movement to the south of the structures for the purposes of cultivation. Alternatively, the physical appearance of layer 40 could be linked to waste disposal rather than cultivation.

Geochemical analysis

Brendan Derham

Chemical analysis, organic and inorganic, was undertaken of a series of sediments from Milla Skerra, aiming to gather evidence to help illuminate patterns of food processing and other agro-industrial activities that may have been carried out there (Braids and Miller 1975; Senesi and Loffredo 1999). Geo-chemical analysis was carried out of inorganic material using portable X-ray fluorescence (XRF).

The main areas of work focused on the settlement's underlying and surrounding sediments (contexts 89, 67 and 40), rake-out debris in house 1 from the hearths used during occupation (contexts 107, 121 and 127), material from the post-occupation use of house 1 as a midden dump (context 122), and the windblown sand that buried the site (context 8). Samples from midden material contemporary with the use of yard 5 (context 224) and midden that built up over its tumbled wall (context 130) were also included in the analysis.

Results of analysis of the soils and sediments

Table 3.3 presents the results of the analysis. Soils and sediments frequently do not contain wax esters or acylglycerols, due to diagenetic effects. However, in this study any present would have been hydrolysed and converted, during the derivatisation step, into their respective esters and ethers. In general, the main organic constituents

Table 3.3 Results of XRF analysis (concentrations in ppm)

Sample		*Context*	*Si*	*Al*	*Mg*	*P*	*S*	*Cl*	*Fe*	*Ca*	*Mn*	*Ti*	*Ni*	*Cu*	*Zn*	*As*	*Sn*	*Pb*
87	Windblown sand	8	175,967	66,454	23,045		2,194		25,708	256,235	557	1,940	62	32			67	
232	Glacial sub-soil	113	218,763	112,807	35,546	12,826	416		56,414	35,351	1,767	3,408	221	70	68	30	41	9
84	Earliest ogs under site	67	214,606	103,476	29,113	17,284	1,326		53,558	49,003	2,580	3,818	124	65	52	59	32	
81	Old ground surface	40	216,074	105,941	28,132	14,277	1,293		54,376	39,084	2,451	4,446	153	48	55	67	28	8
111	Hearth rake-out, house 1	107 (>106)	225,512	94,575	13,236	10,923	1,673	673	43,832	38,513	837	5,663	112	66	23	62		10
119	Hearth rake-out, house 1	121 (<106)	197,090	82,225	14,157	12,940	2,455	1,330	57,605	39,580	854	4,441	140	79	28	73		10
117	Hearth rake-out, house 1	127 (bone)	199,581	101,828	16,608	18,202	1,334		92,823	27,571	1,909	3,686	176	84	43	68	28	9
109	Midden over house 1	122 (pot + tuyere)	204,328	87,245	20,146	15,357	1,881		51,506	42,516	2,491	4,394	158	113	61	66		11
226	Midden outside yard 5	224	196,830	73,979	12,595	26,535	1,529		52,219	80,750	6,031	3,076	185	111	116	48		
170a	Midden outside yard 5	130	171,009	76,531	23,306	22,388	2,156		49,755	109,629	3,896	3,051	207	61	79	55	28	
170b	Midden outside yard 5	130	180,631	73,520	20,898	22,615	1,895		52,455	89,614	3,618	3,385	191	73	91	65	40	

Si; Silicon, Al; aluminium, Mg; magnesium, P; phosphorous, S; sulphur, Cl; chlorine, Fe; iron, Ca; calcium, Mn; manganese Ti; titanium, Ni; nickel, Cu; copper, Zn; zinc, As; arsenic, Sn; tin, Pb; lead in soils and sediments are saturated fatty acids with chain lengths ranging from C_{20}–C_{30}, as well as a C_{14}–C_{18} series. The two series exhibit a clear even-over-odd predominance. Characteristic bacteria-derived lipids such as branched and hydroxy-acids and odd-chain C_{25} and C_{27} fatty acids are present, but at low levels. The even carbon number fatty acids present in the soils are all at fairly comparable amounts. The series of alcohols in the range C_{22}–C_{34} (n-alkanols) are also, like the fatty acids, predominantly even-chained. The absence of extensive bacterial indicators in combination with levels of longer carbon chain (C_{20}–C_{30}) alcohols and fatty acids demonstrate the generally plant-based origin of extractable soil organic matter.

The organic extracts from the underlying, surrounding and overlying sediments and soils from the site contain fairly consistent levels of the even carbon number fatty acids (C_{16}, C_{18}, C_{20}, C_{22}, C_{24}, C_{26}, C_{28} and C_{30}) and high levels of long chain n-alkanes and n-alkanols (C_{22}–C_{34}). The organic component of the windblown sand, for instance, contains 70% n-alkanols and eicosanoic acid (C_{20}). This is in marked contrast to those contexts associated with human occupation and activity which show much more uneven levels of fatty acids, with levels of C_{14}, C_{16} and C_{18} fatty acids dominating those greater than C_{20} in length. In the heavily composted midden deposits and hearth rake-out material, however, a return to a predominance of longer chain fatty acids and n-alkanols is seen, possibly as a consequence of extensive microbial and thermal processes.

The inorganic matrix of sediments and soils generally consists of complex permutations of alumino-silicate, iron and carbonate-based minerals. These bulk matrices also contain lower levels of a much wider range of components derived either from the underlying geology or from anthropological inputs.

In the case of Milla Skerra, the inorganic components of the underlying and background sediments (67, 89, 40) are predictably consistent, as they are derived from the same underlying glacial till. The windblown sand (8), however, is markedly different, having much higher levels of calcium and sulphur combined with lower levels of silicon and aluminium, as well as the heavier metals such as iron, manganese, nickel and titanium. The hearth rake-out deposits (107, 121, 127) contain higher levels of sulphur and chlorine as well as surprisingly low levels of manganese, particularly as this last element has been regarded as a geochemical marker for hearths. The elevated levels of manganese, copper and zinc present in the midden deposit (224) that accumulated outside yard 5 during its use point towards the inclusion of waste material from metal-working processes. This also applies to the loosely dumped, un-trampled post-occupation midden deposit (122) covering the paved floor of house 1, which also contained a steatite tuyère (SF 942). The phase 3A midden deposit (130) that built up against the west wall of yard 5 is particularly rich in calcium and phosphorous, congruent with the large numbers of marine shells it contains.

Chapter 4

Fires and food at Milla Skerra

Ruby Cerón-Carrasco, Brendan Derham, Jennifer Miller, Susan Ramsay and Catherine Smith

The excavations found abundant evidence for what people were burning as fuel at Milla Skerra and the foods they were growing, gathering, catching, cooking and eating. The results of specialist analyses of carbonised plant remains, fish and animal bones, marine shells and residues trapped in pottery sherds illuminate the ways they kept themselves warm and fed, and how these changed over the several hundred years that the settlement was occupied.

The carbonised plant remains

Jennifer Miller and Susan Ramsay

The programme of routine bulk sampling resulted in 211 bulk samples, which were wet sieved on site prior to analysis. In addition, five spot finds of charcoal were identified. As many of the contexts from this site contained similar carbonised plant assemblages, this report provides an overview of the environmental findings and interpretation for the site as a whole.

Native woodland resources and driftwood

Very little evidence was found for the utilisation of native tree types as fuel at Milla Skerra. The only charcoal types that may be from native trees were small amounts of willow, hazel, oak and indeterminate conifers. However, even within these types, it is unlikely that oak would have been growing on Unst, or any of the Northern Isles, at this time. Willow and possibly hazel could have grown locally, but it is clear from the low quantities of charcoal of these types that any local presence must have been severely limited. Indeterminate conifer charcoal could include Scots pine, a native of mainland Scotland, the Western Isles and Orkney, but its native status in Shetland is not proven (Bennett *et al*. 1997). However, the large quantities of non-native spruce and/or fir charcoal recorded from the site suggest that the indeterminate conifer charcoal is probably poorly preserved spruce/fir rather than Scots pine. The lack of any significant tracts of woodland in Unst at this time is not surprising. Pollen evidence from Shetland suggests that, although woodland was present on these islands in the earlier Holocene, by the 2nd millennium BC any significant areas of woodland had been cleared and blanket mire had developed over much of the landscape (*ibid.*).

The largest proportion of charcoal found at Milla Skerra was spruce and/or fir. Neither of these genera is native to Scotland, or even the British Isles as a whole. Both spruce and fir charcoal have been identified from many archaeological sites in the Northern Isles, including Jarlshof (Dickson and Dickson 2000), Papa Stour (Dickson 1992) and Clickhimmin (Hamilton 1968) in Shetland and Knap of Howar (Dickson 1983) and Skara Brae (Dickson and Dickson 2000) in Orkney. These finds have been interpreted as evidence for the use and collection of driftwood, which probably originated in Scandinavia or the eastern seaboard of North America. Dickson (1992) considers North America as the more likely origin for the remains of driftwood found in Scottish archaeological deposits due to the nature of ocean currents during the later Holocene. The oak charcoal from Milla Skerra may also be the remains of driftwood used for fuel, or it may be derived from wood or artefacts brought from mainland Scotland.

Heather, turf and peat

Wood was not the main source of fuel used by the settlement's inhabitants. Heather-type charcoal and/or carbonised stems made up over 10% of the fuel waste found, while burnt peat/turf was over 80% of the total. As woodland was so scarce on Unst, and driftwood was an unreliable source, people would have had to make use of any other combustible material that they could collect. Much of the landscape of Unst would have comprised rough grassland and blanket mire, with members of the heather family growing on both types of habitat.

Peat was, and still is, commonly used in the Highlands and islands of Scotland as fuel, particularly in areas where woodland has been cleared and blanket peat has formed in its place. Archaeological evidence for the use of peat as fuel on Shetland has been found at Jarlshof and the Biggings, Papa Stour (Dickson 1999).

It is also likely that grassland or heathland turves were being burned, as there were frequent finds of carbonised stems and rhizomes of monocots (grasses and sedges), together with numerous finds of heather stems, including underground stems. Above-ground stems from heather-family types may have been collected specifically for fuel or initially for flooring, roofing or bedding but then subsequently used as a fuel source. Underground and above-ground stems of heather type could have been collected accidentally while cutting turves from heathland habitats. Some above-ground material must have been collected, as there were carbonised heather flowers and leafy shoots within the assemblage as well as seeds of crowberry (a heather-like plant). Seeds of grassland habitats were also recorded, including sedges, heath grass, knotweeds, redshank and buttercups, suggesting that a number of different habitats provided turves for burning at Milla Skerra.

An increasing reliance on turf for fuel, in addition to peat, is evident at many other prehistoric sites in the Northern Isles, including Skara Brae (Dickson and Dickson 2000), Howe (Dickson 1994), the Biggings (Dickson 1999) and Knap of Howar (Dickson 1983). At these sites, the emphasis on the use of turf depended upon the age of the site and the availability of other fuel resources. For example, turf was not the primary fuel at Skara Brae, but there woodland and driftwood were prolific enough to use in preference to turf. In contrast, turf was used as the pyre fuel at the Bronze Age cemetery at Linga Fiold (Bunting *et al.* 2001), probably due to necessity rather than choice.

Turf has often been valued in its own right as the fuel of choice for use in drying cereal grain and other situations requiring a fuel that burns with a slow, steady heat (Dickson 1998). In the case of cereal drying, this phenomenon is less likely to result in the grain itself catching fire. When wood is scarce, turf can become the main source of everyday domestic fuel for cooking and warmth, with turf from roofing material and byre waste also re-used in some instances for fuel (Fenton 1978). Wood, either from local sources or driftwood, may have been kept for specific purposes other than everyday domestic fuel, for example when a fire at a higher temperature was required for some industrial process. It would be difficult to maintain high temperatures with peat or turves, which tend to burn slowly, although if the peat was first made into peat charcoal it could then be used for processes requiring hotter temperatures.

Seaweed

A single fragment of brown seaweed was recovered from context 217, silty midden overlying the tumbled wall of yard 5. Seaweed has been used as fertiliser and domestic fuel since antiquity (Dickson and Dickson 2000) and particularly in the Northern Isles, where it has been recorded from multi-period prehistoric sites such as Howe (Dickson 1994). It may often be under-recorded due to small fragment size and the difficulty of identification within carbonised samples dominated by poorly preserved charcoal. As well as being useful for fuel, seaweed is rich in mineral salts, resulting in its use throughout history in many industrial processes, including soap and glass production and the cleaning of wool for cloth manufacture. It also has an important role as a soil fertiliser in areas where other organic resources are scarce (Fenton 1978).

Cereals

Carbonised cereal grain was present in many of the contexts examined, although never in great enough concentrations to suggest storage of grain or processing on any significant scale. The main cereal type present was six-row barley, with the hulled variety present in very small amounts. Only a single grain of wheat was recorded, while oats were entirely absent. Indeterminate cereal grains were the most common cereal type recorded, which suggests that the grains may have undergone several episodes of burning or been severely abraded over time.

Naked barley is the most common cereal type recorded from sites in the Shetland Isles during the Neolithic and Bronze Ages, including Ness of Gruting and Jarlshof (Dickson and Dickson 2000). However, the popularity of naked barley declined throughout the Bronze Age, being replaced by the hulled variety, which could be stored more easily due to the protective outer hulls of the grain (Van der Veen 1992). This progression occurred throughout Scotland, although Alldritt (2003) observed a short resurgence of naked barley during the Iron Age in the Northern Isles.

Only a single grain of wheat was recorded from the Milla Skerra assemblage. Many areas of Scotland are not conducive to the cultivation of wheat because the vagaries of the weather make it impossible to guarantee satisfactory yields. Here it is likely that any wheat was growing as a weed within the barley crop or as part of a system of maslin cultivation (where mixtures of cereal types are grown together) rather than having been grown as a crop in its own right.

Crop weeds were not common among the assemblage. Although several of the weed species recorded could grow in arable fields, particularly if the growing conditions were not at an optimum, only chickweed and corn spurrey would generally be considered as indicators of arable fields. Cereal-processing waste was very rare in the assemblage, with only a single context (175), an occupation deposit in cell 2, containing barley chaff in the form of rachis internodes. This could indicate that small-scale cereal processing was being undertaken in the cell.

The mammal and bird remains

Catherine Smith

The mammal and bird remains from Milla Skerra are fairly well-preserved, showing slight to moderate levels of abrasion, although the average fragment size is generally small. Bones were recovered both by hand-excavation and by sieving of soil samples. The latter contained a higher proportion of bone calcined by heat than the hand-excavated samples.

Species present

The mammalian species present in the hand-excavated component are shown in Table 4.1 (total numbers of fragments in brackets). Indeterminate mammal includes three worked fragments of unknown mammalian origin. Rabbit (*Oryctolagus cuniculus*) was present only in the windblown sand that sealed the abandoned structures. The presence of this species, which was not introduced to the Scottish mainland until the medieval period, is therefore not problematic, particularly given rabbits' well-known propensity to burrow through archaeological deposits. It does, however, flag up the possibility of redeposition of relatively modern material in these layers. Bird species were also plentiful, although the domestic fowl (*Gallus gallus*) was absent. All of the birds, with the exception of the now-extinct great auk, have been recorded in recent times in Shetland.

The sieved samples contained fewer species, but included fragments which may have come from a horse molar, although it was in a poor, degraded condition and a more positive identification could not be made. Also present in the retents were small mammal fragments, one of which was referable to house mouse (*Mus musculus domesticus*).

Table 4.1 Mammalian and bird species present in the hand-excavated component of the assemblage

Species	*Numbers of fragments*
Mammals	
Cattle	181
Sheep/goat	144
Pig	51
Cetacean	66
Seal species	3
Rabbit	9
Small mammal	3
Large ungulate	55
Small ungulage	113
Indeterminate mammal	1320
Birds	
Guillemot *Uria aalge*	12
Razorbill *Alca torda*	2
Black guillemot *Cepphus grille*	1
Little auk *Alle alle*	2
Great auk *Alca impennis*	28
Gannet *Morus bassanus*	21
Cormorant *Phalacrocorax carbo*	1
Shag *Phalacrocorax aristotelis*	19
Cormorant/shag *Phalacrocorax* sp.	13
Goose species *Anser* sp.	1
Eider duck *Somateria mollissima*	6
Duck species	1
Wader species	2
White-tailed sea eagle *Haliaeetus albicilla*	1
Passerine	3
Indeterminate bird species	89

Distribution of bones by phase

Bones accumulated on the ground surface beneath yard 5, indicating activity before its construction (phase 2A). They principally originated from domestic cattle, sheep and pigs and there was evidence that several fragments had been worked, among them several chopped cetacean vertebral fragments.

Cattle, sheep/goat, pig and cetacean bones were all present in deposits that built up during the use of yard 5 (phase 2B and 2C). In particular, the midden outside the yard contained plentiful fragments of bone. For the first time there was evidence of exploitation of seabirds, including great auk (context171, SF 1918), guillemot, little auk, gannet, duck species and sea eagle (context 238, SF 2232). Small mammal long bones were retrieved from a sieved soil sample (context 206, sample 177). The size of the specimens indicated they could have come from field mouse or house mouse, although neither can be confirmed.

The midden deposits that covered yard 5 in phase 3 provided further evidence of exploitation of great auk, as well as razorbill, guillemot, black guillemot and eider duck. In addition, marine species such as seal (context 208, SF 1890; context 217, sample 190) and cetacean were being utilised, as well as domestic cattle, sheep/goat and pig. As the ground level over the former yard was subsequently raised further with the addition of more midden material and stones (phase 4A), bones of cattle, sheep/goat, great auk, guillemot and gannet (context 201, SF 1878) were dumped.

Small numbers of bones, most of them from domesticated cattle and sheep/goat, were present in the occupation deposits that accumulated during the occupation of house 1 (phases 4B and 5A). A maxilla from a house mouse (sample 167, context 196) was found in the packing for the primary hearth. Two fragments of burnt tooth from the heap of midden and hearth waste that lay against the partition wall (sample 117, context 127) may have come from a horse, although this is not certain given the poor condition.

Few bones were associated with yards 3 and 4 (phases 4B and 4C–D), the assemblage consisting only of cattle and sheep/goat remains. In the small cell (2) (phases 5B, 7A, 7B), the mammal remains present were cattle, sheep/goat, pig and cetacean. Great auk, razorbill and gannet continued to contribute to the diet, while three bones, probably from the same individual small passerine bird, may represent a chance casualty (context 25, SF 663).

A collection of cetacean fragments (SF 777) came from a midden deposit (33) that covered the ruins in yard 6 (phase 7B). The largest consisted of a small whale vertebra with two chopped surfaces and hack marks parallel to the chopped surface. Three out of 20 other cetacean fragments were also chopped. Only a few bones were present in the midden which accumulated as the yards fell into disrepair (phase 7B); one bone was from cattle.

As all of the structures went out of use, they seem to have been used for dumping refuse (phase 7C). Cattle, sheep/goat and pig bones were all identified. Cetacean fragments were plentiful in this phase, particularly in context 7 (SF 151) where some of the fragments had been chopped, perhaps to aid oil extraction. A further cetacean fragment (SF 69) may have been part of a worked object. Bird bones were also numerous and included great auk, guillemot, gannet, cormorant, shag, goose and wader species. The great auk bones, 12 in number, were found in context 6 (SFs 24 and 97) and represent two different individuals.

As windblown sand accumulated thickly over the ruined settlement with periods of stabilisation in phase 8, animal and bird bones continued to accumulate in small quantities. Cattle, sheep/goat, pig, great auk, shag, cormorant/shag, and eider duck were present in this phase. Eleven bones of one juvenile individual probably came from a cormorant rather than a shag, based on size, but it was not possible to be more definite (SF 13). This bird had definitely been consumed since there were knife cuts on a femur. Similarly, the eider duck bones (SF 13) were slightly porous and were also probably from an immature bird, implying collection late in the breeding season.

Among the large stones lying above the 2nd–4th-century inhumation burial (phase 9) was a cattle upper molar tooth (context 17, SF 67). This is probably a chance inclusion in the deposit, although cattle teeth are known to have been deliberately included in graves of the later Iron Age.

Age of animals at death

Since only one cattle and one sheep/goat mandible survived, little can be said about the age at death based on tooth eruption and wear pattern. The surviving cattle jaw was from a young calf at Grant's (1982) wear stage 3 (phase 3A, context 130, SF 1844). The sheep/goat mandible had a wear stage of 36 in the scheme of Grant, corresponding to Payne's (1973) stage G, or from four to six years in modern terms. A less-reliable, but necessary, method of assessing age is to determine the state of epiphysial fusion of the long bones. Age categories based on the age range at which the epiphyses (articular ends) ossify and fuse to the shaft of the bones can therefore be assigned.

As might be expected for an island economy where providing winter fodder could be difficult, a high proportion of both cattle and sheep/goat were killed while juvenile or immature. Although there is a degree of overlap between the age categories, 32.7% of the ageable cattle bones came from animals in the youngest age groups, foetal/juvenile (F/J) or juvenile (J). At least 53.4% of the cattle died before reaching maturity and only 15.5% survived until adulthood (A). For sheep/goat the situation was fairly similar. Although fewer foetal/juvenile bones were retrieved, 30.5% of the hand-excavated sheep/goat bones came from animals in the youngest age group, although taken as an average, only 13.8% of the sheep/goat long bones came from adults in category A.

Somewhat surprisingly, no very young pig bones were found, either in the hand-excavated or sieved samples. However, this may be a reflection of the small number of available bones, as only 16 in total were complete enough for assessment of fusion. Of these, however, 43.8% came from animals which died while still immature (categories J/I and I) as opposed to 37.5% which came from fully mature adults.

Of the domestic animals, those which survived to adulthood represented the breeding stock which were kept alive over several winters, while the juveniles represented animals, more probably male than female, which would have been culled before the necessity of providing winter fodder became acute.

As regards the other mammalian species, there was evidence that young seals had died or been killed. Of the four seal bones recovered, three had unfused articular ends and were thought to have come from juvenile/immature animals. A fused proximal radius was dense and solid and probably came from an adult. The younger individuals may have been captured onshore at the breeding grounds.

Most of the bird bones appeared to be from adults, with the exception of an individual cormorant and an eider duck in phase 8. These were probably juveniles, implying collection during the breeding season.

Size of domestic animals

Where possible, anatomical measurements were made on the bones of cattle, sheep/goat and pig, although a high degree of fragmentation limited the number available. One cattle metatarsal (phase 2B, context 224, SF 2224) was estimated to have come from an animal of approximately 101.4 cm at the withers (von den Driesch and Boessneck 1974). The Milla Skerra beast was of small stature, much smaller than Neolithic cattle from Skara Brae, but compared fairly well with animals of Iron Age date. With the exception of the Neolithic animals, all of the examples from Orkney and Shetland would have appeared small by comparison with modern breeds. Platt (1934, 315) quotes a metacarpal length of 17.5 cm for a contemporary specimen from the 'small Shetland ox' in the collection of the Royal Museum of Scotland, which would have stood approximately 107.3 cm at the withers. The Milla Skerra animal would therefore have been slightly smaller.

A single intact sheep/goat radius from Milla Skerra (phase 2B, context 238, SF 2232) with a greatest length of 13.3 cm provided an estimated withers height of 53.4 cm (Teichert 1975). Davis (1996) has published baseline measurements for a modern flock of female Shetland sheep kept at Snelsetter, Orkney, for which the mean radius length is 13.6 cm, range 13–14.5 cm (*ibid.*, table 2, 596). The flock's mean estimated withers height is therefore 54.9 cm, range 52.5–58.5 cm. Iron Age sheep from Howe, Orkney had a mean withers height of 57.1 cm (range 51.9–63.1) based on the radius (Smith and Hodgson 1994, 7.3.1mf). The Milla Skerra sheep specimen, although short, falls within both the modern Shetland range and the Iron Age range. However, as the Milla Skerra radius was the only surviving intact sheep long bone, it is not possible to comment on the proportions of the limbs (for example, whether or not the animals were spindly-legged, with proportionally long metapodia as in the modern Soay). As to whether the Milla Skerra sheep were horned, there is only the evidence of a single horn core (phase 3A, context 130, SF 1921) which is short, with depressions similar to thumbprints at the base and possibly from a female. These depressions are thought to be associated with poor planes of nutrition.

Butchery and worked bone

Although evidence of butchery is limited by factors such as surface abrasion, small fragment size or burning, there was evidence that bones of domestic animals and cetaceans were chopped with sharp implements. Shafts of long bones were cut across during disjointing of carcasses and were also split lengthwise in order to extract marrow. Vertebral centra of cattle and sheep/goat were chopped in the median sagittal plane or were chopped laterally, removing the lateral processes. One skull fragment of a pig, a parietal bone, was chopped in half in the sagittal plane, presumably in order to extract the brain (phase 2C, context 205, SF 2032).

Cut marks were apparent on a few bones, although almost without exception the cuts themselves had become indistinct due to surface abrasion. Bones of cattle, sheep/goat, pig, large ungulate and indeterminate mammal all bore evidence of cut marks. A cattle tibia shaft bore thin parallel cuts on the shaft, thought to have been made by a metal knife (phase 2B, context 206, SF 2159). Deeper parallel cut marks were present on a rib of large ungulate (phase 7B, context 25, SF 669). Bird bones also provided evidence of cut marks, indicating meat removal. These included a femur from a young cormorant (phase 8, context 8, SF 13), a gannet humerus with four cuts at the proximal end (phase 7C, context 6, SF 85) and a great auk humerus with several small nicks along the outer edge, presumably made by a tool (phase 7C, context 6, SF 24).

Pathology

There was no evidence of pathology in the bones of the domestic mammals. Two bird bones, however, showed some degree of abnormality. Thickening of the shaft of a great auk coracoid (part of the shoulder girdle) by deposits of smooth bone, on both the dorsal and ventral surfaces, may be evidence of a healed fracture (phase 2B, context 224, SF 1943). Part of the carpo-metacarpus (a bone of the wing) from a shag appeared to have a misaligned fracture (phase 7C, context 7, SF 315). Whether these injuries allowed the affected birds to be more easily caught cannot be known, but it is possible.

Discussion

The faunal assemblage from Milla Skerra has provided evidence of the diet and subsistence strategies of the occupants of the site as well as an insight into the size and shape of the animals themselves. The people who lived and worked here relied on their domestic animals for meat, wool, hides and the raw materials to make objects for everyday use. If winter fodder was scarce, they must have struggled to keep their animals alive over the winter months, and there is evidence that many younger animals were killed, keeping principally the breeding stock alive until the next season. Fenton (1978, 429), in his classic ethnography of the Northern Isles, has written of the struggle to get the cattle, weakened by winter privation, on their feet in the spring – 'apo [upon] the liftin' – and it is likely that the Iron Age inhabitants of Unst faced the same problems of survival, both for their livestock and themselves.

One domestic creature which was entirely absent from Milla Skerra was the domestic fowl. Apparently chickens did not arrive in any great number to the north of Scotland and the islands until the advent of the Norse, although there is a token presence in the later Iron Age at the brochs of Crosskirk, Caithness (Macartney 1984, 136) and Howe of Howe, Orkney (Bramwell and Ballin Smith 1994, 157).

In addition to the domestic livestock, the people of Milla Skerra were fortunate in their marine resources. Seabirds such as auks of several species, cormorants and gannets were harvested for their meat, eggs and feathers in their season. Although younger birds were easier to catch on the nesting ledges of the islands, their bones were not numerous in the assemblage, which is mainly composed of bones of adults. This is possibly because bones of younger birds are softer than those of adults and are less well-preserved in burial conditions. Cliff nesting species were caught in historical times by setting nets against the rocks in which the birds were trapped. Eggs were also collected, although this was a hazardous occupation, involving as it did climbing down rock stacks while secured by ropes made variously of straw or pig hair which might be cut through by the sharpness of the rocks (Fenton 1978, 512–13).

The great auk (garefowl) seems to have been well used by the islanders, and was found throughout the occupation of the site. Being flightless, this species was easy to trap when at its breeding sites in the spring. The eggs were large, providing a good source of protein, and were also taken by hunters. Unfortunately, each pair laid only one egg annually and sadly it is easy to see, with hindsight, how it came to be hunted to extinction in the mid-19th century. Great auks are recorded from Neolithic Knap of Howar, Papa Westray (Bramwell 1983, 103) and broch sites of the Iron Age, for example at Howe of Howe, Orkney (Bramwell and Ballin Smith 1994, 153–4). They have also been recorded on archaeological sites as recent as the Norse period at Buckquoy, Orkney (Serjeantson 1988, 214).

The smaller auks, the guillemots (or *loom/longvie*, to give the Shetland name), razorbills (*sea craa*), black guillemots (*tystie*) and little auk (*rotchie*) have, however, survived to the present day and are still to be found breeding in the Shetland Isles, although they are no longer exploited for food. Somewhat surprisingly, no bones of puffin were recorded, although this species is eaten today in the Faroes and Iceland. Fenton records hunting of puffins on Unst, using hooked sticks thrust into the nesting burrows (1978, 518). Since the rabbit was not introduced to the islands until relatively recent times, it may be that puffins did not become plentiful until the opportunity to colonise rabbits burrows presented itself. Other factors affecting the food supply are of course highly important, as evident in the current decline in sea bird numbers in tandem with over-fishing of their prey species.

Gannets or Solan geese are still hunted in the Western Isles, although special dispensation from wildlife protection legislation is needed, and is limited to the men of Ness, Lewis, allowing them to make an annual trip to the rocky stack of Sula Sgeir. The young gannets (*gugas*) are captured using long poles with a noose at the end, plucked, singed to remove any stubborn feather quills and salted to preserve the meat (Beatty 1992).

Birds were not the only wild resource available. Besides fish, whales and seals were also utilised by the islanders. Whale (cetacean) bone was present in many of the phases of the site, although only a few fragments were recognisable as particular elements, such as vertebrae. Most of the recovered fragments were small chopped pieces, which were either the detritus from bone working, or from rendering for the oil which they contained. Whale oil was much valued for lighting and was used in rush lights (Fenton 1978, 548), but could also be used as a lubricant. Pilot or ca'in whales, so called because they were driven, or ca'ed, like sheep, were commonly caught off the Northern Isles and there are records of some which were captured in Unst in the late 18th century (*ibid.*, 547). Although the islanders appear not to have eaten the meat in the 18th and 19th centuries, choosing to leave the carcasses stripped of blubber to rot on the beach, this is in contrast to the situation in the Faroe Isles and it is far more likely that in Iron Age Shetland they would also have eaten the meat (*ibid.*, 549; Nicholson 1990,120).

It is notable that, throughout the occupation of the site, there seems to have been little change in the species which were exploited. Seabirds were caught and eaten from the earliest to the latest phases, an indicator of their abundance as much as of the strong nerves of the men who ventured on to the rocks and sea in order to trap them. Small whales were also harvested throughout the life of the settlement.

Finally, the presence of house mouse (*Mus musculus domesticus*) in a phase 4B context, the packing for the primary hearth in house 1, is of interest since there are few known occurrences of this species on the Shetland Isles in the Iron Age. It is believed that the house mouse was introduced to mainland Europe from the Middle East in the Bronze Age, as a consequence of increased cereal cultivation and storage (Yalden 1999, 122–3). Examples are known from Iron Age sites in England, including Gussage All Saints, Danebury and Maiden Castle, although the species may have been present at an earlier date (*ibid.*). On Shetland, the house mouse has been recorded from well-sealed early Iron Age contexts at Old Scatness broch (Dockrill *et al.* 2015).

The fish remains

Ruby Cerón-Carrasco

The fish remains from Milla Skerra were recovered by wet sieving through a 1 mm mesh and by hand during the excavations. The detailed results of the analysis are given in the catalogues (see archive report, Shetland Museum and Archives). The level of preservation of the fish bone was consistent throughout the site, in terms of fragment size and condition. Bones were most frequently 20–70 % complete. Their condition score was generally in the range of 6–9, indicating well-preserved to extremely poorly preserved bone.

Species present

A total of eight taxa were identified, consisting of six identified to species and two to family level. Table 4.2 shows the fish remains by area and phase. Fish remains were most abundant in the deposits that built up during the early use of yard 5 (phases 2B and 2C), including herring and very large cod. The thick midden layers that sealed it in phase 3 included a similar range of species and sizes as well as salmon and plaice. Small quantities of fish remains were recovered from deposits associated with the second

Table 4.2 Fish remains from Milla Skerra, showing the number of identified specimens per phase

Species	*2B–2C*	*3A–3B*	*4A*	*4B*	*5B*	*6A–6B*	*7C*	*10*
Saithe VS	24		19	4	11	21	4	
Saithe S	2	1						
Cod M	3	3					3	1
Cod L	7	4					1	5
Cod VL	3	1						
Ling M		1						
Ling VL		6		1				
Gadidae S	2	5	4					
Gadidae M		6						
Gadidae L	3	2	1					2
Gadidae VL							2	
Plaice		2						
Elasmobranch			1					
Herring adult	2							
Salmon		5						

hearth in house 1 (phase 5A). These were mainly from very small saithe, although a very large vertebra from ling over 150 cm long was also found. Remains of very small saithe were also found in midden deposits sealing the ruins of house 1 (phase 7B).

Discussion

The fishing strategies used by a past community can be inferred from the fish bone recovered at a site, by reference to biological data about the behavioral patterns of different fish and by reference to ethnographic data. Unless otherwise stated, most information on the habitat and size of the species described below derives from Wheeler (1969; 1978). The assemblage comprised five family groups of mainly marine fishes. The main group represented was the cod family group, that is the Gadidae.

Unst has been one of many productive fishing areas in Shetland (Goodlad 1971), so it is not surprising to encounter fish remains from earlier periods. In the Shetland Islands the exploitation of marine resources, particularly of fish, has proved easier than extracting food from the land, and it later developed into a prolific fishing industry. Much of the fishing tradition in Shetland developed from intermittent, local activity conducted in the voes or in tidal races between the islands with rod or handline (Gray 1978). Some of the fish caught, such as young saithe, have traditionally been used for immediate subsistence and for their oil, extracted from their livers. Cod and ling were also caught to be cured for preservation and were, from the Viking period at least, used for export.

Fishing at Milla Skerra appears to have been a broad-based activity, from the range of species and particularly the range of Gadidae (cod family) sizes. This size range implies that fish were caught from rock-pools, inshore and deeper water, probably using boats which would have been required particularly for catching large ling and cod.

Cod (*Gadus morhua*) has been one of the most important food fishes of the British fish fauna, and has been exploited ever since people began to fish the seas of Europe. They are common in all periods in the Northern and Western Isles, but their relative importance did change through time (Barrett *et al.* 1999). Their value as prime food is enormous, as their firm flesh allows for preservation as dried or salted stock fish, and they keep well for winter consumption or trade. In the northern North Sea, cod spawns in February and early March. Its growth rate varies with different populations: in the North Sea it can grow to an average of 18 cm in the first year, 36 cm in the second year, 55 cm in the third year and 68 cm in the fourth year. A mature cod can reach 150 cm in length and weigh up to 40 kg. Cod are widely distributed in a variety of habitats from the shoreline to well down the continental shelf, in depths of 600 m. Younger, smaller fish (less than 60 cm total length) usually live close inshore, while larger individuals tend to inhabit deeper waters. The cod represented at Milla Skerra ranged from small (30–60 cm total length) to very large (> 150 cm total length). The larger cod would have been caught from boats using long lines with multiple hooks (Goodlad 1971; Fenton 1978).

Saithe (*Pollachius virens*) is a common fish in northern inshore waters; some of its most important spawning areas are in the north-west of the British Isles. They are found in shallow water, particularly during their first three to four years. They spawn from January to April and by midsummer the young fish are found close inshore among weed-covered rocks and open bays. This immature phase lasts for at least two years, and mature fish are found slightly offshore. They increase in length by about 15 cm annually for the first three years, followed by approximately 10 cm annual growth for the next three years; they can reach a total length of 100 cm in their eleventh year.

Saithe are a shoaling fish and have been the target of seasonal exploitation from the earliest times and also more recently in the Northern Isles (Low 1813; Fenton 1978). In the recent past, immature saithe were caught by net (the 'poke-net') from rocky locations by simple rod and line or from boats in shallow waters. This was essentially a year-round activity, beginning in August with the catch of the smaller saithe (*sillucks* in local dialect) measuring 15–25 cm; by May they had grown to lengths of 30–35 cm (*kuths*) and were still being caught, after which they retired to deeper water and were less commonly fished (Low 1813, 193–4). In Shetland, from early 19th-century records, it is clear that saithe were the most widespread fish around the shores. The *sillucks* were regarded as 'the staff of life to the inhabitants' (Fenton 1978, 531) and their livers were removed to extract oil (Cerón-Carrasco 1994; 1998a; 1998b). In Shetland, saithe were hung and left to dry by the wind and sun without the use of salt. This dried fish was called *scrae-fish* (Fenton 1978).

The remains of saithe recovered at Milla Skerra came from all phases that produced fish remains and were from specimens of 15–30 cm long. It is likely that hooks used to catch young saithe were also used to catch other, medium-size gadids in the assemblage.

Ling (*Molva molva*) is essentially a deep-water fish occurring in waters of 300–400 m depth. It breeds between March and July, and most of its spawning grounds are north of the British Isles. Ling can attain a total length of 200 cm. Ling of medium to extra large size (200 cm total length) were represented at Milla Skerra, and these would have been taken using boats in deep water.

Herring (*Clupea harengus*) were present in small amounts, with vertebrae from adult specimens of up to 30 cm in length. These may have been caught by line rather than using nets, which would have produced larger catches. The assemblage also included flatfish plaice (*Pleuronectes platessa*) and a few remains of elasmobranch (shark, ray or skate).

Salmon (*Salmo salar*) at Milla Skerra were represented by vertebrae from adult specimens (60–80 cm total length). Salmonids may have been caught using lines with hooks, by spearing, or by using nets in the lochs, at sea or from the shore. Fishing for these could have been a year-round activity. Although several later prehistoric settlements in the Northern Isles have produced salmonid remains, including Scalloway broch (Cerón-Carrasco 1998c), they are relatively rare. Salmon remains have a relatively low density and are therefore more liable to differential preservation, but this alone cannot account for their low occurrence in Scottish sites (Barrett *et al.* 1999).

Although Milla Skerra produced a limited amount of fish remains, these have provided enough information to consider their importance in the exploitation of marine resources by the Iron Age inhabitants of Unst. Fishing at Milla Skerra appears to have been a year-round activity of a subsistence nature. Fishing from rocks or from boats in shallow water would have caught young saithe that could have been eaten fresh or preserved for later consumption, and their livers may have been used for oil. Other species would have been caught while fishing for this species. Boats would have been used to fish in deeper waters for larger gadids, particularly ling and adult cod.

Marine mollusca, with notes on crustacean and echinoidea remains

Ruby Cerón-Carrasco

The marine shell from Milla Skerra was recovered from the processing of bulk samples and collected by hand during the excavations. The results of the analysis, including crustacean and sea urchin remains, are presented in Table 4.3.

The shore is an environment subject to constant change, and different species have adapted to significant ecological variations within the littoral zone. The marine habitat comprises different dwelling and habitat zones, including the sublittoral and intertidal zones, and marine molluscs develop different shapes of shell among the same species in response to environmental factors.

The main species represented at Milla Skerra was the limpet (*Patella vulgata*); this is a species of major importance on most littoral shores and in shallow waters. It is present on all rocky shores from the most sheltered ones dominated by the algae *Ascophyllum nosodum* (L) to the most exposed, mussel- and barnacle-dominated ones.

Growth rates of limpets vary considerably, although studies in Orkney have shown that rates of growth are consistent from year to year (Baxter 1982). Characteristically, limpet growth rates are fastest in the first year, ranging from 5–15 mm, but declining by their third year to 3–10 mm growth. The growth rate then tends to remain relatively constant for several years before its virtual cessation. The Milla Skerra assemblage contains a higher proportion of adult than juvenile limpet.

Variations in limpet shell dimensions and shape are associated with particular environments: limpets on the lower shore are more exposed to the forces of waves than limpets on the upper shore, so the former tend to be flatter while the latter are more conical (Jones and Baxter 1985). A flatter, more streamlined shell has a smaller wave impact area than a more conical shell and is less likely to be knocked off the substrate. The overall size and shape of limpet shells from Milla Skerra suggest that they were gathered from exposed areas, as their flattened shape would have protected them from strong wave action. Fenton (1978) has noted that the early modern occupants of the Northern Isles collected limpets from low tide locations, as these were considered to be more tender and palatable than those collected from higher parts of the shore, which were mainly used as fishing bait.

Table 4.3 Marine mollusca at Milla Skerra, showing numbers per phase

Species	*2A*	*2B–2C*	*3A–3B*	*4A*	*4B (house 1)*	*4B (yards)*	*4C–4D*	*5B*	*6A–6B*	*7B*	*7C*	*8*	*9*	*10*
Limpet adult			388	31		1	3	19	17	18	52	20	9	18
Limpet juvenile			289	29		1		15	15	14	24		20	2
Crushed limpet shell	*	**	****	****	*	****	**	***	****	****	***	**	**	***
Crushed burnt limpet shell		*	**	**		**		**	**	**	**			
Periwinkle adult			148				56	65	1	1	69	3	4	4
Periwinkle juvenile			73					20			22	4	14	14
Perwinkle crushed shell			****	*			**	***	***	**	****	**		*
Periwinkle burnt crushed shell								*	**					
Oyster adult							1		1					
Crushed oyster shell						*		****	***	*	**			
Icelandic cyprine clam adult								2	**		18	13		3
Icelandic cyprine clam crushed shell			**					***		1	**	***	**	**
Icelandic cyprine clam burnt crushed shell								*		****				
Cockle adult			1					2		**	2	1		
Crushed cockle shell			*								*			
Crushed burnt cockle shell								**						
Crushed prickly cockle shell									**		1			
Prickly cockle burnt crushed shell								**	*		**			
Mussel adult			4					***			1			
Mussel crushed shell		*	***					*			*		*	*
Mussel burnt crushed shell			*											
Razor shell crushed														
Carpet shell adult			1											
Whelk adult			1											
Flat periwinkle adult									1		1			2
Rough periwinkle adult								2			4		3	

Table 4.3 Marine mollusca at Milla Skerra, showing numbers per phase (Continued)

Species	*2A*	*2B–2C*	*3A–3B*	*4A*	*4B (house 1)*	*4B (yards)*	*4C–4D*	*5B*	*6A–6B*	*7B*	*7C*	*8*	*9*	*10*
Dogwhelk adult							10				1	1		
Dogwhelk juvenile							16							
Dogwhelk crushed shell							**							
Oyster adult														
Crushed oyster shell														
Oyster burnt crushed shell														
Icelandic cyprine clam adult														
Icelandic cyprine clam crushed shell														
Crustacean claw fragment									***					
Sea uchin spines														

For crushed shell, quantities are indicated thus: * = rare; ** = present in low quantities compared to main species (<10); *** = present in large quantities, similar to other species within sample; **** = present in large quantities and predominant species within sample.

The edible periwinkle (*Littorina littorea*) was also plentiful in the assemblage. Mature periwinkles are slightly more abundant, although the quantity of juvenile specimens is also significant. It is therefore concluded that periwinkles were gathered mainly to be consumed by humans. Both limpets and periwinkle inhabit rocky locations, which would also explain the occasional dogwhelk (*Nucella lapillus*), which may have been caught accidentally while gathering periwinkles. The flat periwinkle and rough periwinkle specimens may have been gathered along with the seaweed with which these species are usually associated. Limpets, periwinkles, whelk and dogwhelk are gastropods with very sturdy shells, which survive well in archaeological deposits.

Mussels present in the assemblage would also have been gathered from rocky locations. Unlike the gastropods, this bivalve has a very fragile shell which breaks easily and is recovered generally as fragments.

Species from muddy/sandy substrates were also present. These were mainly bivalves such the Icelandic cyprine clam, prickly and common cockles, which have quite strong shells. Razor shell and banded carpet shell were recovered, although both species have quite fragile shells, particularly the razor shell, and would break easily. Oysters, a bivalve, were also present; these are mainly found in shallow waters and due to their fragile and layered structure they are mostly recovered as fragments, although some whole specimens were found. The whelk (*Buccinum undatum*) (a gastropod found in muddy/sandy substrates) was also present.

Discussion by phase

The greatest quantity of shells was found in contexts relating to the use of yard 5. The main species were limpet and periwinkle, with large numbers of specimens from mainly adult individuals. Abundant crushed shells, including burnt shells, occurred throughout all the phases and particularly in those relating to yard 5 (phases 2B and 2C), yard 3 (phases 4B, 4C and 4D) and cell 2 (phase 5B), and in the stony midden that was piled up over the obsolete yard 5 before yard 3 was built (phase 4A). Such fragments may represent the debris from molluscs used as food. Apart from limpet and periwinkle, other important edible species occurred throughout this part of the settlement, including oyster, mussel, razor shell, clams, cockles and mussel. All of these would have constituted an important part of the diet and would have been easily available. Only three non-edible species were recovered and in very minimal numbers: dogwhelk, flat periwinkle and rough periwinkle.

Very little shell was recovered from deposits relating to the occupation of house 1, although claw remains of the edible crab *Cancer pegurus* were recovered in hearth-waste deposits. The fragments were burnt, so the claws may have been roasted. Domestic hearth waste from phase 5A also contained remains of edible sea urchin (cf *Echinus esculentus*), which is common throughout Scotland. Sea urchin remains have been recorded at the Bronze Age site of Northton, Harris and in the late Iron Age settlement at Cnip on the Isle of Lewis (Cerón-Carrasco 2006). Sea urchin may be prepared by boiling or roasting on hot stones, although

Table 4.4 Results of organic residue analysis

21 samples		*Context*	*C14*	*C16:1*	*C16:0*	*C18:2*	*C18:1*	*C18:0*	*C20*	*C22*	*C24*	*C26*	*C28*	*C-30*	*n-ROH*	*Comments*
87	Windblown sand	8	5.6		6.7		5.2	5.1	11.7						59.2	
232	Glacial sub-soil	13	0.9		5.8		3.3	4.8	4.0	3.3	4.3	4.1	3.2		32.6	
84	Old ground, under site	67			5.9		3.1	5.8	6.0	3.9	1.1	2.4	3.6		21.0	
81a	Old ground, next to site	40			3.3		1.2	3.3	4.0	3.4	5.4	6.5	7.7	6.2	26.6	
81b	Old ground, next to site	40			3.9		1.3	3.8	4.6	3.5	4.9	4.9	10.5	7.5	22.0	
111	Hearth rake-out, house 1	107 (>106)	0.7		4.0		2.7	2.5	4.1	3.5	3.2	5.2	8.4		23.9	Large pottery sherds
119	Hearth rake-out, house 1	121 (<106)	1.2	0.7	4.8		2.4	2.8	4.1	3.3	3.4	2.0	7.9		16.5	Large pottery sherds
117	Hearth rake-out, house 1	127		2.8	7.9		7.2	4.9	7.0	4.7	4.7	2.4	5.1		12.3	Large pottery sherds; lots of bone
109	Midden in house 1	122	1.0		4.5			3.4	4.7	3.3	0.8	3.9	1.4		12.3	Lots of pottery + tuyere
226	Midden outside yard 5	224			5.8			6.7	7.0	5.3	2.7	2.7	10.4		18.0	Lots of bone and pottery
170a	Midden outside yard 5	130		3.3	5.0		3.0	5.3	6.1	3.7	1.0	2.2	7.6		17.8	Lots of shells
170b	Midden outside yard 5	130	1.0	4.3	5.0		2.3	4.2	4.5	3.0	0.8	2.1	7.2		28.9	Lots of shells
968	Sherd; probably not	127	0.7		4.1			1.4	1.4	3.4	4.5	4.6			12.1	Lots of bone. Organic rich, mainly intractable
1789	Sherd (sooty outside)	137 (Waste in hearth 1)	3.2	1.3	16.1		5.4	13.4	1.6	1.5	5.9	1.8			19.2	Lots of pottery
931	Sherd (sooty outside)	106 (Hearth rake-out Str 1)	9.4		41.9		3.5	37.4	2.3	1.5						Lots of pottery
1006	Sherd (sooty outside)	127 (Hearth rake-out Str 1)	9.7		42.5	2.2	5.8	35.8	0.9							Lots of bone
985	Sherd; large lump	122 (Midden overlying Str [illegible])			10.7		9.8	12.1	1.5	1.5		1.6			20.6	
955	Sherd; large lump	122 (Midden overlying Str [illegible])	5.4	2.3	41.2		2.9	48.2								
1900	Sherd; rough ware	224 (midden, outside Str 5)	9.2		10.8		6.1	6.8							34.4	
2022	Sherd; rough ware	224 (midden, outside Str 5)	5.0		19.8		5.0	19.9	5.0	4.4	5.2	3.3			6.8	Organic rich but mainly intractable
1500	Sherd; rough ware	130 (midden, after Str 5)	5.8		32.6		9.1	50.5								Organic rich but mainly intractable

Table 4.5 Fatty acid composition of plant and animal foodstuffs; weight percent of total fat based on data from Food Standard Agency 1998

	C<10:0	C10:0	C12:0	C14:0	C15:0	C16:1	C16:0	C17	C18:3	C18:2	C18:1	C18:0	C20:5	C20:1	C20:0	C22:6	C22:5	C22:1
Wheat	–	–	–	–	–	Tr	11.4	–	3.6	37.7	9.5	0.5	–	Tr	0.5	–	–	–
Greens[1]						3	13		56	16	7	Tr						
Pig	–	Tr	Tr	1.2	Tr	2.1	21.6	0.4	1.3	14	35.8	12.3	Tr	Tr	0.2	0.2	0.2	–
Beef	–	–	–	2.9	0.6	4.4	22.6	1	0.4	2	37.5	11.6	–	–	Tr	–	Tr	–
Lamb	–	0.2	0.5	5.3	0.7	1.6	19.9	1.1	1.6	1.9	34.3	16.8	Tr	0.2	Tr	–	0.2	–
Milk (cow)	7.1	2.8	3.8	10.3	1	1.8	26.5	0.5	0.5	1.8	20	10.3	–	0.3	–	–	Tr	–
Milk (sheep)	5.8	7.1	3.8	9.1	1.6	1	20.5	0.7	1	2.6	19.3	10.5	–	0.2	0.3	–	–	0.2
Hens eggs	–	–	–	0.3	–	2.2	19.9	0.4	0.7	14.3	35.4	7	–	0.3	0.4	–	–	–
Fish	–	–	–	3.7	0.4	5	12.9	0.2	1.2	6.5	17.3	3.8	4.4	5.6	–	16	1.7	5.4
Deer	–	–	0.3	4.9	1.6	3.2	19.2	1.1	3.2	9.2	14.1	16.2	1.1	–	0.3	–	2.4	–

[1] based on data from Gurr and Harwood 1991, 166

they can also be eaten raw. Like most marine species, this is a food rich in iron and must have been important to the diet of the inhabitants of coastal areas in prehistory. The fact that it has not been more widely recorded may be due to poor retrieval practices or other taphonomical losses.

Larger amounts of shell occurred in midden deposits that covered house 1 before and after its collapse (phases 6A and 6B). These included both whole specimens and fragments of limpet and periwinkle; a specimen and fragments of the Icelandic cyprine clam; common cockle; and fragments of the spiny cockle and oyster. Most of the shell was very fragmented or crushed, with a large amount of crushed burnt shell. All of these are edible shellfish.

The marine shell remains from Milla Skerra point to the exploitation of an easily accessible food source from the coast, obtained from rocky shores as well as sandy/muddy substrates. The large concentrations of limpets and their characteristic shell shape are consistent with an exposed situation, indicating that they were collected at low tide. It may also be assumed that shellfish were predominantly harvested during summer months, when the weather was milder, and that although some of the smaller specimens of limpet and periwinkle may have been used as bait, most of the shellfish was gathered and used for human consumption.

Geochemical analysis of pottery residues

Brendan Derham

Chemical analysis was undertaken of organic residues in several pottery sherds from Milla Skerra, aiming to gather evidence to help illuminate patterns of food processing and other agro-industrial activities that may have been carried out there (Gunstone *et al.* 1994; Heron *et al.* 1991). Organic residue analysis (ORA) was carried out using gas chromatography (GC) and gas chromatography-mass spectrometry (GC-MS).

Analysis of the pottery organic residues

Organic material associated with archaeological pottery sherds may be from a variety of sources: charcoal formed during maufacture or grease used in the manufacture that has survived a low-temperature firing; the post-firing addition of a sealant to the pottery surface; residues from the use of the pot; assimilation from the surrounding soil after deposition; and finally contamination during and after excavation. Analysis of the sherds produced a range of results (Tables 4.4 and 4.5).

The midden deposit (224) that built up outside yard 5 during its use in phase 2 contains two sherds (Small Find (SF) 1900 and SF 2022) which were rich in n-alkanols and with a fairly even distribution of fatty acids. These are therefore likely to represent heavily degraded organic material. One sample (SF 2022) is also rich in intractable organic material such as charcoal or burnt food.

In contrast, SF 1500 from the later midden deposit (130) that formed outside yard 5 contains a fatty acid profile rich in C_{16} and especially C_{18} fatty acids, but also with some C_{14} and $C_{18:1,}$ suggesting a ruminant animal fat such as sheep tallow. This sherd also contains intractable organic material that might be charcoal residual within the ceramic matrix and left *in situ* from the low-temperature firing of a pot rich in fibres or grease.

The loose midden (122) that covered the paved floor of house 1 contained SF 985, a sherd with a residue profile compatible with heavily degraded material, that is rich in n-alkanols and a fairly even distribution of fatty acids. In contrast, SF 955 from the same context contains few longer chain n-alkanols and fatty acids but near equivalent levels of C_{16} and C_{18} fatty acids as well as some C_{14}, $C_{18:1}$ indicating a ruminant fat. It is significant that palmitoleic acid $C_{16:1}$ is present, as it only commonly occurs in butterfat from cows.

The analysis included three sherds from cooking pots associated with the occupation of house 1, all from layers making up the thick mound of ash-midden behind the hearth: SF 1789 (context 137), SF 931 (106) and SF 1006 (127). SF 1789 contains mainly n-alkanols and fatty acids with only a limited excess of C_{16} and $C_{18,}$ suggesting that it does not contain residues associated with its use. In contrast, SF 931 and SF 1006 contain fatty acid profiles, the largest component of which is C_{16} as well as C_{14}, $C_{18:0}$ and $C_{18:1}$. The fact that SF 1006 even contains the readily degraded $C_{18:2}$ implies particularly good preservation in this sample. The evidence suggests that these two sherds were used to cook a seed-based material such as grain or nuts to make some kind of porridge.

The analyses provide evidence for the use of distinct foodstuffs, such as the cooking of porridge and the storage of butterfat, during the occupation of house 1. The presence of sheep tallow in a low-temperature-fired pot in the post-abandonment midden deposit outside yard 5 is open to two interpretations: either as storage of a foodstuff or grease, or its use as a binder in the manufacture of the pot. Chemical evidence for the dumping of debris from metal-working was also identified in the midden overlying the house 1 floor and in the midden outside yard 5.

Chapter 5

The making, using and breaking of pots

Olivia Lelong and Beverley Ballin Smith

The pottery recovered from the excavations at Milla Skerra reveals a great deal about how pots were made and used; the different forms and fabrics that potters were using over time, and how vessels were treated after they broke.

The pottery assemblage comprises 2,037 sherds and 2,793 fragments of pottery, with fragments defined as sherds which are missing one or both surfaces. Of the sherds, 1,755 are body sherds, 201 are from rims and 87 from bases; they represent up to 1,323 vessels. The pottery was recovered from 127 contexts and from all phases of the site. Most if it came from thick occupation and midden deposits associated with the yards and house.

Methods

The assemblage was analysed by context following the guidelines of the Prehistoric Ceramics Research Group (1995) along with those of Rice (1987) and Orton *et al.* (1993). A fabric series was developed for the assemblage and vessels were identified by diagnostic and/or conjoining sherds of the same fabric or by groups of sherds sharing the same fabric (and form, where it could be determined) – usually within Small Find (SF) numbers, but occasionally across them. This may have resulted in some sherds from different SF numbers being assigned to different vessels when in fact they originated from the same pots.

Sherds within each vessel group were counted and weighed by type (body, rim and base). The longest axis of the largest sherd was measured, along with average wall thickness and degree of abrasion. Firing profile, surface treatment, decoration, evidence for manufacture and alterations such as residues or sooting were noted. Vessel form and size were recorded where possible through descriptions of rim, base and body forms, measurement of rim and base diameters and recording the percentage of a rim or base present. Vessels with diagnostic sherds and those with distinctive characteristics such as perforations or evidence of re-use went through a second phase of more detailed recording to refine understanding of form, function and manufacture. The data were entered into a Microsoft Access database which forms part of the project archive, which has been deposited with Shetland Museum and Archives.

Fabrics

The fabrics fall into six main groups according to their predominant inclusions. Fabrics containing steatite are by far the most dominant, followed by sandy fabrics. Those containing mica, other rock inclusions, bone and shell are rare.

Table 5.1 sets out the fabric series. Table 5.2 shows the number of vessels in each fabric across the different phases of the settlement, along with the number per fabric in the three main external ground surfaces identified during excavation, differentiated by the phases to which they appeared to relate (contexts 40/75, 53 and 25). (Micromorphological analysis has interpreted these as ploughed middens and identified no distinctions or boundaries between them (see Ellis, Chapter 3); however, they were distinguished on excavation by differences in texture, colour and constituents and by their association with different structural phases (see Chapter 2).)

As discussed further below (see *Vessel forms* and *Making, using and breaking pottery at Milla Skerra*), some of the fabrics were consistently used to make vessels of certain forms and size ranges, apparently for particular uses.

Evidence for manufacturing and firing

While fabrics containing steatite dominate the assemblage, the coarseness and density of steatite inclusions vary considerably across them. Some may have occurred naturally in the clay (for example, the relatively sparse, pale inclusions in fabric S7). Others, like vessels made

Table 5.1 Fabrics identified in the assemblage

Fabric	Description
Steatite-rich fabrics	
S1:	A range of soft fabrics with sparse to moderate, well-sorted angular steatite grits, fine sandy texture and often a slightly sparkly appearance.
S2:	Medium-hard, fine, smooth fabric with moderate medium-size rounded steatite inclusions and sparse very coarse ones. Consistently used to make thin-walled (<8–10 mm) vessels, often burnished on the exterior, usually smoothed and sometimes burnished inside, well-fired in reducing conditions.
S3:	A range of soft, coarse, chunky fabrics, often with a rough, soapy texture but can feel smooth in better-finished examples. They contain moderate very coarse, well-sorted steatite grits, and sometimes also rare clay pellets and rock fragments which may occur naturally in the clay. Used to make large, heavy, thick-walled vessels. Includes three distinctive sub-groups:
S3a:	Soft, rough and soapy with an irregular fracture and common, well-sorted steatite grits. Fairly consistent firing profile with reduced core and oxidised surfaces, although one surface may also be reduced, in pale colours ranging from buff to light grey. Sherds are almost always highly abraded, indicating low durability.
S3b:	Soft and soapy with an irregular fracture and modern medium to coarse steatite grits. Usually oxidised throughout or on both surfaces. The exterior surface is typically smoothed so the inclusions lie flush with or just break the surface, giving sherds a brick-like appearance.
S3c:	Soft fabric with a soapy to smooth texture and moderate fine to medium steatite grits. Can be oxidised or reduced on exterior, and surfaces (especially exterior) are usually at least smoothed and often highly burnished.
S4:	A distinctive, smooth, medium-hard fabric with common very coarse angular steatite grits. Interiors are well-smoothed to make the steatite inclusions lie flush with the surface; the exterior may be smoothed or burnished. Pots are consistently reduced on the interior and core and either reduced or oxidised on the exterior. On a few examples (recorded as S4c), interiors are crudely burnished over a roughly wiped surface. This fabric was a favourite for cooking pots, suggested by frequent burnt residues.
S5:	A range of silvery, soapy, soft fabrics with moderate to common very coarse, poorly sorted steatite grits and often very common, fine, powdery steatite inclusions. May derive from steatiferous clays. Vessels may be oxidised or reduced.
S5a:	A sparkly-silvery, medium-hard, distinctive fabric with both very coarse and fine steatite inclusions and a soapy texture. Consistently used to make pots of medium wall thickness (average 11–13 mm) with smoothed and/or burnished interiors and exteriors, fired in reducing conditions.
S6:	A range of soft fabrics with a soapy, rough texture and hackly fracture. It appears packed with steatite grits (very common, very coarse, poorly sorted, sub angular). Vessels made in these fabrics are usually large, heavy and thick-walled and often fired in reducing conditions.
S7:	A smooth, medium-hard fabric containing sparse to moderate, coarse, sub angular steatite grits and sometimes rare rock inclusions. Pots made in S7 are frequently burnished on the interior and smoothed or burnished on the exterior, masking the inclusions.
Sandy fabrics	
Q1:	A range of soft fabrics with sparse to moderate, fine to medium, well-sorted quartz sand grains and sometimes rare dark rock inclusions. Vessels are usually oxidised throughout or oxidised with reduced cores, but occasionally reduced throughout.
Q2:	A range of medium-hard fabrics with fine, sandy texture containing sparse, moderately sorted sand grains that may occur naturally in the clay.
Q3:	A range of fine, sandy, medium-hard to hard fabrics with sparse, well sorted sand grains. Vessels are thin-walled and well-made and fired in a range of conditions.
Micaceous fabrics	
M1:	Soft fabric with a smooth, sandy texture, containing sparse, medium to very coarse, poorly sorted mica inclusions which may occur naturally in the clay.
Rock-bearing fabrics	
R1:	A hard fabric with a hackly fracture and rough texture, containing sparse, poorly sorted, fine, sub angular inclusions of shiny black rock which may occur naturally in the clay.
R2:	A hard fabric with a hackly fracture and rough texture, containing sparse to moderate, poorly sorted, coarse, sub angular inclusions of shiny black rock.
Bone-gritted fabrics	
B1:	A soft fabric with a fine, sandy texture and sparse, coarse, dull white inclusions which are thought to be bone fragments.
Shell-gritted	
SH1:	A soft fabric with a fine, sandy texture containing rare to sparse dull fragments of shell with a curved or plate-like structure.

Table 5.2 Numbers of vessels in each fabric according to phase

Phasing key												
5th–4th C BC		*4th–3rd C BC*	*2nd–early 1st C BC*			*1st C BC–1st C AD*		*1st C AD*		*late 1st–2nd C AD*		*5th–6th C AD*
Yard 5 - before and during use		*Midden heaped over yard 5*	*Midden & ground prep over yard 5*	*Yards 3 & 4 & house 1 built*	*Yard 3 altered, yard 4 obsolete*	*House 1 in use*	*Yard 3, cell 2 built*	*Midden over house 1*	*House 1 collapses, more midden*	*Yard 3, cell 2, yard 6*	*Structures tumbling*	*Temporary occupation*
2A	2B/C	3A/B	4A	4B	4C/D	5A	5B	6A	6B	7B	7C	10

PHASE	*2*		*3*		*4*		*5*		*6*		*7*		*10*	*External ploughed middens*		
Fabrics	*2A*	*2B/C*	*3A/B*	*4A*	*4B*	*4C/D*	*5A*	*5B*	*6A*	*6B*	*7B*	*7C*	*10*	*75/40*	*53*	*25/32*
B1											2					
M1		3		11		3						1	1	1	3	
Q1		16	54	65		34	7	4	1	3	33	18		33	34	28
Q2		2	2	1		4				1	4	1		1	4	4
Q3													13			
R1			3	3		1			1			1		2	1	2
R2		1	1	3				1								
SH1		1		1	1			1							1	1
S1	6	70	91	46	11	6	43	23	51	26	20	81		52	73	69
S2	2	26	16	3	7	2	30	10	9	11	6	16		24	34	52
S3		5	19	10	7		25	14	14	11	6	2		14	19	19
S3a		1	1	2	1		5	1	1	13	15	3				3
S3b		5	3		1					3	1					
S3c					5		7									
S4	2	6	7	8	6	2	37	17	15	25	11	5		5	12	14
S4c								1	4							
S5	5	16	40	3	18	6	20	38	10	12	19	69		19	35	42
S5a	1	40	3	3	1			1		1	1	2	1		4	1
S6	1	2				1			4			1				
S7			1				23		3	2	4	1			4	

in fabrics S2 and S4, contain steatite grits of consistent density and coarseness which are more likely to have been added as temper. Analysis of steatite recovered during the excavations identified a high proportion of raw material; this was interpreted as working debris from the crushing and grinding of steatite, possibly to use in pottery production (see Forster, Chapter 6; MacSween 2009). Added as temper, steatite would have increased the capacity of pots to absorb, store and evenly radiate heat, making them more resistant to thermal shock from cooking fires (Rice 1987, 229).

Fabric groups dominated by sand, rock and mica may derive from sandy or micaceous clays or where rock fragments occurred naturally in the matrix, rather than indicating deliberately added temper. A few examples (mainly S1 and Q1) contain grog inclusions, where pottery sherds have been ground up and mixed into the wet clay. The bone and shell fragments found in a few fabrics are likely to have been added as filler in order to increase resistance to thermal stress (ibid). No vesicular pottery (in which organic temper has burned out during firing, leaving voids in the fabric) was observed. There is some evidence from across the site of pots having been packed with dry grass before firing. Grass marks are visible, for example, on V 242, V 263, V 275, V 285 and V 283 from post-collapse midden in house 1 (phase 6B), and on a few other vessels from phase 2A, 2B/C, 3 and 5B deposits.

The assemblage displays considerable evidence of manufacture. Coil joins (both N- and H-shaped) were noted on 150 vessels (11% of the total), indicating they were constructed from the base to the rim by the progressive addition of slabs or coils of clay. Failed joins are common throughout all phases, as many pots broke horizontally along the coil join. About 79% are N-shaped in section, where the edges of the slabs were thinned, placed side by side and pressed together. The other 21% are H-shaped in section, where a tongue at the edge of a coil or slab fitted into a groove on the corresponding piece. The coils that could be measured average 40 mm in height. A thin slip or mask of clay was applied over joins, but this was often not strong enough to keep the vessels intact when they were knocked or otherwise put under stress.

The manufacture of rims to neck or body, and bases to base edges, often failed due to poor finishing of the join. Some rims were secured more firmly by finger moulding (for example, V 208 in phase 6A), grooving (V 220, phase 6A), finger nicks (V 262, phase 6B) or finger tucks (V 483 and V 463, phase 2B/C). On V 283 (phase 6B), it is possible to see how the base was joined to the wall: the coil for the wall was thickened at this point, with an applied layer that was smoothed down over the outside of the base. On the large, bucket-shaped V 286 (Fig. 5.4) from the same context, the joint between the wall and base is visible where the potter did not completely smooth it over. On V 79 (phase 5A), two or three finger dimples are visible externally at the junction of the base with the wall, where the potter pressed the pieces together. Fingertip and nail impressions are visible on a number of pots – for example, V 321 (phase 7B), V 29 (phase 4B) and V 437 (phase 2B/C). These marks are rare evidence of manufacturing methods for steatitic pottery, which is relatively soft and easily abraded.

The assemblage shows interesting evidence of its firing conditions. About half of the pots (50.2%) were fired upside down, so that oxygen reached the external surfaces. The other half (49.8%) were fired in reducing conditions, but again most of the pots were placed upside down in the kiln or clamp, with the internal surfaces of 73% reduced. The variety of colours noted is largely a product of the manufacturing process, but some were produced through a vessel's prolonged use on the hearth. For example, the fabric of V 553 (Fig. 5.2), a large, globular cooking pot, is quite friable with surface cracking around the temper and erosion of the surface. It was found on the midden (151) piled over the obsolete yard 5 in phase 3, and most of the vessel is represented. It appeared to have been tossed nearly whole onto the midden, perhaps after fracturing on a cooking fire.

Surface treatments and decoration

A high proportion of vessels show evidence for surface finishing. About 5% exhibit wiped striations on their exterior (71) or interior (68). About 18% (243 vessels) have smoothed exteriors, while 30% (397) have smoothed interior surfaces. Burnishing is evident on the exteriors of 23% (309 vessels) and on the interiors of about 7% (96). A few (102, over 7%) have what appears to be an external slip; most of these are thin-walled cooking pots made in fabric S2. A possible interior slip was identified on four vessels.

Some show evidence of knife trimming to remove protruding grits and other irregularities while the pots were drying to leather-hard state. For example, V 30 (phase 4B, house 1) displays marks of knife trimming beneath its burnished surface. It is quite possible that three narrow incised lines, *c*. 10 mm apart on the top of the rim of V 89 (phase 4B), are the result of knife trimming rather than decoration. Some vessels, such as V 767 (phase 4C/D), had surface bumps that were not removed prior to burnishing or by the burnishing process. Other pots were well-burnished but the finish was lost as the surface flaked and laminated due to low-temperature firing (for example, V 114, phase 4B).

Burnishing of exterior surfaces was the most common surface treatment. Some interior surfaces may have been burnished to increase impermeability to liquids rather than for aesthetic reasons; the roughly wiped, crudely burnished interiors of pots made in fabric S4c are probably examples of this.

A few sherds bear incised marks, although those on V 89 (described above), the two grooves on V 1201 (phase 7), and the shallow incised line on V 906 (phase

7C) could have been incidental, acquired during knife trimming or use. One vessel – V 675 (phase 4A) in a Q1 fabric – has what looks like an incomplete incised star (Fig. 5.2). The assemblage is striking for the almost complete absence of decoration. This may be partly due to the prevailing use of steatite temper; decorative motifs would have worn away quickly through the handling and use of pots made in soft, steatitic fabrics. Even so, some traces might be expected to have remained and thus the general lack of decoration appears to a real attribute of the assemblage.

Vessel forms

The forms evident from the diagnostic sherds indicate a broad trend from squared, flared and everted rims in the earlier phases of the settlement towards plain, upright rims in the later phases (Table 5.3). Understanding how vessel forms changed over time is complicated by the degree to which many deposits, especially middens, were reworked and moved around during the lifetime of the settlement.

Where a diameter to height ratio can be assessed, vessels are described as jars (where the height exceeds the maximum diameter) or bowls (where the height is less than the maximum diameter) (Downes and Lamb 2000, 40). Several broad, shallow vessels were also among the Milla Skerra assemblage and these are described as dishes, bowls or platters.

Phase summary

Tables 5.4–5.10 and Figures 5.1–5.6 show the vessel forms identified from contexts associated with each phase. These contexts represent when sherds reached their place of final deposition, which may have occurred some time after pots broke and in a different place altogether. In other words, some sherds were found not where vessels broke (primary context of deposition) nor where they were first discarded after having been gathered up (secondary context of deposition), but where they were subsequently moved along with other midden material (tertiary context of deposition). That said, there are some clear differences in form and fabric between phases.

Phase 2A: Earliest activity

Sherds from up to 11 vessels were found in the ground surface (234) pre-dating the construction of yard 5, and all are in steatite-rich fabrics. They are represented by sharply

Table 5.3 Overview of rim and base forms according to phase (see Table 5.2 for phasing key)

Rim/base form	*2A*	*2B/C*	*3A/B*	*4A*	*4B*	*4C/D*	*5A*	*5B*	*6A*	*6B*	*7B*	*7C*	*10*
Everted rim		1	9	13	4	3	3	5	1	1	3	1	
Sharply everted rim	1		5			1							
Slightly everted rim		1	2	2	1	1	2						
Everted rim, flat top		6						1					
Flat rim			1						1				
Flared rim		2	3	2	1	1					1		
Plain rim	1	6		1	5	9	7	12	5	10	10	7	
Plain rim, internal bevel		1				3	2	2	5	2			
Plain rim, external bevel							1			1			
T-shaped rim		1											
Upright rim, flared, external bevel					1								
Beaded rim		1		1						1			1
Splayed rim									1				
Shallow dish with plain rim, rounded base		1											
Shallow dish with plain rim, flat base, angled walls					1	1		1					
Flat base						1							
Flat base, angled walls	1	3	2	2	3		7	1	2	2	1		
Dished base		1											
Flat base, straight walls		1					1			1			
Rounded base									1				

Table 5.4 Rim and vessel forms from phase 2 contexts

Sub-phase: contexts of deposition	*Vessel nos*	*Fig.*	*Rim/base type – vessel form*	*Rim diam. (mm)*	*Sooting/residue*
2A: pre-yard 5(context 234)	**391**	5.1	T-shaped rim – carinated	150	
2B: external	405 **407** 410	5.1	plain rim – barrel-shaped	50	Y
middens (contexts 206,	438 **531**	5.1	flared rim – open-mouthed bowl	50–130	Y
224, 238) and ground	439 480		plain rim	60	Y
surfaces (contexts 236,	**490**	5.1	plain rim, interior bevel	60	
237) contemporary with	496		slightly everted rim		Y
use of yard 5	**430**	5.1	sharply everted rim – globular	50	
	443 **463** 471	5.1	everted rim, flat top – globular	130-150	Y
	483 442	5.1	T-shaped rim	130	
	411	5.1	plain rim – shallow bowl	65	

Numbers of illustrated vessels are shown in bold.

Table 5.5 Rim and vessel forms from phase 3 contexts

Sub-phase: contexts of deposition	*Vessel nos*	*Fig.*	*Rim/base type – vessel form*	*Rim diam. (mm)*	*Sooting/residue*
3A: over yard 5	**553** 573	5.2	everted rim – globular	130–170	Y
(context 171)	**552 563**	5.2	sharply everted rim	70–80	Y
	532	5.2	slightly everted rim	150	Y
3A: outside	640 616		flared rim	60	Y
yard 5 (contexts 129, 130, 208)	578 581 **598** 623 637	5.2	everted rim	45–120	Y

Numbers of illustrated vessels are shown in bold.

Table 5.6 Rim and vessel forms from phase 4 contexts

Sub-phase: contexts of deposition	*Vessel nos*	*Fig.*	*Rim/base type – vessel form*	*Rim diam. (mm)*	*Sooting/residue*
4A: midden under	**675 676** 687 693	5.2	everted	50–60	Y
yards 3 and 4	699 702 730				
(100, 102, 161, 162)	688 690		slightly everted	35	
	705		plain		
4B: house 1 construction,	15 **30**	5.3	everted	55–140	Y
early use	**25**	5.3	beaded – globular	170	Y
(124, 137, 169, 189)	26		flared	250	Y
	21		plain		
	14	5.3	plain – shallow bowl	170	Y
	87	5.3	rolled – globular/barrel	120	Y
	89	5.3	plain, internal bevel	75	
4B: yards 3 and 4	**749 756**	5.2	everted	60–100	
construction, early use	**754**	5.2	beaded	130	
(26, 42, 86, 99)	**750** 757 762 764	5.2	plain	85–125	
	767	5.2	plain	110	

Numbers of illustrated vessels are shown in bold

Table 5.7 Rim and vessel forms from phase 5 contexts

Sub-phase: contexts of deposition	*Vessel nos*	*Fig.*	*Rim/base type – vessel form*	*Rim diam.(mm)*	*Sooting/ residue*
5A: house 1 ash-midden	60 77 78 108 109		plain rim	100–160	Y
(contexts 105, 108, 125, 127,	113 **122** 173	5.3	flat base – barrel-shaped	115	Y
132, 138, 145, 150)	131		plain rim, external bevel	80	
	107		plain rim, internal bevel	60	
	125 168 787		everted rim	70	Y
	130 172		slightly everted rim	130–210	Y
5B: cell 2 construction	806		plain rim, internal bevel		
(185, 187)	745		globular form		Y

Numbers of illustrated vessels are shown in bold

Table 5.8 Rim and vessel forms from phase 6 contexts

Sub-phase: contexts of deposition	*Vessel nos*	*Fig.*	*Rim/base type – vessel form*	*Rim/base diam. (mm)*	*Sooting/ residue*
6A: house 1	**220**	5.4	everted rim – globular jar	120	Y
abandoned	186 189 206 **207**	5.4	plain rim – barrel-shaped	50–180	Y
(contexts 122, 123)	228				
	193 219 **231**	5.4	plain rim, internal bevel	70–135	
	208		splayed rim – globular jar		
	184	5.4	flat rim – shallow bowl	120	
6B: house 1	**266**		everted rim	150	Y
post-collapse	**262**	5.4	beaded rim – barrel-shaped	60	
(contexts 47, 49,	235 242 246 263		plain rim	80–130	Y
104)	264 273 **275** 281	5.4	plain rim – barrel-shaped		
	282				
	255 **288**	5.4	plain rim, internal bevel – barrel-shaped	195	
	286	5.4	flat base, angled wall – bucket-shaped	140	
	301	5.4	plain rim, external bevel	100	

Numbers of illustrated vessels are shown in bold

everted, squared, T-shaped and plain rims – for example, V 391 (Fig. 5.1; fabric S2) (see Table 5.4) Several of the rims are comparable to forms from late Bronze Age to early Iron Age vessels found elsewhere in Shetland (see *The wider context* below).

Phase 2B/C: Yard 5 occupation

The contexts associated with the use of yard 5 and deriving from nearby domestic activity (phases 2B and 2C) contained much larger quantities of pottery – from up to 147 vessels – in various forms and fabrics, although steatite-rich ones still dominated (see Tables 5.2 and 5.4). Many were thin-walled, well-fired, burnished cooking pots made in fabrics S2 and the sparkly S5a, which made its strongest appearance in this phase. Straight(er)-sided or barrel-shaped pots had plain rims (for example, V 407) and the internal bevel on the plain rim of V 490 could have supported a lid, although the actual shape of the pot is not clear (see Fig. 5.1). Others were jars with distinctive T-shaped or flattened, everted rims (V 463 and V 483 in Fig. 5.1). There were also more open-mouthed bowls with flared rims (V 531, Fig. 5.1). A shallow bowl or platter with a rounded base (V 411 in Fig. 5.1) could have been used for communal meals. This appears to be a long-lived form, with examples also found in deposits that formed in phase 4B (V 14, Fig. 5.3) and phase 6A (V 184, Fig. 5.4).

Phase 3A/B: Midden covering yard 5

Of the sherds from *c.* 150 vessels found in midden that covered yard 5, many were from cooking pots with flared or everted rims (Table 5.5). Some were thick-walled and heavy-bodied with rim diameters of 70–170 mm, such as the large, globular, burnt cooking pot found on a phase 3 midden (V 553, Fig. 5.2). In contrast, V 552 (S2) and V 563 (Q1) are both finer, almost biconical vessels with residues

Table 5.9 Rim and vessel forms from phase 7, 8 and 10 contexts

Sub-phase: contexts of deposition	*Vessel nos*	*Illus.*	*Rim/base type – vessel form*	*Rim/base diameter (mm)*	*Sooting/ residue*
7A/B: cell 2 late use	789		everted rim		Y
(contexts 51, 54, 57)	809 812 814		plain rim	70–110	Y
	839	5.5	plain rim	70	
7B: yard 6 (context 33)	**321** 327	5.5	everted rim	60	Y
	358	5.5	flared rim	80	
	332 336 337 343 344 345 348 349 350 353	5.5	plain rim	80–150	Y
	342	5.5	flat base, angled walls	60	Y
7B: final use of yard 3, cell 2	834		everted rim	120	
(contexts 27, 35)	**819**	5.5	slightly everted rim	70	
7C: sandy midden	**869**	5.5	everted rim	50	
(context 7)	868 898 902		plain rim		Y
	870		plain rim – barrel-shaped		
	920 930 938				
8: innundation (context 8)	948		plain rim – barrel-shaped	70	
10: temporary camp (context 5)	**956**	5.5	beaded rim – barrel-shaped		

Numbers of illustrated vessels are shown in bold

Table 5.10 Rim and vessel forms from ploughed middens outside the yards and house

Sub-phase: contexts of deposition	*Vessel nos*	*Fig.*	*Rim/base type – vessel form*	*Rim diam. (mm)*	*Sooting/ residue*
Formed by start of phase 4B:	976 **979** 982 984	5.6	everted rim – globular	60–80	
ploughed middens (contexts	989 1004				
40, 75) pre-dating yards and	987 **992**	5.6	flared rim	60–120	Y
house construction	**986**	5.6	flared rim, beaded	70	
	1155		plain rim	120	
	1156		everted rim	80	Y
Formed by start of phase 5B:	1071 1075 1096		everted rim	75	Y
ploughed middens (contexts					
53, 72, 98) pre-dating cell 2	**1079**	5.6	sharply everted – carinated	95	Y
construction	**1088**	5.6	slightly flared rim	55	
	1068		flared rim	35	
	769 1050 1059		plain rim	50–115	Y
	1084 1087 1097		plain rim	50	
	1112		plain rim		
	1129		plain rim, carinated	80	
	768 803 1083 1098		plain rim, internal bevel	130	Y
Formed by start of phase 7C:	**1242** 1246	5.6	everted rim, beaded	80–150	Y
ploughed midden (contexts					
25, 32, 120) pre-dating	**371**	5.6	slightly everted	60	Y
accumulation of sandy middens	784		everted rim, flat top	100	Y
	1171 1174		plain rim	60	Y
	1178 1195 1196		plain rim	60	Y
	1205 1250		plain rim		
	1224		plain rim, internal bevel		

Numbers of illustrated vessels are shown in bold

around their narrow mouths (Fig. 5.2). These smaller, better-made pots may have been used for drinking soup or other liquids. V 532 and V 598 (both fabric S1) are thicker-walled jars with short, flared rims (Fig. 5.2), both bearing burnt residues. Sandy Q1 fabrics were very much in use, along with a range of steatite-rich fabrics (see Table 5.2).

Phase 4A/4B: Thick, stony midden underlying yards 3 and 4

More than 100 pots were represented by sherds found in the midden material piled up before the construction of yards 3 and 4 (phase 4A). Several were small, thin-walled vessels with everted rims of only 50–80 mm diameter (Table 5.6). Pots made in fine, highly burnished S2 and S5 fabrics were also abundant, and some have burnt residues. One thin-walled pot bears what appears to be an incised star on its rounded shoulder (V 675, Fig. 5.2).

Phase 4B: Construction and early use of house 1

Sherds from two highly burnished pots were set into the yellow clay that formed the base for the first hearth in the house (see Table 5.6). V 25 was a thick-walled, heavy cooking pot (fabric S3c) with a thick, rolled rim, while V 30 was a finer, smaller vessel (fabric S2) (see (Fig. 5.3). The sherds were set into the clay with their burnished surfaces facing up. The majority of rims from this phase are flared or slightly everted, with a few plain examples. Part of a heavy, shallow, flat-based bowl or dish (V 14, Fig. 5.3), made in fabric S6 and thickly tempered with steatite grits, was found in a basal deposit in the house. It is very similar in form to V 411 (Fig. 5.1) and V 184 (Fig. 5.4). External sooting and residue indicate it was used for cooking, perhaps for frying fish. Other cooking pots in steatiferous fabrics include V 87 (Fig. 5.3), a thin-walled cooking pot with an internal residue, and V 89 (Fig. 5.3), which has parallel incised lines on top of its plain rim; both were found in early hearth waste deposits.

Phase 4B: Construction and early use of yards 3 and 4

Sherds from up to eight pots were incorporated in the south wall of yards 3 and 4, perhaps having been scooped up with midden that was used to pack the rubble wall core or deliberately tucked into the core while it was being built (see Table 5.6). They include vessels with plain, flared and everted rims, such as V 749, 750 and 754 (fabric S5) and V 756 (fabric S3) (see Fig. 5.2).

Phase 5A: House 1 in use

As house 1 continued in use, sherds from up to 147 pots were piled up along with ashes and food waste to the south of the hearth and behind it to the east, against the internal partition. These were mostly cooking pots – thick-walled, flat-based vessels with straight or angled walls, some bearing residues (Table 5.7). They were generally tempered with steatite, probably to increase thermal strength, although the high percentage of base sherds suggests many broke during cooking. Vessel bases range from 60 to 130 mm in diameter, while rims range from 70 to 201 mm. A large, barrel-shaped jar (V 122, Fig. 5.3) was perforated near its rim and suspended, probably over a fire; the cord on which it hung wore a V-shaped notch in the fabric (not illustrated).

Phase 5B: Construction of cell 2

Parts of several vessels were placed in the wall of cell 2 during its construction. They include a large body sherd from a small, globular cooking pot with a lustrous, burnished exterior (V 745, fabric S2), which was set into the yellow clay used to bond the wall, and part of a plain-rimmed pot with an internal bevel (V 806) (see Table 5.7).

Phase 6A/6B: Abandonment and collapse of house 1

After house 1 ceased to be occupied, the midden spread over its floor included sherds from up to 58 pots along with stone tools, food waste and ashes. Sherds from a further 86 pots were later left, along with more organic and hearth waste, over the collapsed walls (phase 6B). Most of the vessels had plain rims, some with internal or external bevels (Table 5.8). Some were clearly barrel-shaped jars like V 207 (Fig. 5.4). Everted, beaded and splayed rims occur on a few examples, such as a large, globular cooking pot thickly tempered with steatite (S4) (V 220, Fig. 5.4). Some of the heavy bases came from thick-walled, bucket-shaped pots (for example, V 286, Fig. 5.4). Part of a shallow bowl or platter, perhaps used for communal meals (V 184, Fig. 5.4), was also left there. It appears very similar to V 411 (Fig. 5.1, phase 2B/C) and V 14 (Fig. 5.3, phase 4B).

Phase 7A/7B/7C: Final use of the settlement

Small, straight-sided and barrel-shaped jars with rather modest plain, flared, beaded or slightly everted rims dominate the up to 382 vessels represented among sherds from the final phases of the settlement (Table 5.9), when people were piling midden in the roughly built yard 6, leaving bog ore and hearth waste in the older yard and cell, and finally letting walls fall into disrepair. V 332 (Fig. 5.5), for example, is a coil-built, thin-walled cooking pot with a plain rim (S2). V 869, a silvery, soapy (S2) jar with an everted rim above a straight wall (Fig. 5.5), appears identical in form and similar in size to V 676 from phase 4A (Fig. 5.2). Radiocarbon dates for material from these different phases indicates a span of at least 225 years between them (see Table 2.1). This seems to suggest either the longevity of certain pottery forms or the long curation and much later re-use of midden at the settlement.

Exterior ploughed middens

A much larger and more varied assemblage (representing up to 238 vessels) was recovered from successive layers of cultivated infield outside the buildings. Ploughing evidently mixed older and newer constituents, producing this variation, but there are some clear distinctions between the cultivated soils of different phases (Table 5.10). The earliest ploughed midden layers (contexts 40 and 75, which extended beneath the walls of yards 3 and 4 and house 1) contained a number of everted and flared rims, including V 979, V 986 and V 992 (Fig. 5.6). Those which formed after the house and yards were built, but before the cell was constructed (contexts 53, 72, 98) , produced more plain rims. One also contained the sharply everted rim of a large, carinated cooking pot (V 1079, Fig. 5.6) which is more akin to forms popular in phases 2 and 3 and was probably residual from earlier activity. The last ploughed middens (25, 32, 120), which were sealed by midden-rich sand, again had plenty of plain rims but also some everted examples that may have been residual. A large, thick-walled cooking pot with a rolled, flared rim (V 1242, Fig. 5.6) was similar to a vessel from the earliest use of house 1 (V 25, Fig. 5.3).

Phase 10: Temporary camp

In the mid-1st millennium AD, sherds from up to 13 vessels were left during a phase of temporary occupation over the dune-covered remains of the settlement (Table 5.10). These were quite different in both form and fabric: much thinner-walled and built using sandy clays. A beaded rim came from a small, barrel-shaped jar made in fabric Q3 (V 956, Fig. 5.5).

Discussion

Making, using and breaking pottery at Milla Skerra

The pottery reveals much about craft activity at the settlement; practices relating to cooking, eating, drinking and storing, and the incidental and deliberate uses of broken pottery. The interpretation of how both practices and pottery changed over time must be hedged with some caution, given the nature of the site. The excavated area was a relatively small space that was intensively used and re-used over hundreds of years. It formed part of a larger settlement, the full extent and character of which are unclear, where deposits (especially middens) were built upon, ploughed or moved around and often put to secondary uses. That note of caution notwithstanding, some of the midden heaps were primary deposits, indicated by the presence of relatively unabraded, conjoining sherds (for example, the phase 2B middens 206/224/238). In other cases, sherds of pottery were deliberately placed for certain purposes. It is thus possible to discern some evidence for clear trends and specific acts around the making, using and breaking of pots.

Milla Skerra's inhabitants used steatite-tempered pottery throughout the lifetime of the settlement (see Table 5.2), although sandy clays made a strong appearance in the earlier phases (2–4) and again towards the end. The abundant tiny bits of steatite recovered through sieving samples of excavated deposits (see Forster, Chapter 6) suggest that pottery production was taking place at the site, with steatite grits mixed into sandy or steatitic clay to enhance vessels' ability to withstand heat. It could have may have been for aesthetic reasons as well: a new, highly burnished pot in a steatite-rich fabric would have looked striking, like a pewter vessel.

Ground-up shell, bone and grog were also added occasionally. The rock and mica inclusions identified in a few fabrics may have occurred naturally in the clay. The glacial till underlying the site is a rather coarse sandy clay and people may have been quarrying it to make pottery, but equally they may have used other, better-quality sources of clay.

Most of the more loosely defined fabrics (Table 5.1) remained in constant use. Vessels made in silvery-soapy S5 were found in all phases, but especially in contexts associated with house 1 and following its collapse (phases 4B, 5A and 6), and in the final phase of midden deposition over the tumbling settlement (phase 7C). About 14% of them bear sooting or residues. Large, heavy pots were made throughout the life of the settlement, often in rough, chunky S3 fabrics. Big, highly burnished vessels (S3c) like the one whose sherds were set in the clay of the first house 1 hearth (V 25 and V 30, Fig. 5.3) were found only in deposits associated with the construction and early use of this building, along with the residual example from a ploughed midden (V 1242, Fig. 5.6).

Analysis of rim forms displays a general trend from everted rims in the earlier phases to plain ones in the later phases. This must reflect changing potting techniques to some extent, but it could also relate to changes in cooking practice. Vessels with rims that were flared, everted, squared and T-shaped – prevalent in earlier phases – would have been easy to grip below the rim and lift on or off a fire. Of these pots, 46% have sooting or residues. However, this would have put stress on the rim-wall join and indeed many broke just below the rim. Of the vessels with plain rims, including those with internal or external bevels, where form could be discerned they tend to be barrel- or bucket-shaped; 24.2% have sooting or residues. The plain-rimmed vessels were much more common during phases 4C/D to 7C (see Table 5.3), from the 2nd century BC to the 2nd or early 3rd century AD. A barrel- or bucket-shaped pot would have had to be gripped around the sides to lift it on or off the fire, with no stress on the rim. Either form would have meant the cook had to protect their hands from heat conducted through the fabric (as well as radiating from the fire), although perhaps more so with the barrel- or bucket-shaped pots.

Three vessels have perforations, indicating either that they were suspended (probably over a cooking fire) or that they broke and repairs were attempted. The best example of a perforated vessel is V 122 (phase 5A midden and hearth waste; Fig. 5.3). This well-preserved vessel has a plain, flattened rim *c.* 115 mm in diameter and was bag- or barrel-shaped. The sooting and food deposits on its surface and near the rim, the change of colour down the body of the pot, and the loss of surface near the base all indicate that it was a cooking pot. There is a small perforation 25 mm (not illustrated) below the rim and another rim sherd is notched, indicating wear from the cord on which it hung. Some sherds have distinct internal grooving, such as V 107 (phase 6A), perhaps worn by repeated stirring of the pot's contents with a bone or wooden spoon.

Three vessels were shallow dishes or bowls, with short sloping sides above wide bases: V 411 (phase 2B, Fig. 5.1), V 14 (phase 2B, Fig. 5.3) and V 184 (phase 6A, Fig. 5.4). These may have been used to cook and serve dishes that were shared among members of a household as they sat together for meals. Parallels for this form have not so far been identified among contemporary, published Shetland assemblages, yet it was long-lived at Milla Skerra.

Potters' wares

Several groups of vessels were made with certain fabrics, wall thicknesses, surface finishes and firing conditions of such consistency that they have been termed 'wares'.

Sparkly cooking wares

During the early phases of the settlement, especially 2B/C, people used and broke many sparkly, steatite-rich cooking pots. The medium-hard S5a fabric was consistently used to make vessels of medium wall thickness (averaging 11–13 mm) with smoothed and/or burnished interiors and exteriors, fired in reducing conditions (silver grey). They made up over a quarter of the vessels deposited in phases 2B and 2C and about 70% of the pots represented in the midden heaps outside yard 5. About a third of them display sooting or residues. They more or less fell out of use as yard 5 became covered in midden, with only a few, probably residual examples found in deposits relating to later phases (Table 5.2).

Burnished mugs

Vessels made in fabric S2 were overwhelmingly small, thin-walled jars with rim diameters under 90 mm (mostly 50–60 mm) and bases of up to 65 mm diameter. They were well-fired in reducing conditions (black or dark grey), with burnished exteriors and smoothed and sometimes burnished interiors. About a third have soot or residues and, where form can be distinguished, they were globular or barrel-shaped. Similar in size and shape to modern mugs, they may have been used for individual hot or cold drinks. They appear in nearly all phases of the settlement, but especially in the domestic middens piled around and over yard 5 and in house 1 occupation deposits (Table 5.2).

Grey-buff coarse wares

The distinctive coarse, soapy, buff-grey fabric S3a was always used to make large, thick-walled pots, with sherds from up to 46 vessels found. Of these, 78% were in house 1 occupation deposits and the midden that sealed it, with the highest concentration in phase 7B (yard 6) and only a light scattering in other phases and areas. Just one bears a residue. These may have been used for storing dry foodstuffs (such as grain) in the domestic sphere.

Waterproofed wares

Three groups of vessels made in three different steatite-tempered fabrics had consistently burnished and/or well-smoothed interiors. The interior finishing may have been for functional reasons, designed to make the less porous. The two most prevalent groups – those made in fabrics S4 and S7 – were mainly found in deposits associated with house 1, from its use as a dwelling all the way through the post-abandonment phases of midden deposition (phases 4, 5 and 6).

The striking S7 pots, with their buff and dark grey smoothed exteriors and dark burnished interiors, were generally large and thick-walled. Only 10% of the S7 vessels have sooting or burnt residue. The pots made in S4 had interiors that were consistently smoothed to make the large steatite grits lie flush with the surface; 74% came from house 1 occupation and later midden deposits, although some appeared as early as phase 2A. One quarter of them have sooting or residues. These pots may have been used especially to store liquids or heat liquid-based foods like soup, with the steatite filler making them more resilient to the boiling and cooling of the contents.

Only four vessels were recorded in fabric S4c, with crude burnishing over reduced, roughly wiped interior surfaces. All were found in the midden (122) spread over the floor of house 1. These might have come from a single batch of pots.

The wider context

There are both similarities and differences between the Milla Skerra assemblage and pottery from contemporary excavated settlements in Shetland. Reference to periods here follows the structure outlined for Shetland and adjusted in light of dating evidence from Old Scatness, Dunrossness (Dockrill *et al.* 2015). Early Iron Age here refers to the period *c.* 700–300 cal BC, Middle Iron Age to *c.* 300 cal BC– cal AD 0, Later Middle Iron Age to *c.* cal AD 0–400 and Late Iron Age/Pictish to *c.* cal AD 400–900.. The settlement at Milla Skerra spanned at least part of the Early Iron Age, all of the Middle Iron Age and part of the Later Middle Iron Age, with a subsequent phase of activity (phase 10) in the Late Iron Age/Pictish period.

The closest excavated site, in both geographical and chronological terms, is Bayanne on the neighbouring island of Yell. Bayanne lay near the head of Basta Voe on the east side of Yell, a distance of 13 nautical miles or 10 km as the gull flies. It was occupied from the mid-2nd millennium BC to the mid-1st millennium AD; Phases 2B and 3 overlapped with Milla Skerra's occupation, with Phase 3 at Bayanne broadly contemporary with phases 4–7 (Moore and Wilson 2014, 89). At both settlements, the inhabitants re-worked earlier deposits and structures, and some structural similarities are apparent. Much of the Bayanne pottery from these phases was steatite-tempered or made using steatitic clays, and vessels were sometimes smoothed, burnished and polished.

In terms of forms, splayed and T-section rims like those from Milla Skerra's phase 2 middens were found at Bayanne in Phase 3 (MacSween 2014, fig. 3.35, V 181). They are also comparable to Downes' Jar 1 from Early Iron Age contexts in South House at Sumburgh Airport on mainland Shetland (Downes and Lamb 2000, fig. 15, Jar 1.3). Downes (2000, 40) identifies similar vessels from early Iron Age contexts at Mavis Grind (Cracknell and Smith 1983), Jarlshof (Hamilton 1956, 37–8) and Clickhimin (Hamilton 1968, fig. 19, 1–5). Globular vessels with short, everted rims such as V 553 (phase 3, Fig. 5.2) are similar to ones from Phase 4 at Bayanne (MacSween 2014, fig. 3.37, V 334). Vessels with everted rims and sharp shoulders (for example, V 1079, Fig. 5.6) were also found at Bayanne (ibid., fig. 3.38, V 853). Gently globular pots with thickened rims (for example, V 25 from the phase 4B hearth in house 1, Fig. 5.3) and V 1242 (Fig. 5.6) appear comparable to vessels from Phase 6 at Bayanne (ibid., fig. 3.38, V 760).

The excavations at Old Scatness (Dockrill *et al.* 2015) have provided a sequence of dates for the occupation and by extension for pottery associated with dated contexts (Brown 2015b). Murray (2016) has conducted comparative analysis of a number of later prehistoric pottery assemblages from excavated sites on Shetland, using the Old Scatness sequence to identify and date broad trends to re-interpret pottery sequences from less well-dated excavations. Rounded, everted, squared and beaded rims were common at Old Scatness during the Middle Iron Age, and there were many shouldered vessels. Potters were using steatite temper, as well as quartz grits sometimes mixed with steatite, burnishing vessels and adding incised decoration (parallel and diagonal lines). Steatite temper was used through the 4th century AD, and grass temper began to be added between AD 200 and 400. Rims with internal bevels and rims with applied or moulded decoration (applied, slashed cordons and pinched pie-crust decoration) were features of the first four centuries AD at Old Scatness, as well as the brochs of Clickhimmin and Upper Scalloway on mainland Shetland and Underhoull on Unst (ibid.).

While the Milla Skerra assemblage is broadly consistent with contemporary trends in potting across Shetland, it lacks any applied decoration and only one certain example of incised decoration (V 675, Fig. 5.2). This is striking in comparison to other assemblages, including the one from Underhoull, which lay only several hours' walk or boat journey away on the south-west coast of Unst. Three main types of pottery, contemporary with each other, were recovered from a series of Early and Middle Iron Age structures downhill from Underhoull broch (Small 1966). The first were large, ovoid cooking pots with everted rims and applied decoration below, including pinched pie-crust and slashed lines. The second were finer-quality vessels with rolled rims and slight incisions below the rim. The third were termed 'native ware' - steatite-tempered pots with straight, flattened and slightly everted rims, mostly undecorated. This third type is the most similar to the pottery in use throughout the Milla Skerra sequence.

The Milla Skerra assemblage is striking mainly for its internal consistency and conservatism. The lack of decorated vessels may reflect a more local, inward-looking economy than those of larger, wealthier, more socially complex settlements like Old Scatness and Underhoull. It seems likely, from the abundance of ground steatite, that people were making pottery at or near the settlement, although they may have also sometimes traded for it. Certain traditions of fabric and form had considerable longevity, such as the Burnished Mugs and Grey-Buff Coarse Wares. One or two others, such as the Sparkly Cooking Wares, were ubiquitous for a few generations and then abandoned.

Analysis of the distribution of different kinds of pottery across the settlement and through the stratigraphic sequence has helped clarify how some spaces were used and some deposits formed. The relatively rare occurrence of pottery in contexts associated with the use of yards 3 and 4 and cell 2 lends support to the interpretation that these were spaces for craftwork and storage. The condition and size of sherds in some midden deposits indicate these were secondary contexts of deposition, while other middens were evidently quarried and deployed in another location. The mixed character of assemblages from exterior contexts and the presence of much residual material suggests they were indeed ploughed middens, as micromorphological analysis concluded (Ellis, Chapter 3). More detailed analysis of formation processes at Milla Skerra could be conducted, using the data collected on sherd:vessel ratio and sherd size, weight and degree of abrasion as indicators of residuality and movement.

Catalogue of the illustrated pottery

Phase 2A – before construction of yard 5

V 391, SF 2202, context 234 (Fig. 5.1)

Squared, sharply everted rim sherd from a thick-walled vessel with a carinated shoulder. The fabric is soft, soapy and silvery with up to 20% very coarse steatite inclusions and up to 30% fine steatite inclusions (S5). The profile is unoxidised throughout (grey). Wall thickness 13 mm, rim diameter 130 mm

Phase 2B – yard 5 in use

V 407, SF 2131, context 236 (Fig. 5.1)

Plain rim with a hint of an external bead from a small, barrel-shaped cooking pot, represented by two rim and two body sherds. The interior and exterior are smoothed with

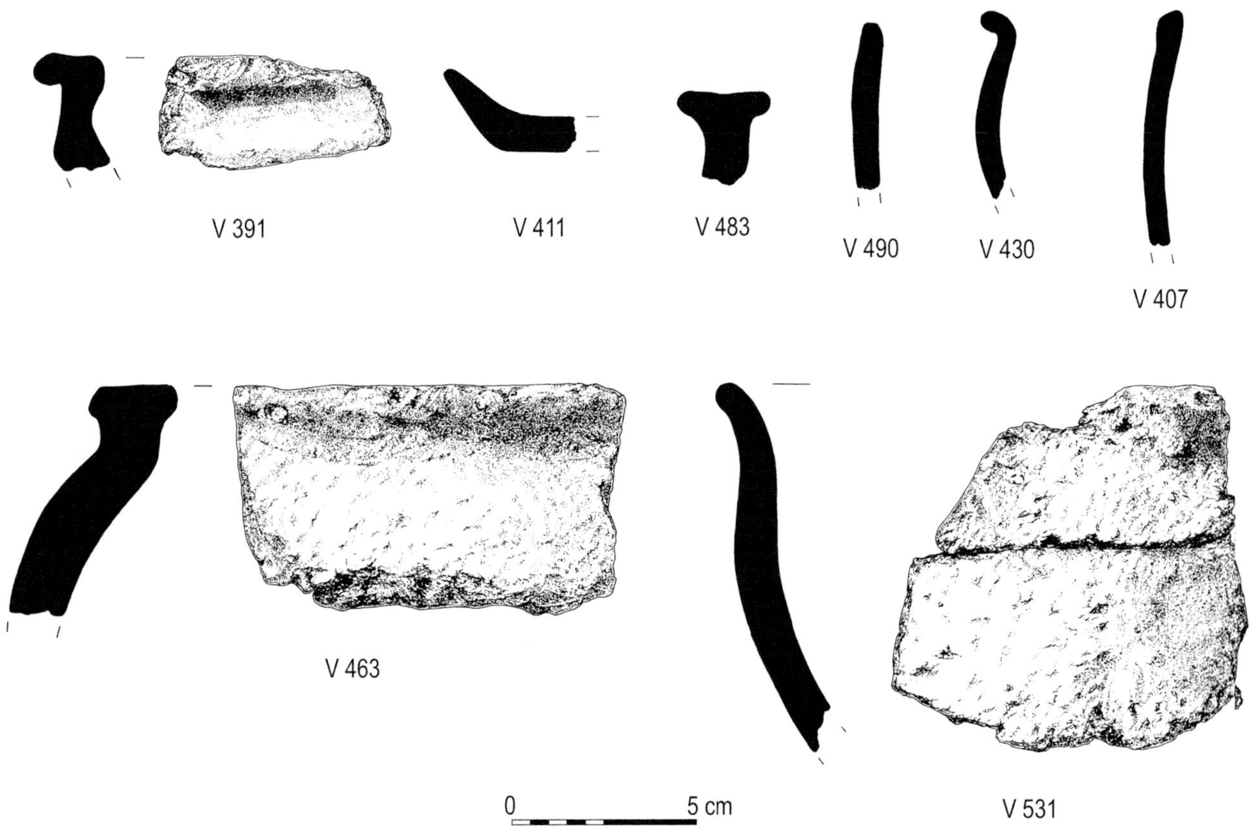

Figure 5.1 Some diagnostic vessels from the ground surface pre-dating yard 5 (phase 2A) (V 391) and phase 2B deposits contemporary with its use (V 407, 411, 430, 463, 483, 490, 531)

fingertip impressions visible, and there is burnt residue and sooting on the exterior. The fine, medium-hard fabric has up to 15% medium steatite inclusions (S2) and is unoxidised throughout the profile (dark grey). Wall thickness 6 mm, rim diameter 50 mm

V 411, SF 2426, context 237 (Fig. 5.1)
Rim and base sherds from a shallow, open bowl 32 mm high. The rim is plain and tapering and the base is flat. Both the interior and exterior are wiped. The fabric is soft, fine, sandy and slightly soapy with up to 10% well-sorted steatite inclusions (S1), inconsistently fired (grey). Wall thickness 8 mm, rim diameter 65 mm, base diameter 55 mm

V 430, SF 2178, context 238 (Fig. 5.1)
An everted rim from a small, globular pot, represented by two rim and three body sherds. It has a wiped and smoothed interior and smoothed exterior. The fabric is fine and sandy with up to 10% well-sorted steatite inclusions (S1), oxidised throughout the sherd profile (orange). A well-made vessel, better fired than most others in this fabric. Wall thickness 6 mm, rim diameter 50 mm

V 463, SF 2114, context 224 (Fig. 5.1)
Flattened, expanded rim with slight external bevel from a globular cooking pot. The exterior surface is smoothed so that the inclusions lie flush with or just break the surface. The fabric is soft, soapy and coarsely gritted with up to 10% steatite inclusions (S3b). The profile is oxidised throughout (orange). Burnt residue on the exterior. Wall thickness 13 mm, rim diameter 150 mm

V 483, SF 2207, context 224 (Fig. 5.1)
Flat, T-shaped rim sherd, with fingertip impressions indicating it was pinched to create the horizontal overhangs, and three body sherds. The fabric is medium-hard with a soapy texture and irregular fracture, with both very coarse and fine steatite inclusions (S5a). It is unoxidised throughout (dark grey). Wall thickness 13 mm, rim diameter 130 mm

V 490, SF 2166, context 238 (Fig. 5.1)
Plain rim sherd with a subtle internal bevel from a small, barrel-shaped vessel. Both the interior and exterior are wiped and the exterior is burnished. The fabric is medium-hard with a smooth texture and up to 15% medium-sized steatite inclusions and up to 5% very coarse steatite fragments (S2). Unoxidised throughout the sherd profile (dark grey). In the thinness of the walls and firing quality it is consistent with other pots in this fabric, but unlike most others it was very crudely finished, with lumps of clay protruding from the burnished surface. Wall thickness 8 mm, rim diameter 60 mm

V 531, SF 1743, context 206 (Fig. 5.1)
Conjoining rim and body sherds from a heavy, coil-built cooking pot with an open, globular form and gently flaring rim. The vessel broke along an H-section coil join and fingertip impressions are visible. The fabric is soapy, steatitic clay, rough and hackly with up to 40% very coarse, poorly sorted steatite inclusions (S6). The exterior is unevenly fired (grey) and both the core and interior are unoxidised. Burnt residue on the exterior. Wall thickness 12 mm, rim diameter 130 mm

Phase 3 – midden over yard 5

V 532, SF 1752, context 171 (Fig. 5.2)
Short everted rim sherd from a thick-walled cooking pot with a smoothed interior and exterior and external residue. The fine, sandy fabric has a sparkly appearance with *c*. 10% well-sorted steatite inclusions (S1), unoxidised throughout (silver-grey). Wall thickness 14 mm, rim diameter 150 mm

V 552, SF 1815, context 171 (Fig. 5.2)
Sharply everted rim sherd from a small, well-made, ?globular cooking pot with a smoothed interior, burnished exterior and external residue. The fabric is fine and medium-hard with up to 15% medium steatite inclusions (S2), unoxidised throughout. Wall thickness 7 mm, rim diameter 80 mm

V 553, SF 1801, context 171 (Fig. 5.2)
Short everted rim from a massive, globular cooking pot bearing an external residue, represented by two rim and 15 body sherds. The fabric is soft and very coarse with up to 15% very coarse, well-sorted steatite inclusions (S3), inconsistently fired on the exterior and unoxidised on the core and interior (grey/orange). The exterior surface is burnt and eroded. Wall thickness 16 mm, rim diameter 170 mm

V 563, SF 1750, context 171 (Fig. 5.2)
Sharply everted rim sherd from a small cooking pot with a smoothed interior and burnished exterior, bearing an external residue. The sandy fabric (Q1) is inconsistently fired externally and unoxidised at the core and internally (orange/grey). Wall thickness 9 mm, rim diameter 70 mm

V 598, SF 1965, context 130 (Fig. 5.2)
Gently everted rim sherd from a large cooking pot bearing external residue. The fabric is soft, sandy and slightly

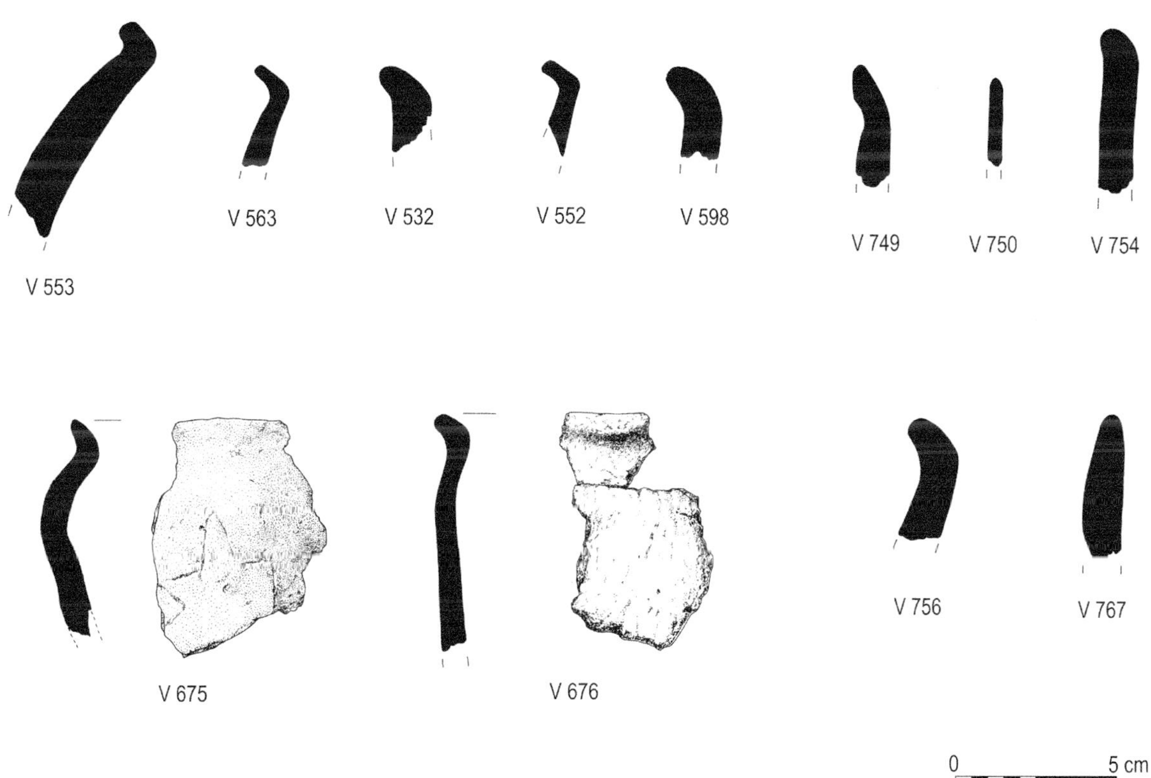

Figure 5.2 Some diagnostic vessels from middens deposited in phase 3A (V 532, 552, 553, 563, 598) and phase 4A (V 675, 676), and from contexts associated with the construction and early use of yards 3 and 4 (V 749, 750, 754, 756, 767) in phase 4B/C/D

soapy with up to 10% well-sorted steatite inclusions (S1), unoxidised throughout. Wall thickness 13 mm, rim diameter 120 mm

Phase 4A – stony midden underlying yards 3 and 4

V 675, SF 1201, context 102 (Fig. 5.2)
Everted rim sherd from a vessel with a pronounced, curving shoulder, smoothed on the interior and exterior. There is an angular incised motif on the wall below the shoulder like the upper part of a star. The fabric is micaceous and sandy (Q1), with an oxidised exterior and interior (orange) and unoxidised core (grey). Wall thickness 10 mm, rim diameter 60 mm

V 676, SF 1195, context 102 (Fig. 5.2)
Everted rim from a straight-walled vessel, very similar to V 675 from the same context; represented by three conjoining rim and body sherds. The fabric is micaceous and sandy (Q1) with an oxidised exterior and interior (orange) and unoxidised core (grey). Wall thickness 9 mm, rim diameter 60 mm

Phase 4B – house 1 construction and early use

V 14, SF 1222, context 169 (Fig. 5.3)
Conjoining rim and base sherds from a shallow, open bowl 40 mm high. The rim is plain and tapering and the base is flat. The interior and exterior are wiped and the exterior has both burnt residue and sooting. The fabric is steatitic clay with up to 40% very coarse, poorly sorted steatite inclusions (S6), unoxidised throughout the profile (dark grey). Wall thickness 15 mm, rim diameter 170 mm, base diameter 60 mm

V 25, SF 1522, context 190 (Fig. 5.3)
Plain rim with a deep, flattened external bead from a large cooking pot, coil-built with a fracture along an N-joint and a highly burnished exterior and internal residue. The four rim and three body sherds are in a soft, soapy fabric with up to 15% fine to medium steatite inclusions (S3c), oxidised on the exterior (orange), unoxidised in the core and interior. Wall thickness 12 mm, rim diameter 170 mm

V 30, SF 1568, context 196 (Fig. 5.3)
Flared rim from a thin-walled vessel with a burnished exterior, represented by one body and three rim sherds.

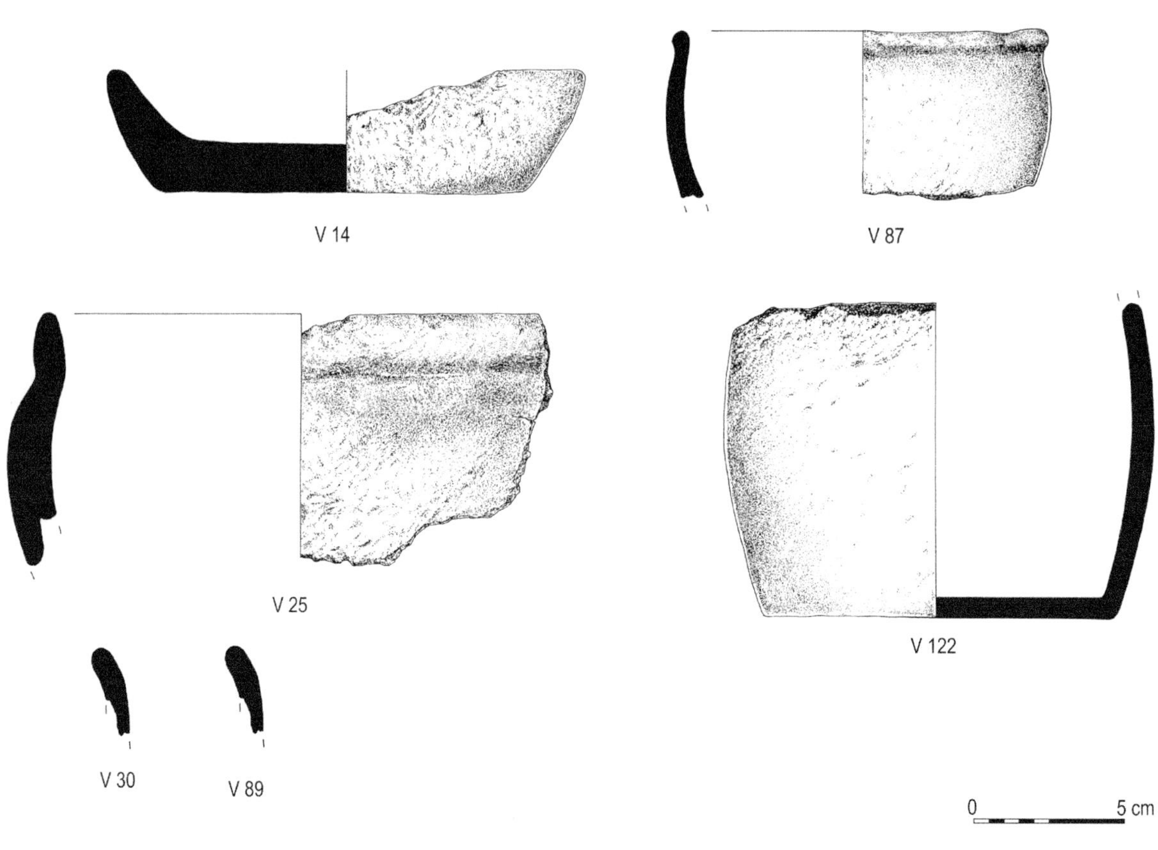

Figure 5.3 Some diagnostic vessels from contexts associated with the construction and early use of house 1 in phase 4B (V 14, 25, 30, 87, 89) and its occupation in phase 5A (V 122)

The fabric is medium-hard with a fine fracture and up to 15% medium steatite inclusions and sparse, very coarse ones (S2), unoxidised throughout the sherd profile (dark grey). Wall thickness 7 mm, rim diameter 140 mm

V 87, SF 1189, context 137 (Fig. 5.3)
Rolled rim above the gently swelling body of a large cooking pot. The interior is wiped so that the inclusions lie flush with the surface; there is internal residue. The conjoining rim and body sherds are in a medium-hard fabric with up to 25% very coarse, poorly sorted steatite inclusions (S4); the exterior is unoxidised (dark grey), the core oxidised and the interior inconsistently fired. Wall thickness 6 mm, rim diameter 120 mm

V 89, SF 1194, context 137 (Fig. 5.3)
Slightly flaring rim in a smooth, fine, medium-hard fabric with up to 15% medium steatite inclusions and sparse very coarse ones (S2); two rim and three body sherds. Oxidised throughout profile (dark grey). Similar to V1088, context 53. Wall thickness 8 mm, rim diameter 75 mm

Phase 4B/C/D – yard 3/4 construction and early use

V 756, SF 932, context 26 (Fig. 5.2)
Everted rim sherds (two conjoining) from a large vessel. The fabric is soft, sandy and heavily gritted with steatite inclusions (S3), also containing some large, shiny inclusions of black rock (S3), unoxidised throughout (dark grey). Wall thickness 13 mm, rim diameter 100 mm. From a secondary context (wall core of yards 3/4)

V 749, SF 822, context 86 (Fig. 5.2)
Upright, slightly flaring rim sherd from a vessel with a wiped and smoothed interior and smoothed exterior. The fabric is silvery, soft and soapy with up to 30% fine, well-sorted steatite inclusions and up to 20% very coarse, poorly sorted ones (S5), unoxidised throughout (silver-grey). Wall thickness 9 mm, rim diameter 60 mm

V 750, SF 822, context 86 (Fig. 5.2)
Plain rim and four body sherds from a small, well-made, barrel-shaped vessel with a smoothed interior and exterior, very bright and silvery. The fabric is medium-hard with up to 15% medium-size steatite inclusions (S2). Wall thickness 6 mm, rim diameter 70 mm

V 754, SF 810, context 86 (Fig. 5.2)
Plain rim with an internal bevel from a barrel-shaped vessel, very silvery in appearance. The two rim sherds are made in a soft, soapy fabric with up to 20% very coarse, poorly sorted steatite inclusions and up to 30% fine powdery ones (S5), oxidised throughout the sherd profile (silver-grey). Wall thickness 14 mm, rim diameter 130 mm

V 767, SF 859, context 42 (Fig. 5.2)
Plain rim in a soft, soapy, silvery fabric with both coarse and fine steatite inclusions (S5). Smoothed interior and burnished exterior; unoxidised on interior and core but inconsistently fired on exterior.
Wall thickness 11 mm, rim diameter 110 mm

Phase 5A – house 1 in use

V 122, SF 1265, context 150 (Fig. 5.3)
Plain rim from a barrel-shaped, flat-based cooking pot. The fabric is medium-hard and steatite rich (S2), oxidised on the interior and core and inconsistently fired on the exterior. Interior is smoothed and exterior is wiped and burnished with an external residue adhering. Oval perforation (not illustrated), 3.6 mm wide 24 mm below top of rim. Wall thickness 8 mm, rim diameter 115 mm

Phase 6 – midden in abandoned house 1, before (6A) and after (6B) collapse of the walls

V 184, SF 1219, context 122 (Fig. 5.4)
Flat rim and base (two conjoining sherds) from a shallow platter 25 mm high, made in a hard fabric containing sparse, poorly sorted, fine shiny black rock inclusions (R1). Unoxidised (grey) throughout the firing profile. The exterior is roughly burnished, and the rim is either highly burnished or polished through use. Wall thickness 10 mm, rim diameter 120 mm

V 193, SF 992, context 122 (Fig. 5.4)
Plain rim (two conjoining sherds) with an internal bevel from a probable jar. The fabric is medium-hard and heavily gritted with steatite (S4), burnished on both the interior and exterior and unoxidised (grey) throughout the profile. Fingertip impressions are visible. Wall thickness 10 mm, rim diameter 135 mm

V 207, SF 955, context 122 (Fig. 5.4)
Plain rim (two conjoining sherds) from a barrel-shaped vessel, made in a medium hard, fine fabric (S2) with sparse coarse steatite inclusions and moderate medium-size ones, unoxidised (grey) throughout the profile. The interior is smoothed and the exterior is burnished and wears a possible slip. Wall thickness 8 mm, rim diameter 65 mm

V 220, SF 911, context 123 (Fig. 5.4)
Slightly everted rim with an internal bevel, from a large, globular cooking pot. Three rim and four body sherds made in a medium-hard, well-fired fabric gritted with steatite (S4c), unoxidised (grey/black) throughout. The exterior is burnished and the interior is also burnished over a roughly wiped surface. Sooting is evident on the exterior. Wall thickness 11 mm, rim diameter 120 mm

V 231, SF 991, context 123 (Fig. 5.4)
A plain rim from a barrel-shaped jar made in a soft, silvery, soapy fabric heavily gritted with steatite (S5)

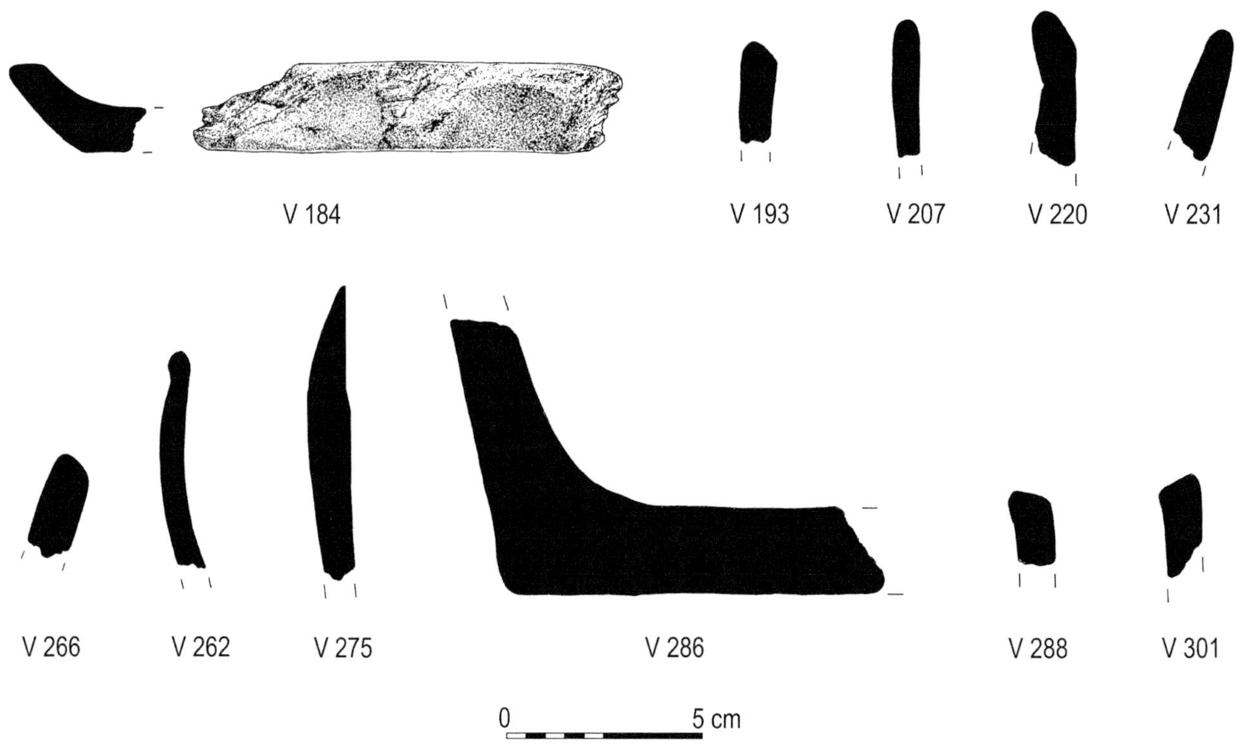

Figure 5.4 Some diagnostic vessels from house 1 contexts that formed after its abandonment in phase 6A (V 184, 193, 207, 220, 231) and after its walls collapsed in phase 6B (V 262, 266, 275, 286, 288, 301)

and unoxidised (grey) throughout the firing profile. The exterior is burnished. Wall thickness 10 mm, rim diameter 70 mm

V 266, SF 819, context 49 (Fig. 5.4)
Plain rim with an internal bevel from a large cooking pot. Two rim sherds made in a soft, sandy fabric with moderate steatite inclusions (S1), oxidised throughout the firing profile. Both the interior and exterior are smoothed, and there is burnt residue on the interior. Wall thickness 12 mm, rim diameter 150 mm

V 262, SF 818, context 49 (Fig. 5.4)
Short beaded rim from a small, fine, globular jar. Two rim sherds, made in a medium-hard fabric with moderate medium steatite inclusions and sparse very coarse ones (S2), unoxidised (dark grey) throughout the firing profile. The exterior is burnished and may wear a slip. Wall thickness 4 mm, rim diameter 60 mm

V 275, SF 773, context 49 (Fig. 5.4)
Plain rim from a small, barrel-shaped cooking pot with a plain rim. Six rim and body sherds (three conjoining), made in a smooth, medium-hard fabric with common very coarse angular steatite grits (S4), unoxidised (black) on the interior and core and unevenly fired on the exterior. It is wiped on the interior and exterior, and the upper part of the exterior is burnished. Sooting and residue are visible on the exterior. Wall thickness 10 mm, rim diameter 80 mm

V 286, SF 791, context 49 (Fig. 5.4)
Flat base and angled wall sherd from a large, bucket-shaped pot made in a soft, sandy fabric (Q1), oxidised (orange) on both surfaces with a reduced core. The exterior is smoothed. On the base, the joint with the slab used to form the wall is visible where the potter did not quite smooth it over. Wall thickness 22 mm, base diameter 140 mm

V 288, SF 792, context 49 (Fig. 5.4)
Plain rim sherd with an internal bevel from a vessel made using a sandy clay (Q1), unoxidised (dark grey) throughout the firing profile. Very well-finished and well-fired. Wall thickness 12 mm, rim diameter 140 mm

V 301, SF 909, context 104 (Fig. 5.4)
Plain rim sherd with an external bevel from a vessel made in a soft, sandy fabric with sparse to moderate, well-sorted, angular steatite inclusions (S1). Unoxidised (grey) throughout the firing profile with fingertip impressions visible. Wall thickness 12 mm, rim diameter 100 mm

Phase 7 – final uses of the structures

V 839, SF 334, context 31 and SF 432, context 51 (Fig. 5.5)
Plain rim from a barrel-shaped vessel. The 19 rim, base and body sherds are in a medium-hard fabric with common

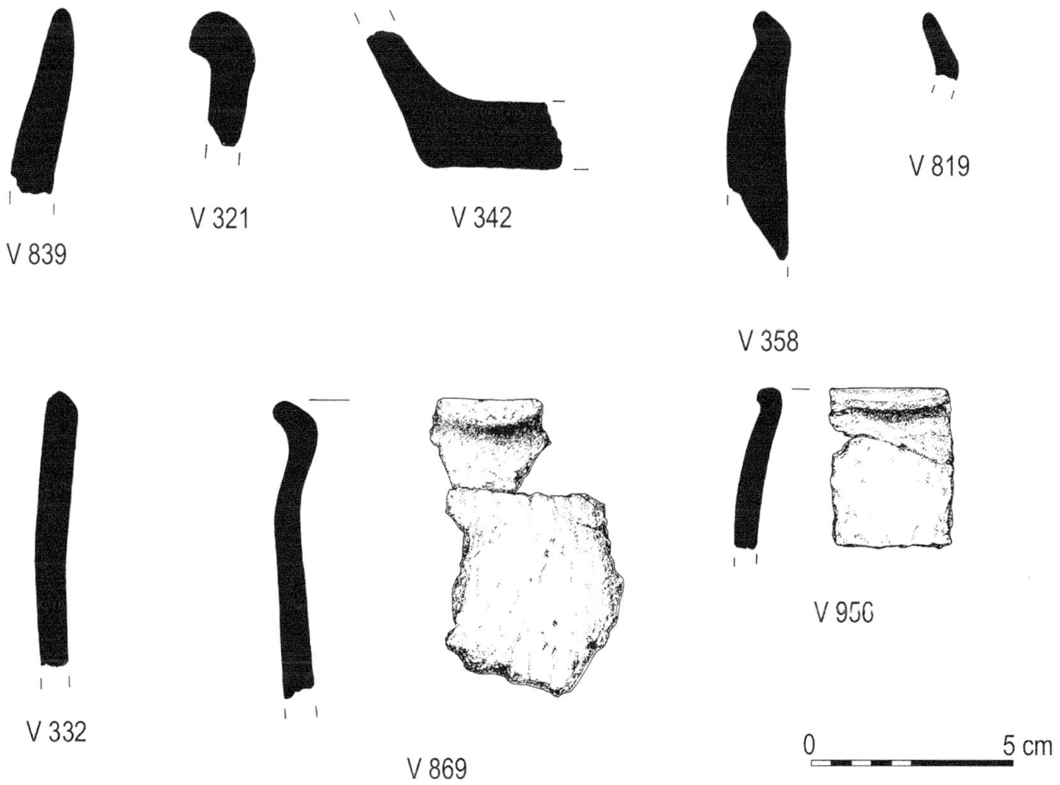

Figure 5.5 Some diagnostic vessels from contexts associated with the phase 7A/B use of cell 2 and yard 3 (V 819, 839) and midden deposited in yard 6 (V 321, 332, 342, 358); from midden-rich sand that covered the tumbling structures in phase 7C (V 869), and from an occupation deposit relating to the phase 10 temporary camp (V 956)

(25%) very coarse, sub angular steatite inclusions (S4c). Oxidised interior, unoxidised core and inconsistently fired exterior. The exterior is smoothed and the interior is rough and crudely burnished. Wall thickness 11 mm, rim diameter 70 mm

V 321, SF 636, context 33 (Fig. 5.5)
Small sherd from a rolled, everted rim. Made in a soft fabric with a fine, sandy texture tempered with sparse, coarse bone fragments (B1). Coil built with N-section join visible. There are at least two fingertip impressions in a row beneath the rim on the exterior. Unoxidised on the core and interior and inconsistently fired on the exterior. Wall thickness 13 mm

V 332, SF 433, context 33 (Fig. 5.5)
Rim and 15 body sherds, several conjoining, from a well-made, barrel-shaped cooking pot. The plain rim has a slight internal bevel. The fabric is medium-hard, fine and smooth with moderate medium-size steatite inclusions and sparse very coarse ones (S2). Smoothed on the interior and burnished on the exterior. Unoxidised (grey) on the interior and core, inconsistently fired on the exterior. The pot broke horizontally along the coil joins, and a N-section join is visible. The exterior bears a residue. Wall thickness 6 mm, rim diameter 110 mm

V 342, SF 427, context 33 (Fig. 5.5)
Flat base and angled wall sherd from a cooking pot made using sandy clay tempered with sparse to moderate steatite inclusions (S1). Unoxidised (grey) on the interior and core, inconsistently fired on the exterior. Smoothed on the interior and burnished on the exterior. Sooting is visible on the exterior. Wall thickness 16 mm, rim diameter 60 mm

V 358, SF 335, context 33 (Fig. 5.5)
Large slightly everted rim sherd from a thick-walled pot made in a soft, sandy fabric tempered with sparse to moderate steatite inclusions (S1). A N-section coil join is visible. Unoxidised (grey) throughout the firing profile. Smoothed on the interior and exterior. Wall thickness 14 mm, rim diameter 80 mm

V 819, SF 209, context 35 (Fig. 5.5)
Rim and body sherds (several conjoining) from a small pot made in a soft, soapy fabric with common steatite inclusions, both coarse and fine (S5). Unoxidised (grey) throughout the firing profile. Burnished on the interior and exterior, very silvery in appearance. Wall thickness 8 mm, rim diameter 70 mm

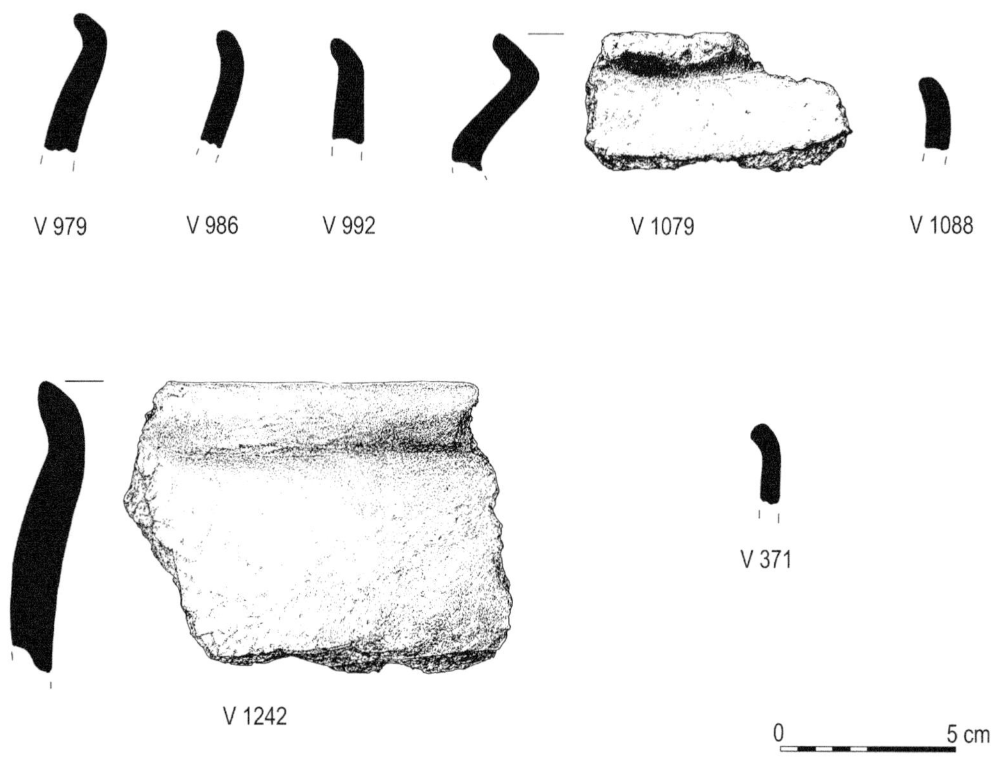

Figure 5.6 Some diagnostic vessels from exterior ploughed middens pre-dating the phase 4B construction of the yards and house (V 979, 986, 992), the phase 5B construction of cell 2 (V 1079, 1088) and the accumulation of phase 7C midden-rich sand (V 371, 1242)

V 869, SF 131, context 7 (Fig. 5.5)
Rim and body sherds from a finely made pot with a short everted rim above a rounded shoulder and straight wall. Made in a soft fabric tempered with fine steatite inclusions, silvery in appearance and soapy in texture (S2). Unoxidised throughout the firing profile, smoothed on the interior and burnished on the exterior. Wall thickness 6 mm, rim diameter 50 mm

Phases 2B-7B – exterior ploughed middens

V 979, SF 1710, context 75 (Fig. 5.6)
Short everted rim sherd from a ?globular cooking pot with a smooth interior, burnished exterior and exterior residue. The fabric is fine and medium-hard with up to 15% medium steatite inclusions (S2), unoxidised throughout (dark grey). Wall thickness 8 mm, rim diameter 60 mm

V 986, SF 1745, context 75 (Fig. 5.6)
Flaring, subtly beaded rim sherd. The fabric is fine, medium-hard with up to 15% steatite inclusions (S2), unoxidised throughout the profile (dark grey). Wall thickness 8 mm, rim diameter 70 mm

V 992, SF 676, context 75 (Fig. 5.6)
Slightly everted rim from a straight-walled cooking pot with both internal and external residues. The fabric is soft and sandy with up to 10% steatite inclusions (S1), inconsistently fired on the exterior and otherwise unoxidised. Conjoining rim and body sherds. Wall thickness 13 mm, rim diameter 120 mm

V 1079, SF 906, context 53 (Fig. 5.6)
Sharply everted rim and base sherds from a carinated cooking pot, smoothed on the interior and exterior with an external residue. The fabric is fine, sandy and slightly soapy with up to 10% well-sorted steatite inclusions (S1), oxidised externally and unoxidised in the core and interior. Wall thickness 8 mm, rim diameter 95 mm

V 1088, SF 912, context 53 (Fig. 5.6)
Slightly flaring rim sherd. The fabric is smooth, fine and medium-hard with up to 15% medium steatite inclusions and sparse very coarse ones (S2), unoxidised throughout the sherd profile (dark grey). Wall thickness 8 mm, rim diameter 55 mm

V 1242, SF 628, context 25 (Fig. 5.6)
Rolled, everted rim from a large coil-built vessel, represented by two rim and body sherds in a medium-hard fabric with common (25%) very coarse, sub-angular steatite inclusions (S4). Unoxidised (grey) throughout the firing profile. Interior is smoothed and exterior is burnished with a possible slip. External residue. Wall thickness 15 mm, rim diameter 150 mm

V 371, SF 403, context 32 (Fig. 5.6)
Slightly everted rim sherd from a small, finely made cooking pot in a smooth, medium-hard steatite-tempered fabric (S2). Unoxidised (dark grey) throughout the firing profile. What may be a slip is visible on the exterior, as well as burnt residue. Wall thickness 7 mm, rim diameter 60 mm

Phase 10 – temporary occupation

V 956, SF 10, context 5 (Fig. 5.5)
Rim and body sherds from a well-made, barrel-shaped vessel with a beaded rim, in a hard, sandy fabric (Q3). Unoxidised exterior, reduced core and interior. Smoothed on the interior and burnished on the exterior. Wall thickness 6 mm

Chapter 6

Craftwork at Milla Skerra: metalworking and bone, stone and iron tools

Beverley Ballin Smith, Torben Bjarke Ballin, Ann Clarke, Amanda Forster, Martin Goldberg, Fraser Hunter, Richard Jones, Olivia Lelong, Dawn McLaren and Anthony Newton

At Milla Skerra, objects made from pumice, bone, stone, steatite, quartz and iron were found in the stratigraphy from all phases of occupation, along with raw materials and the by-products of manufacture. The results of specialist analysis of these diverse assemblages are presented in this chapter. They reveal much about the nature of craft work in the settlement – the tools and other objects that people made, the uses to which they put them, and where in the settlement different processes took place.

The bog ore and slag

Dawn McLaren

Over 27.5 kg of unprocessed bog ore was recovered during excavation, the majority derived from a discrete pile of material in cell 2. A scatter of small fragmentary pieces, with no evidence of modification or vitrification, was also recovered from across the settlement.

Bog ore is formed in bogs, marshes and peat mosses when impure, iron-rich sediments within ground water settle to form compact layers or pockets of porous consolidated pan, often spongy in appearance and yellow or red-brown to black in colour. Bog ore formation is widespread in Scotland, and it occurs in both upland and lowland regions (Campbell 1998, 95). On the whole it remains understudied from an archaeological perspective, although it is often assumed to have been the dominant iron source in later prehistoric Scotland. The presence of bog ore has only been recognised on a few other sites in Shetland, such as Wiltrow, Dunrossness (Curle 1936, 167) and Underhoull (Small 1966, 133).

The bog ore found at Milla Skerra is intriguing because such a large quantity remained unprocessed. In contrast, only very small quantities of ferrous metalworking residues were found, all in residual contexts. These residues comprised less than 100 g of amorphous unclassified iron slag fragments. Such small, fractured vitrified fragments are common within slag assemblages and can be formed during both primary (smelting) and secondary (bloom- or black-smithing) ironworking; they are commonly referred to as unclassified or undiagnostic iron slags (Starley 2000, 337–8). Also recovered were two small vitrified spheres, possible slag spheres, one (0.1 g) from post-abandonment midden (context 7) and the other (0.1 g) from an old ground surface (163) pre-dating the construction of house 1. Slag spheres are produced during smithing when droplets of molten slag are ejected from the bloom by hammering and form into spheres on contact with the air. Their small size and light weight mean that they can easily be transported onto or across a site in small quantities; only when found in significant quantities or concentrations do they indicate *in situ* ironworking activities.

Small quantities (less than 5 g) of magnetic residue were also recovered, all from secondary contexts. Although highly magnetic, no flakes or spheres were identified among the material to confirm this as metalworking residues, and it could equally be corroded fragments of a disintegrated iron object.

The presence of bog ore, iron slag and part of a tuyère (SF 942) together suggest that ferrous metalworking was taking place at the settlement or close by, although not in the excavated area.

Bog ore heap (SF 305) from context 59

A deposit of over 25.5 kg of ore was recovered from the cell (2), which was built over the south-east end of yard 3 in phase 5B. The ore was deposited in a heap during phase 7A, not long before the settlement was finally abandoned (see Figs 2.22 and 8.6). It lay over and around a large, flat-topped stone block (142) which may have served as a working surface; an anvil (SF 597) was found in hearth waste beside it.

It consisted of amorphous fragments, spongy in appearance and porous throughout, with frequent irregular holes caused by formation around rootlets or other organic matter. The pieces range in colour from light orange-brown to dark red-brown, reflecting the varying level of surface oxidation. Generally, but not exclusively, those pieces which are lighter in colour are also lighter in weight and density than the darker fragments, suggesting that they were exposed for longer, resulting in a higher level of oxidation. These probably lay on the surface of the heap. The fragments vary in size from 19.5 to 118 mm in length, 14–102.5 mm in width and 13–65 mm in thickness. None of the material is magnetic.

Many of the fragments display fresh broken surfaces, suggesting the ore was broken up during collection. Although it is not possible to pinpoint its source, examination confirms it was in its natural state; there is no evidence of roasting or vitrification to indicate it had been prepared for smelting.

Why over 25 kg of ore was collected and left in a heap without being processed is difficult to discern. It may represent deliberate storage of raw material or a dump of unused debris. Adjacent to and overlying the heap of bog ore were deposits of hearth waste and midden, suggesting that the latter is more likely.

Isolated fragments from across the settlement

In addition to the heap of bog ore in cell 2, 1960.3 g of small, fragmentary pieces were found scattered across the settlement. Most of these derived from house 1, particularly from later midden and hearth waste deposits left over the abandoned building. These small fragments of bog ore may have been brought to the site accidentally, within peat that had been cut to be used as fuel or building material.

Discussion

It is likely that most of the unprocessed bog ore found at Milla Skerra was collected deliberately in order to produce iron – particularly the heap of bog ore left in cell 2 (context 59). A steatite tuyère (SF 942) found in house 1, along with the presence of a small amount of unclassified iron slag from across the site, supports this interpretation. The tuyère (SF 942), fractured and discoloured by heat, was left along with food waste and other midden on the paved floor of the house (context 122) soon after it ceased to be occupied (see below). This object, used to shield the bellows from heat during a high-temperature pyrotechnic process, would have been used in non-ferrous or ferrous metalworking activities.

Why was the dump of ore from context 59 not processed? Was the ore rejected after collection, perhaps due to impurities? Were the inhabitants waiting for a specialist smelter? Or could the ore have been collected for smelting elsewhere, either at a part of the settlement since eroded away and lost, or somewhere beyond the immediate locale? This last explanation seems the simplest and most plausible.

The block tuyère

Amanda Forster and Dawn McLaren

The tuyère from Milla Skerra is only the fourth example of a block tuyère recovered from the Northern Isles, with comparable ones found at Burland and Old Scatness broch in Shetland and Skaill, Deerness in Orkney. The dating of the Skaill tuyère is unclear, as it was built into the wall of an essentially Norse house (House 2, Site 2) and is therefore likely to pre-date the occupation of the house (Edwards 1997, 73). The Old Scatness example was also recovered from an ambiguous context, and though well-stratified could be Iron Age or Norse in date (Forster 2015). The Burland tuyère was recovered from a metalworking area, dated to AD 400–600, along with evidence of both ferrous and non-ferrous metalworking in the form of iron slag, ingot moulds and hearth lining (Heald and McLaren 2014). The Milla Skerra tuyère came from a well stratified context – the midden that was deliberately spread over the floor of house 1 in phase 6A.

SF 942, context 122 (Figs 6.1 and 2.16)
1401 g, 130 105 75 mm
Fragment from a sub-rectangular block tuyère, manufactured from very blue steatite, which has fractured down the centre. The end which would have been in contact with the furnace or hearth has been lost, leaving a reddened, heat-affected, fire-cracked surface which suggests that the tuyère fractured through use. The

Figure 6.1 The steatite tuyère (SF 942)

perforation would have run longitudinally through the centre of the block. It has been carefully worked, with peck marks and abrasion visible from manufacture. The perforation decreases from 70 mm at the mouth to 17 mm at the end point, where it has become smooth from contact with the wooden bellows. The purpose of a tuyère was to protect bellows from the heat of the fire during use. Although the thermal qualities of steatite make it an ideal material for such objects, they remain relatively rare finds in the Northern Isles.

Pumice artefacts

Beverley Ballin Smith

This report details the results of the analysis of 38 pieces of pumice found within the structures of Milla Skerra and in external contexts associated with them. The majority of pumice pebbles (34/ 89.5%) have been used, with only a small number showing no sign of surface changes (4/10.5%). This is a small to medium-sized assemblage for the Northern Isles, but shows the importance of this intermittently available sea-borne resource to the inhabitants of the settlement.

Most of the pumice pieces are rounded pebbles, naturally abraded by the action of sea, stone and sand. Newton (below) describes the likely origins of the pumice, which was transported by ocean currents and deposited on beaches across the north of Scotland. Pumice pebbles, mostly smaller than hand-sized, are occasionally found washed-up on island beaches today. This lightweight material was collected and brought back to settlements from the Neolithic period onwards – a useful and easily won resource. Although fairly soft and porous, it fulfilled a useful function in being light and easy to handle, and it could be used to smooth organic objects or tools denser than itself, such as bone and wood. Its modern-day equivalent is sandpaper. In areas where pumice was not available, a mixture of quartz sand and water would have been commonly used to abrade tools and smooth objects.

The average weight of the pebbles is 14 g, and the majority of pieces are quite small. It is likely that most pumice pebbles in this assemblage were utilised without prior modification. Their generally rounded or irregular shapes fitted the hand, so they could be used directly on the tool or object that needed smoothing or working,

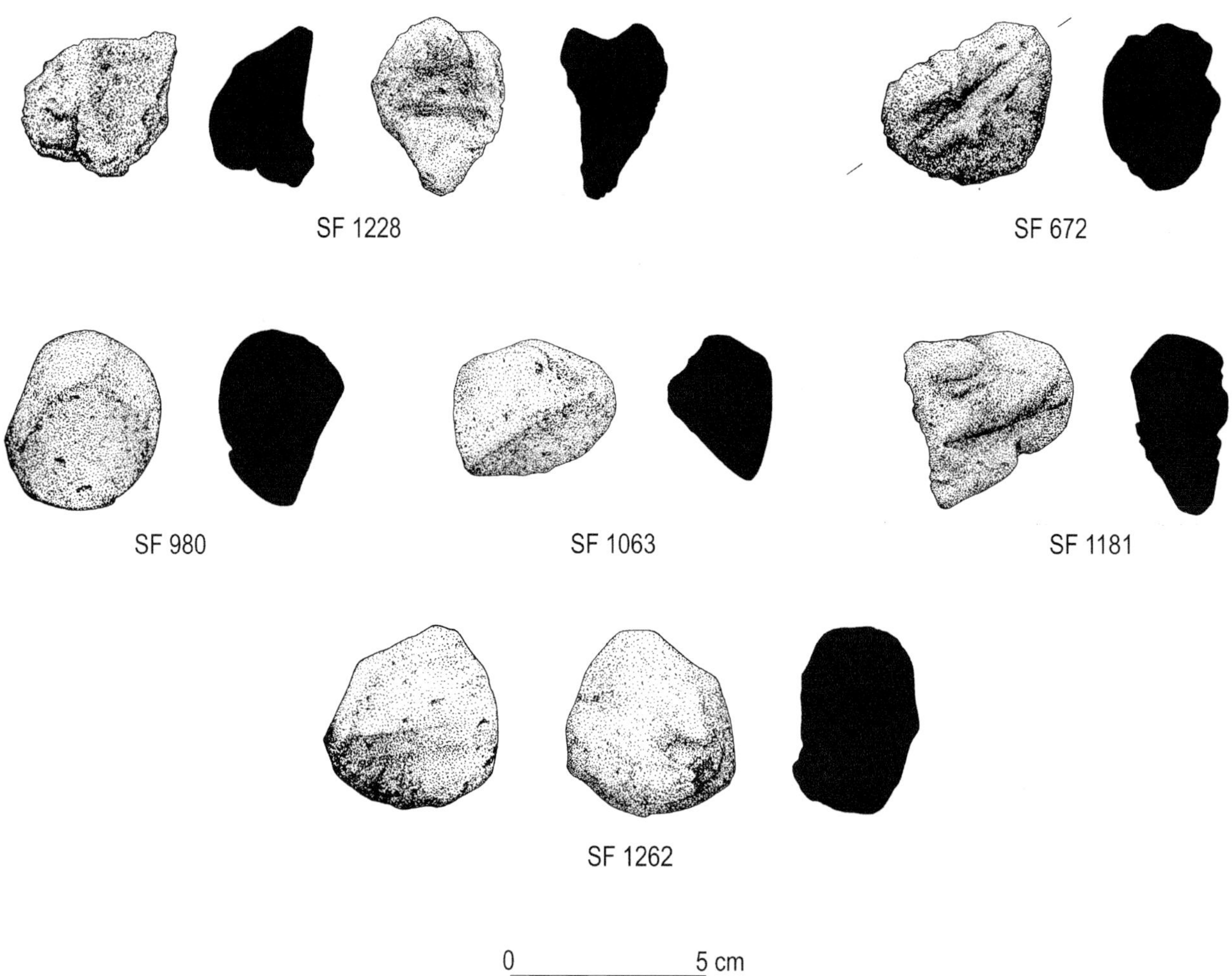

Figure 6.2 Pumice from phases 4A (SF 1228), 4C/D (SF 672) and 5A (SFs 980, 1063, 1181 and 1262 – all from hearth waste in house 1)

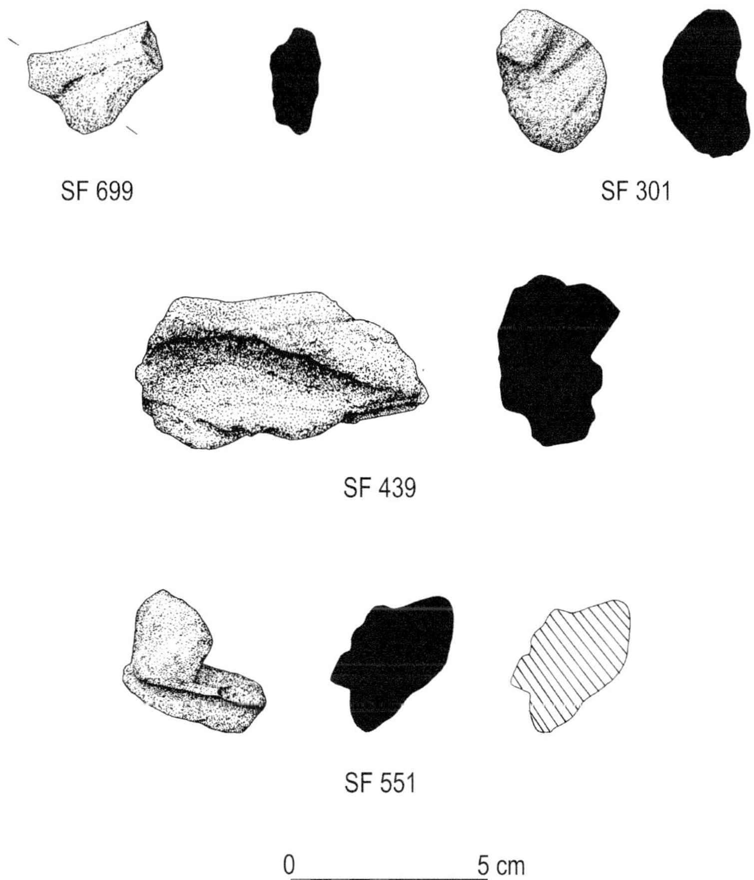

Figure 6.3 Pumice from phases 7A (SFs 301, 439) and 7B (SFs 551, 699), all from yard 3, cell 2 and exterior

Table 6.1 Types of surface alteration of the pumice pieces

Abrasion type	*Number*	*%*
Unworked	4	10.5
Grooved	23	60.5
Notched	4	10.5
Smoothed surfaces	14	36.8
Facets	4	10.5
Flattened surfaces	4	10.5

creating the various types of abraded surfaces found in this assemblage (Figs 6.2 and 6.3; see Table 6.1). Over 60% of pieces are grooved, with another 10.5% notched. The deepest groove is 13 mm wide by 11.5 mm deep and is V-shaped in section (SF 551, Fig. 6.3). The rest are narrower, down to *c.* 5.3 mm in width. Their profiles vary between a slight concavity to distinct U and V shapes. SF 706 not only has a groove, but one of its unworked edges has three small notches. One other piece (SF 201) has a partial notch or groove.

Just over one third of the assemblage (36.8%) has smoothed surfaces, sides or edges, which are often slightly hollowed or concave through use, and are distinct from the grooves which are confined in extent. Related to this category of smoothed pieces are the 10.5% of pieces whose surfaces had been flattened (for example, SF 980 and 1063, Fig. 6.2). The flattening may have been the result of either use or modification prior to use, the former being the most likely. In four cases this flattening was taken to an extreme, resulting in facetted sides or surfaces. Pieces such as SF 706, 850, 1262 (Fig. 6.2) and 1648 not only have facets but also grooves and sometimes notches.

Different types of use-wear indicate the shapes of the objects on which the pumice was used. The common thinking (see below) is that grooves were produced by using the pumice to smooth thin, cylindrical or rounded wooden or bone objects such as pins, arrow shafts and fishing hooks; facets were formed by working on flat surfaces like hides. There were probably many other uses to which pumice was put. Finishing pottery vessels with a high percentage of steatite temper (Lelong and Ballin Smith, Chapter 5) would have been easily and efficiently accomplished using a pumice pebble. Some of the flattened, facetted and smoothed pieces could have been used for this purpose although – unlike examples recorded elsewhere (see below) – none of the pumice retains clay or steatite in its vesicules.

In contrast to other assemblages, none of the pumice from this site is perforated or made into artefacts and there are no fishing weights, whorls or beads.

Catalogue

Table 6.2 Catalogue of the worked pumice

SF no.	*Context*	*Description*	*Colour*	*Weight (g)*	*Measurements (mm)*
59	6	Unworked piece.	Dk grey	4.5	85 × 62 × 61
105	7	Unworked irregularly rounded pebble.	Dk grey-brown	48.7	70.3 × 53.4 × 36.6
201	7	Largely unworked irregularly rounded pebble with a notch or partial groove on one surface.	Dk grey-brown	17.5	47.4 × 37.4 × 25.4
301	31	Pebble. Three roughly parallel grooves on concave surface. Grooves are shallow with a U-shaped profile. Max width of groove 6.5 mm.	Dk grey-brown	5.8	33.5 × 26.8 × 19.2
439	51	Irregular pebble. Concave surface and one side each have broad grooves; max length 57 × 12 mm. Shorter, narrower grooves also other side and on convex surface, 27 mm long × 5.3 mm.	Dk grey-brown	16.5	70.5 × 37.3 × 24.3
440	51	Larger irregular piece with groove on one surface 27.2 × 8.2 × *c.* 4 mm deep. Square profile to base of groove.	Dk grey-brown	31.4	62 × 53.3 × 25.5
544	25	Unworked rounded pebble.	Dk brown	15.6	50 × 31.2 × 28
550	57	Pebble with one surface smoothed and made slightly concave.	Dk grey-brown	25.6	72 × 41 × 26
551	57	Highly grooved irregular pebble. One surface has a long, broad and deep groove 34.5 × 11 × 6 mm. Perpendicular to this on the lower surface is broader and deeper groove 13 × 11.3 mm. Both V-shaped in section.	Dk grey	6.8	40.5 × 25.4 × 24
576	53	Irregular piece with one concave surface with shallow groove close to one edge.	Dk grey	4.5	33 × 28.3 × 14.4
672	53	Pebble with three grooves, one 29.7 × 5.8 mm on otherwise unworked surface, one shallow groove on adjacent surface with perpendicular groove on edge between them.	Dk grey	17.8	45.5 × 37.1 × 28.2
699	25	Irregular piece with worked and smoothed surfaces & sides. Irregular shallow groove on concave surface.	Dk grey	3.6	34.6 × 25.3 × 11.5
706	25	Pebble with one facetted edge and adjoining surfaces, with one U-shaped groove and three notches on an unworked edge. Complex piece.	Dk grey	20.3	52.2 × 38 × 26.2
850	53	Pebble with one smoothed facet and a possible broad groove.	Dk brown	13.3	40 × 36 × 26.7
913	53	Sub-rounded piece with one V-shaped groove on one surface and two fine V-shaped grooves on another.	Dk grey	13.7	41.5 × 33.3 × 32
980	127	Pebble with one flattened surface.	Dk brown	17.2	42 × 34.3 × 28.7
993	123	Largely unworked piece, one surface very slightly grooved or hollowed.	Dk brown	7.7	35.3 × 35.4 × 26
1063	138	Facetted piece with three flattened or slightly hollowed surfaces and one smoothed and convex edge.	Dk brown	9.6	39.8 × 32 × 39
1181	151	Pebble with one smoothed & hollowed surface. Has three grooves on another surface and two U-shaped notches on edge between the surfaces, one prominent and the other less prominent.	Dk grey	11.4	41 × 40.5 × 23.2
1215	131	Probably unworked pebble, but possible slight indentation on one surface.	Dk brown	12.5	50 × 31.5 × 28
1217	102	Irregular piece with one slightly concave & smoothed surface.	Dk grey	9.4	51.4 × 28.2 × 16.5
1228	102	Irregular piece with concave, slightly grooved & smooth surface.	Dk grey	8.3	42.3 × 34.3 × 21.6

Table 6.2

SF no.	Context	Description	Colour	Weight (g)	Measurements (mm)
1231	57	Small fragmentary pebble with smoothed surfaces flattened and convex, possibly worked.	Dk grey	11.6	39 × 27 × 21
1251	53	Fragmentary wedged-shaped piece with two surfaces smoothed and slightly flattened	Dk grey	5.6	30 × 24.3 × 18.8
1262	150	Pebble with obvious facetting of one surface and one side and a possible U-shaped indentation or groove(s) on another surface.	Dk brown	18.5	43 × 43 × 27
1317	163	Pebble with partial shallow groove on either side of one edge.	Dk brown	6.8	49.7 × 21 × 20
1327	163	Small tapering square piece with two smoothed surfaces with a slight hollowing or groove on the edge between them.	Dk brown	4.2	26 × 19 × 23
1355	25	Largely unworked piece, but part of one surface and edge is smooth.	Dk grey	12.7	44 × 37.6 × 23.4
1427	53	Pebble with part of one surface and one edge smoothed.	Dk grey	3.8	32.2 × 16.5 × 26.2
1478	53	Slightly wedge-shaped pebble with one particularly smooth surface, with a V-shaped notch at one end.	Dk grey	12.9	44.3 × 30.5 × 19
1543	53	Irregular fragment with partial groove.	Dk grey	0.7	19.7 × 13.8 × 7.3
1583	53	Pumice pebble with one surface with a wide, shallow groove and one edge with two close-set U- & V-shaped grooves.	Dk brown	4.8	37.6 × 28.5 × 16
1648	234	Pebble block with slightly faceted, smoothed and tapering sides with one flattened & slightly concave surface. Rubbing tool (left handed).	Dk grey	34.8	64.8 × 37 × 31.5
1747	75	Almost triangular piece with smooth surfaces, one especially smooth and concave.	Dk grey	5.7	33 × 26.5 × 15
2070	224	Small irregular lump with a shallow V-shaped groove.	Dk grey	2.3	24.5 × 19.6 × 12.2
2100	224	Pebble with a slightly concave worn area on the edge of one surface.	Dk brown	10.6	38.7 × 29 × 21.5
2117	224	Sub-rounded, dense and unworked piece.	Dk brown	65.7	64 × 68.4 × 45.8
2299	129	Pebble with one side and one surface smoothed and slightly hollowed. Side has one slight scratch running across it.	Dk brown	6.4	40 × 26 × 15.5
38 SFs		TOTAL		*528.8*	

Comparison and dating

As pumice occurs frequently on prehistoric sites of all periods in the Northern and Western Isles and its use-wear is not particularly datable to specific periods, it cannot be used to date sites.

One of the largest collections of pumice published recently was that from Pool, Sanday, Orkney (Smith 2007a, 404–12). Approximately 50% of its 182 pieces were worked and they were concentrated in Neolithic, Iron Age and Norse levels. In contrast to Milla Skerra, the majority of pieces were flattened and smoothed (abraded) rather than grooved, with few pieces having more than one type of wear. Very narrow grooves (notches) were noted, but otherwise grooves tended to be narrower than those in this assemblage. Due to the deep stratigraphy at Pool, it was noted that pumice occurred more frequently in the Neolithic and that it steadily declined in use till the Norse period. Perforated pumice objects were found in Iron Age levels at Pool and also at Scalloway, Shetland (Clarke 1998b, 119).

At Tofts Ness, Sanday in Orkney, pumice occurred more frequently in later phases (Late Bronze Age and Early Iron Age) than in earlier ones, but the numbers of worked pumice were lower than at Pool (Smith 2007b, 290). The site at Barnhouse, Orkney, generally of Late Neolithic date, produced a collection nearly double the size of that from Milla Skerra. Analysis of these pieces showed that the pumice assemblage was similar to that of Pool, with abraded, faceted and concave pieces and others with U-shaped grooves (Clarke 2005, 335). An assemblage from Kebister, Shetland showed the same common traits of wear, but the pumice was distributed across the site in mostly redeposited contexts (Clarke 1999, 167).

A collection of 75 small pieces of pumice was found at the Sands of Breckton, Yell, Shetland (Carter and Fraser

1996, 290) from occupation dating from the Neolithic to the Norse, but they were naturally abraded by the sand and no wear was confirmed. An interesting small collection was found at Mavis Grind, Shetland in the late 1970s (Cracknell and Smith 1983, fig. 18). Among the 20% of used pebbles, one of the most interesting was a piece with adhering clay, identified as a pottery burnisher.

At Sumburgh, two-thirds of the pumice had evidence of use-wear, but there the concave and convex worn pieces are thought likely to have smoothed the sides (and insides) of bowls or vessels (Barrowman 2000, 109–11). Barrowman also thought that finer-pored pebbles were used to smooth bone, wood and pottery, with the coarser pumice used for other materials. Most of the pumice was found in contexts inside structures dated to the Late Bronze Age through to the Iron Age.

At Bayanne on Yell, pumice was relatively scarce until Phase 3 (1st and 2nd century AD). Most of the pieces from this phase were found in midden or soil dumps or in secondary contexts. The few pumice objects from earlier phases are generally simpler with concave worked faces, but the pumice from Phase 3 onward was used more heavily, with many pieces having multiple worked faces and also grooves (Clarke 2014, 181–3).

Provenance of the pumice

Anthony Newton

All of the 49 pieces identified as pumice are brown dacitic pumice, which is a common find in Scottish coastal archaeological sites (for example, Dugmore and Newton 1999; Newton 1999a; 1999b; 2006; Newton and Dugmore 1995). Of 141 sites in Scotland where pumice has been found, 131 were archaeological sites (Newton 1999a). Of these, the highest concentrations are in the Western Isles (47), Orkney (27) and Shetland (26). The Iron Age site at Underhoull on Unst contained 'many pieces' of black pumice in Iron Age and Norse contexts (Small 1966). Iron Age contexts are the most common source of pumice in Scotland; over 50 of the 131 sites are from that period, as are 12 out of 26 sites on Shetland (Newton 1999a). This means that the pumice found at Milla Skerra is typical of similar deposits found around Scotland and in the Western Isles and Northern Isles in particular.

All of the pumice found on archaeological sites in Scotland would have been originally collected from the contemporary beach or from raised beach deposits (where they occur). Whether the pumice was actually used probably depended on its size and shape. There is plenty of evidence that many of the pumice pieces from Milla Skerra were utilised (see Ballin Smith, above).

Origins of pumice

Iceland has long been identified as the probable source of most of the dacitic pumice found around the North Atlantic (Binns 1972). A programme of work involving 1500 electron probe microanalyses and 200 Secondary Ion Mass Spectrometry analyses has been carried out of pumice from across the North Atlantic, including pumice from 14 archaeological sites in Scotland and Ireland (Newton 1999a). Analyses were also undertaken on tephra layers and pumice deposits in Iceland to provide correlation back to possible sources.

The vast majority of the pumice analysed was of the type found at Milla Skerra. This is often described as being brown, black to grey in colour. There were no significant geochemical differences between the colours; they are all dacitic in composition (ibid). Analyses of 98 pieces of the majority dacitic pumice produced average weight percentage SiO_2 abundance of 65.7%, TiO_2 of 1.2%, FeO of 5.5%, MgO of 1.1% and CaO of 3%. All of this pumice has been found in archaeological sites ranging from the Neolithic to the modern day in age.

In contrast, the Mesolithic sites of Staosnaig, Colonsay (Newton 2001) and Camas Daraich, Skye (Newton 2004) contain pumice which is geochemically distinct. It is either light brown or black in colour and has a different texture. This older pumice forms two distinctive geochemical groups: one with around 68% SiO_2 and the other around 70%.

A third group is composed of white pumice, found at medieval contexts at The Biggings and Scalloway (Newton 1999b) and the reworked Sands of Breckon (Newton 1999a) on Shetland. This pumice is physically different from that found elsewhere in archaeological sites in the British Isles, because of its white colour and high vesicularity (which makes it relatively fragile). It is the most silicic of the ocean-transported pumice found across the North Atlantic, with around 72% SiO_2.

Earlier authors (such as Binns 1972) identified the source of most of the pumice as Hekla, perhaps Iceland's most famous volcano. However, recent work has established that most of the pumice actually comes from a series of eruptions of Katla in southern Iceland (see Larsen *et al.* 2001; Newton 1999a; Newton and Dugmore 1995). In fact, all of the analysed pumice found in the British Isles comes from Katla, apart from the white pumice.

The dacitic pumice can be geochemically correlated with a number of dacitic tephra layers from Katla termed SILK layers (Larsen *et al.* 2001; Newton 1999a). Eruptions prior to around 5700 BC are more silicic and can be correlated to the pumice found at Mesolithic sites on Colonsay and Skye. After 5700 BC until around AD 400, a series of less-silicic eruptions produced the widespread dacitic pumice. Unfortunately, it is not possible at present to tie an individual piece of pumice to a particular eruption. This is partly due to the geochemical similarities between individual tephra layers and the fact that dating of pumice pieces themselves is problematic, as it can never be clear whether they were picked up from a contemporary beach, reworked or found in an older deposit.

More recent work by Smith *et al.* (submitted) has identified dacitic pumice in deposits on or close to

Katla itself. These were deposited by glacial floods (*jökulhlaups*), produced by subglacial eruptions of Katla, which transported pumice from the volcano to the sea. Ocean currents then transported the pumice to Unst and other coastlines around the North Atlantic. This dacitic Katla pumice is relatively robust and is widely found around the North Atlantic, partly because it is not easily broken up. Pumice from Hekla tends to be more friable and would probably break into small fragments and sink before it reached a distant coastline.

The more recent medieval pumice found in Shetland was produced by the AD 1362 eruption of Oræfajökull in south-east Iceland. This relatively fragile pumice could have floated across to Shetland, but could also have been transported by boats.

Conclusions

The pumice found at Milla Skerra is typical of the dacitic pumice found not only in Shetland and Scotland but around the North Atlantic. The Iron Age date of the contexts obviously provides a minimum age for the pumice, which means that the pumice was erupted from one of around nine subglacial eruptions from the Katla volcano in southern Iceland. It is likely that the younger of these eruptions (*c.* 1400–1100 BC) produced the pumice found at Milla Skerra, but precise dating is not possible.

The relatively robust and abrasive nature of the pumice means that it would have been a useful tool. Pumice has been used from the Mesolithic to the modern day as an abrasive tool. As it obviously floats, it can also be used as a float on fishing nets.

Re-worked pottery sherds

Olivia Lelong and Beverly Ballin Smith

Seventeen sherds of pottery had been re-used. Twelve have edges that are worn smooth, indicating that they were used to polish or burnish something – perhaps even newly made, leather-hard pots. They were found in middens, wall cores and other secondary contexts rather than in contexts of use: three from the external midden heap in phase 2B; two from midden piled up over yard 5 in phase 4A; four from a phase 4 exterior ground surface; one from a phase 5 exterior ground surface; and two from the matrix of the yard 6 wall (phase 7B).

One of these (SF 1107, V 307), Fig. 6.4) also has grooving on one edge, as do two other body sherds (V 306, V 313), redeposited with midden in yard 6. The grooving is only *c.* 10 mm long and occurs on the broken edge of the external surface, not across the thickness of the sherd. The incisions do not appear to have been made by metal, and it is possible that bone or thread/twine may have been responsible for the marks. These may have been used to finish and smooth bone artefacts.

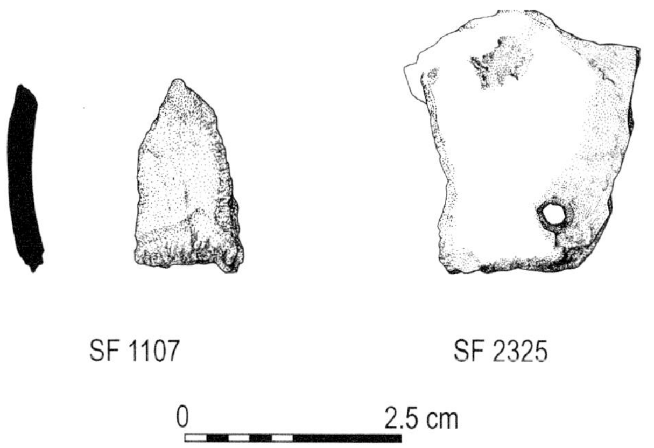

Figure 6.4 Re-worked pot sherds

Three sherds were perforated in order to re-use them. The edges of a sherd from V 1144 (SF 2325; phase 5B) were smoothed and rounded and it was perforated (Fig. 6.4). V 1057 (phase 4B) is a well-fired sherd used as a weight, as it is grooved above the perforation; the edges are not smoothed. V 815 (phase 5B) is a base sherd, the edges of which were smoothed to round it. It was pierced centrally and is scored around the perforation. Both this and V 1057 are likely to be loom weights.

Steatite artefacts

Amanda Forster

The small assemblage of steatite artefacts recovered includes raw material and possible working debris, along with several worked objects. The assemblage indicates that steatite was only rarely worked to produce objects. The numerous fragments of raw material found may be the result of using steatite as a temper in coarse pottery made at the settlement.

In total, 64 finds of steatite were recovered from Milla Skerra, including 31 Small Finds collected during the excavations, with a further 33 fragments recovered from bulk samples. The total assemblage weighs 4.75 kg. Of the 64 pieces making up the assemblage, 59 (2.5 kg) are fragments of raw material (approximately 90% of the assemblage by fragment number). The worked objects include two perforated pieces, along with a tuyére which is discussed separately (see Forster and McLaren, above). The majority of the finds were associated with house 1 and the midden deposits that overlay it.

Perforated disc

Two perforated objects were recovered from the excavations. Both could have been functional rather than ornamental objects (whorls rather than beads), although it is impossible to make a firm identification; one was associated with the later burial and is discussed in Chapter 7.

Steatite beads and whorls have been a feature of Shetland's material culture since early prehistory. Of

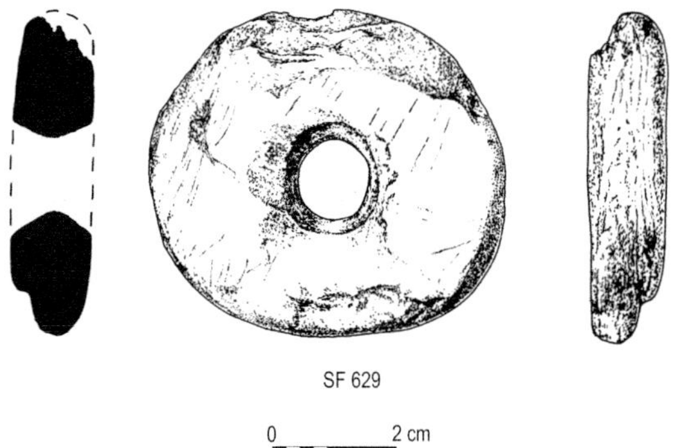

Figure 6.5 The perforated steatite disc (SF 629)

the ten whorls recovered from Scalloway, seven were of steatite (Sharman 1998, 150). A large collection of whorls from more recent excavations at Old Scatness has allowed greater consideration of the morphology of these artefacts (see Forster 2015).

SF 629, context 76, house 1, phase 4B, Fig. 6.5_
58 g, 55 mm diam by 12 mm thick
Large flat disc with a large central perforation measuring 11 mm in diameter. The disc is well-used and polished on all surfaces, probably through use. The laminations are now splitting, and the object looks as if it was well-worn prior to deposition. It was well-stratified – recovered from the matrix of the wall of house 1. Both the size of the perforation (12 mm) and the weight of the disc (58 g) suggest that it is too large to be a spindle whorl. From the large collection of whorls recovered from excavations at 16–22 Coppergate in York, the majority had a perforation of between 9 and 11 mm and a weight of between 9 and 55 g (Walton Rogers 1997, 1736).

NB: During the excavations at Milla Skerra, two steatite artefacts were also collected from the surface at the sites of two previously excavated Norse farmsteads on the same beach (Canmore IDs 141 and 126). A heavily tooled vessel fragment (SF 2322) from the corner base of a flared, four-sided vessel, dating from the 10th–14th century (see Forster 2009), was recovered from the deflated sandy surface at the Norse farmstead excavated in the 1980s (Bigelow 1978), *c.* 100 m from Milla Skerra. A small rim fragment from a bakestone (SF 2338), bearing evidence of faint working and some sooting, was recovered from the spoil heap of the excavation of a much-eroded Norse settlement at the north end of the beach (Hansen 1995). The bakestone may have been either rectangular or semi-circular in shape (see Weber 1999).

The raw material

The 59 fragments of raw material recovered at Milla Skerra must represent working debris from a particular process. Given the paucity of steatite objects from the settlement, the fragments are probably a by-product of pottery making. In assemblages of prehistoric pottery from Shetland, steatite is found frequently as temper in vessels and also as part of the finer fraction, indicating that steatitic clays were being used (MacSween 2009). A high percentage of the Milla Skerra pottery contains steatite fragments which were added as temper (Lelong and Ballin Smith, Chapter 5). This would involve grinding it up and mixing it into the clay in order to aid the firing process, increase the ability of the pots to withstand ranges of temperature, and also perhaps enhance their burnished appearance. It is worth pointing out that even the number of fragments is low and they probably represent a local pottery industry, with clays being prepared on or near the site.

The distribution of the raw material across the site also suggests some trends. Most of the fragments were associated with house 1, including occupation deposits and post-abandonment midden, and these were generally small (weighing less than 9 g). Fragments found in primary middens and ground surfaces outside the house were much larger, often weighing 80–100 g and up to 887 g. Very few fragments were associated with other structures: three in yard 5 and five in yard 3 (all weighing less than 13 g) and two in cell 2 (weighing 15 g and 57 g).

Discussion

Given that steatite outcrops at several places on Unst, it seems unlikely that the rarity of worked steatite objects at Milla Skerra can be attributed to a lack of raw material. It seems more likely that, during the period of the settlement, steatite vessels, lamps and bracelets were simply not in use.

Excavations at Bayanne, Yell, and in the south mainland at Jarlshof and Sumburgh Airport have demonstrated that contemporary sites can have significant differences in material culture across Shetland – especially in terms of steatite finds (see Forster and Sharman 2009). All three sites excavated in the south mainland of Shetland (Old Scatness, Sumburgh Airport and Jarlshof) had relatively limited access to steatite quarries, but steatite objects were recovered from prehistoric contexts at all of them (Forster 2015; Sharman 2000; Hamilton 1956). At Old Scatness, only the Pictish period saw a significant reduction in the employment of steatite to manufacture goods, but even here there was evidence for the use of lamps, gaming devices and beads. At Bayanne in Yell, later phases showed a distinct reduction in the use of steatite on site during the late 1st millennium BC (see Forster and Sharman 2009).

Rare earth element analysis of steatite artefacts

Richard Jones

Fifteen steatite artefacts and lumps from the excavations at Milla Skerra were selected for chemical analysis by ICP-MS (inductively coupled plasma-mass spectrometry). The compositions were then examined in order to assess whether or not the artefacts had a similar origin and to make some statement about the possible identity of the origin(s). The programme of analysis was carried out within the context of the on-going chemical characterisation of northern British and Norwegian steatite described by Jones *et al.* (2007) and Jones *et al.* (2006). Of immediate relevance are the results from Fetlar (Jones 2007) and Bronze Age Bayanne on Yell (Jones 2015).

Brief reference is given at the end of this report to the mineralogical examination of two soil samples collected during the excavations, both of which were whitish in colour and soapy in texture. Sample SW 36 was a thick, discrete lens of very fine, creamy white, soapy sediment with orange mottles (context 63), founding lying on a large slab that had collapsed from the upper wall of house 1. Sample SW 22-1 was a concentration of sticky, soapy white sediment found adhering to the underside of the polished stone disc (SF 222) next to the mouth of the burial. Were they weathered/degraded steatite, perhaps mixed with coarse clay, or derived from some other substance?

The artefacts are of varied typology. Before sampling, which was accomplished by drilling, the appearance of the fabric was noted. Having cleaned an area of the cross-section of each artefact, multiple drillings were taken with a tungsten carbide drill head (2.5 mm diameter) and the pooled powder was collected. The sample weight was at least 500 mg. The same procedure was applied to the lumps of steatite. In two cases, SFs 61 and 907, it was possible to take an additional sample in the form of a cleaned fragment which was then crushed to powder in an agate mortar. The ICP-MS analyses were carried out by Valerie Olive at the Scottish Universities Environmental Research Centre, East Kilbride using an Agilent 7500ce instrument. The analytical procedure and acid dissolution method have been described by her in Jones *et al.* (2007). Table 6.3 lists the artefacts. Assessment of the compositions was achieved by examining the graphical display of the rare earth element (REE) *pattern* and *concentration range* in chondrite-normalised form (Fig. 6.6).

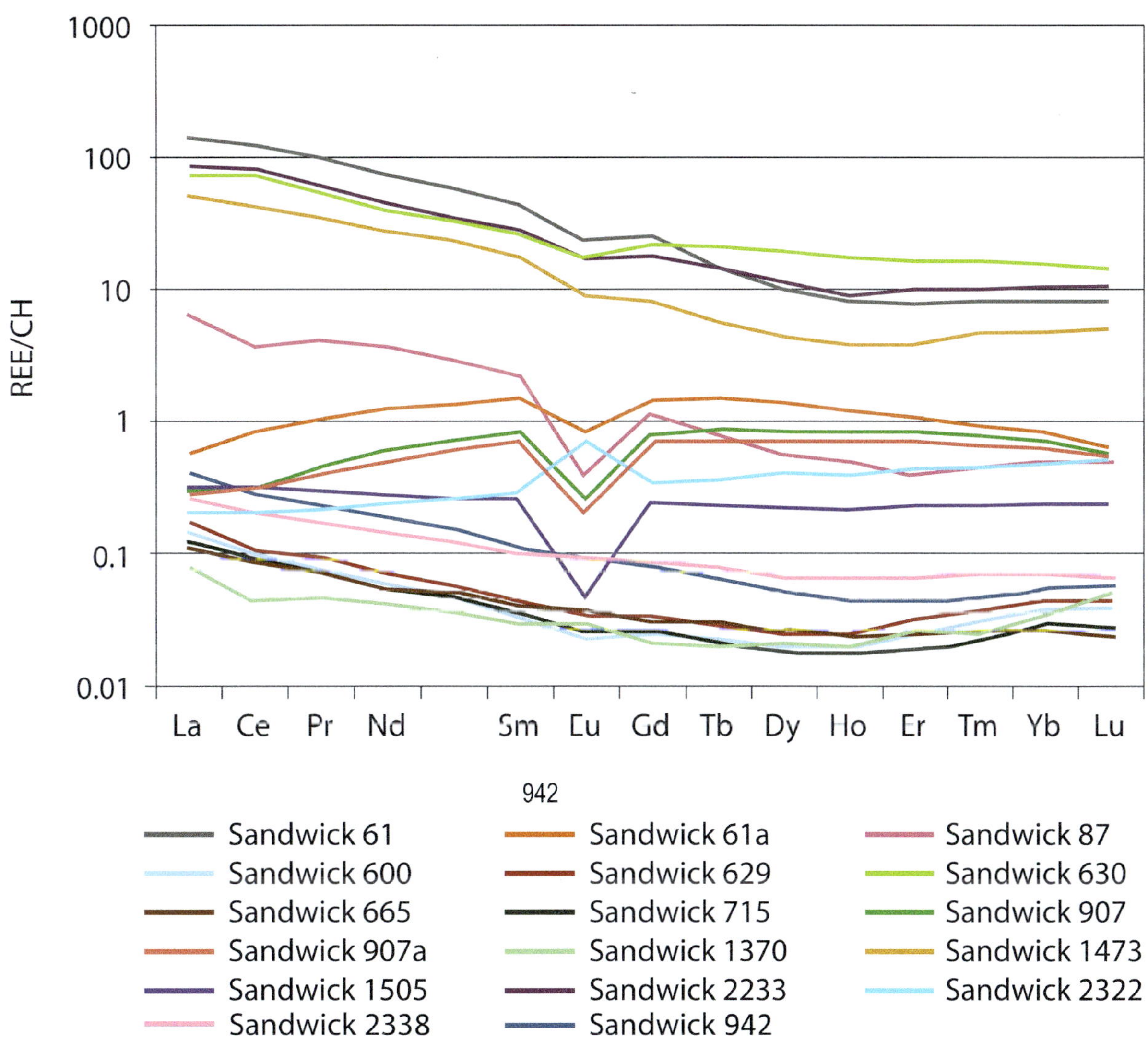

Figure 6.6 Results of rare earth element analysis of steatite objects and deposits

Table 6.3 Steatite pieces subjected to rare earth element analysis

SF number	*Description*
61	Chip – crushed sample
61a	Chip – drilled sample
87	Large bead with burial
600	Fragment
629	Perforated disc
630	Body sherd; hard, brownish fine fabric
665	Fragment
715	Fragment
907	Tool blade – drilled sample
907a	Tool blade – crushed sample
1370	Scoop
1473	Lump
1505	Large lump
2233	Fragment
2322	Large body sherd of large vessel (Norse)
2338	Vessel fragment (Norse)
942	Tuyère

Looking at the rare earth element patterns in Fig. 6.6, three groupings are apparent:

1. 61, 600, 630, 1473 and 2233 have high REE concentrations
2. 61a, 87, 907, 907a, 1505 and 2322 have intermediate REE concentrations
3. 629, 665, 715, 1370, 2338 and tuyère have low REE concentrations

In terms of origin, it is the REE pattern which is most important. In that respect, groups 1 and 3 are similar, their REE patterns apparently resembling those obtained for Fetlar better than those, for example, at nearby Clibberswick or Bayanne.

Group 2 is not uniform. For example, SF 2322, which is macroscopically different from the majority of the other artefacts examined from Milla Skerra, has a positive Europium anomaly. No match has yet been found for it; interestingly, this vessel fragment was found (unstratified on the deflated sand surface) at the Norse-period farmstead on the same beach (see Forster above). The others in this group have negative Europium anomalies and in that sense are not significantly different from those in groups 1 and 3.

The most economic interpretation of the data is that all three groups have a common or related origin. Two scenarios are possible: *either* a single source close to Milla Skerra that has naturally wide concentration ranges, *or* a number of neighbouring sources, again close to Milla Skerra. In support of the former scenario is the presence of 61a in group 2 and 61 in group 1. The exception is vessel fragment SF 2322, which is from a different source.

Table 6.4 Heavy stone artefacts

Artefact	*No.*
Smoothers	31
Polishers	5
Polished pebbles	4
Pebbles	3
Burnisher	1
Plain hammerstones	13
Flaked hammerstones	4
Pounder/grinders	3
Faceted cobbles	3
Anvils	3
Perforated pieces	4
Ard points	2
Heart-shaped object	1
Saddle quern	1
Grinding slab	1
Natural stone 'trough'	1
Pivot stone	1
Architectural fragment	1

Soil samples SW 86 and SW 022-1 were analysed by X-ray diffraction in the Earth Sciences Department at Glasgow University. Their compositions appear similar to each other but at the same time they are complex. Neither of them shows the presence of talc. Their composition and origins could possibly be established with further analysis.

Heavy stone tools

Ann Clarke

A total of 82 heavy stone artefacts were recovered in the excavations (Table 6.4). Most are cobble tools of various types, with smoothers and plain hammerstones the most common. The rest of the assemblage consists of small numbers of other tools such as perforated weights, ard points, anvils, a heart-shaped object and several single pieces such as a saddle quern, grinding slab and hollowed stone. The assemblage is discussed here with reference to raw material selection, manufacture, use and context. Figures 6.7–6.13 show the most diagnostic tools from the different phases.

Raw material

As is common to prehistoric stone assemblages from the north of Shetland, a wide range of stone types is represented. This is a result of the complex local geology of Unst, which comprises metamorphosed sediments (meta-sediments) such as schist, gneiss and phyllite and metamorphosed igneous rocks (meta-igneous) such as granite and serpentinite. Close identification of the rock was not undertaken and instead the broad categories of 'meta-sediment' and 'meta-igneous' rock were used to describe and encompass the wide variation of geological rock types.

There is some evidence for the selection of particular rock types for different jobs. The smoothers tend to be made of softer meta-igneous rock, such as serpentinite; this stone may have been selected for its fine grain, which gives a smooth finish to the material being worked. Schists were chosen for the larger plain hammerstones and the flaked hammerstones, perhaps because cobbles of this rock type had weathered into suitable elongated shapes and were tougher. The only tools made from a rock that may not have been found in the immediate vicinity of the site were the two ard points. Metamorphosed sandstone was probably selected for these cultivation tools because it was more easily shaped by flaking and pecking into a suitable form and it was more tractable in the soil. The location of a suitable source for this metamorphosed sandstone on Shetland is not known at present.

Cobble tools that have been worn by rubbing

Cobbles that have been used as smoothers are the most common type of tool in the Milla Skerra assemblage, with 31 in total. The cobbles are from a variety of meta-igneous rocks ranging widely in shape and size (up to 46 mm by 210 mm). Despite the wide selection criteria for the original blanks, the wear traces left on these tools are quite consistent, comprising one cobble face that has been worn to a flattish and smooth finish or occasionally a slight concave cross-section. These worn faces vary in surface finish, as some are shinier than others and four bear visible multi-directional striations; this is most likely a function of the original raw material – where the softer rock such as serpentinite was more easily damaged by striations and took a polish more readily. Traces of a glossy residue or colour from the substance being worked are present on three of these tools.

Just over half the smoothers bear additional wear traces in the form of rough pecking and/or flaking on one or both ends. This would seem to be at odds with the actions of rubbing that produced the worn faces, and it is likely that some of the smoothers were re-used as hammerstones. Evidence from one smoother (SF 1927, Fig. 6.7) supports this observation, as the flaking damage on the ends clearly truncated the smoothly worn face. It is also clear that only smoothers above *c.* 100 mm in length were re-used as hammerstones; smaller examples have no additional end damage. Another tool (SF 78, Fig. 6.8) has had a complex history of use, as it appears to have originally been a pounder/grinder which was then re-used as a smoother, creating shiny faces with black colouring. It was subsequently used as a hammerstone, as it is heavily flaked over the original pecked facets.

The polishers (five in total) comprise three small pebbles with one polished face (SFs 1521, 2129, 2123) and two larger pebbles with visible striations and high polish on one face (SFs 2030 (Fig. 6.7) and 2282).

The single burnisher (SF 668, Fig. 6.9) is distinguished from the polishers and smoothers purely on the basis of shape. It is a spatulate-shaped schist pebble that was lightly worn by rubbing on one end, possibly through being used to burnish leather-hard pots.

Four polished pebbles (SFs 111, 1937, 1978, 2151) are included in this larger group because of the high all-over polish that they bear. Whether this polish was the result of their use as tools or whether they were selected for their (potential) surface finish is not known for sure. Three of them have similar dimensions (27 mm 25 mm) and the other is smaller. They have attractive colours in common, including a mottled green/brown rock and a blue/green rock; this latter material is serpentinite and is the same rock as the two smallest polishers.

Rubbing the cobble back and forth over a substance or material has clearly produced the wear on these tools. The lack of visible striations on most of the smoothers would indicate that a soft material such as leather was worked to produce such little damage to the surfaces of the stones. Several smaller cobbles were selected as polishers; these bear patches of high polish and were clearly used for a different job, most likely for burnishing smaller areas of leather or perhaps pottery. The four all-over polished pebbles may, by virtue of their similar size, be some form of gaming counter, marker or token, but their association with the polishers in yard 5 suggests that they were all used to finish the material being worked.

Smoothers and polishers were in use throughout the Iron Age of the Northern Isles (Clarke 2006). At the Bronze Age and Iron Age site at Bayanne on Yell, these tools were initially used during the first Iron Age occupation, though they form a smaller component of the assemblage than at Milla Skerra and were found together with a wider range of other tool types. The Middle Iron Age site at Mine Howe, Orkney contained a significant number of smoothers and polishers that are closely associated with a multi use workshop, and this is discussed in more detail below.

Cobble tools that have been worn by bashing, pecking and flaking

This group includes simple forms of hammerstone, most commonly made from schists or coarser-grained metamorphic rocks; eight quartz hammerstones were also recovered and are described here by Torben Ballin. The flaked hammerstones (four in total) are at the larger end of the size range for the plain hammerstones, and their use as heavy hammers has left rough flaking on one or both ends. The plain hammerstones (13 in total) have also been used rather heavily, leaving rough pecking and some flaking on one or both ends (SFs 995 and 164, Fig. 6.8). Of the site's

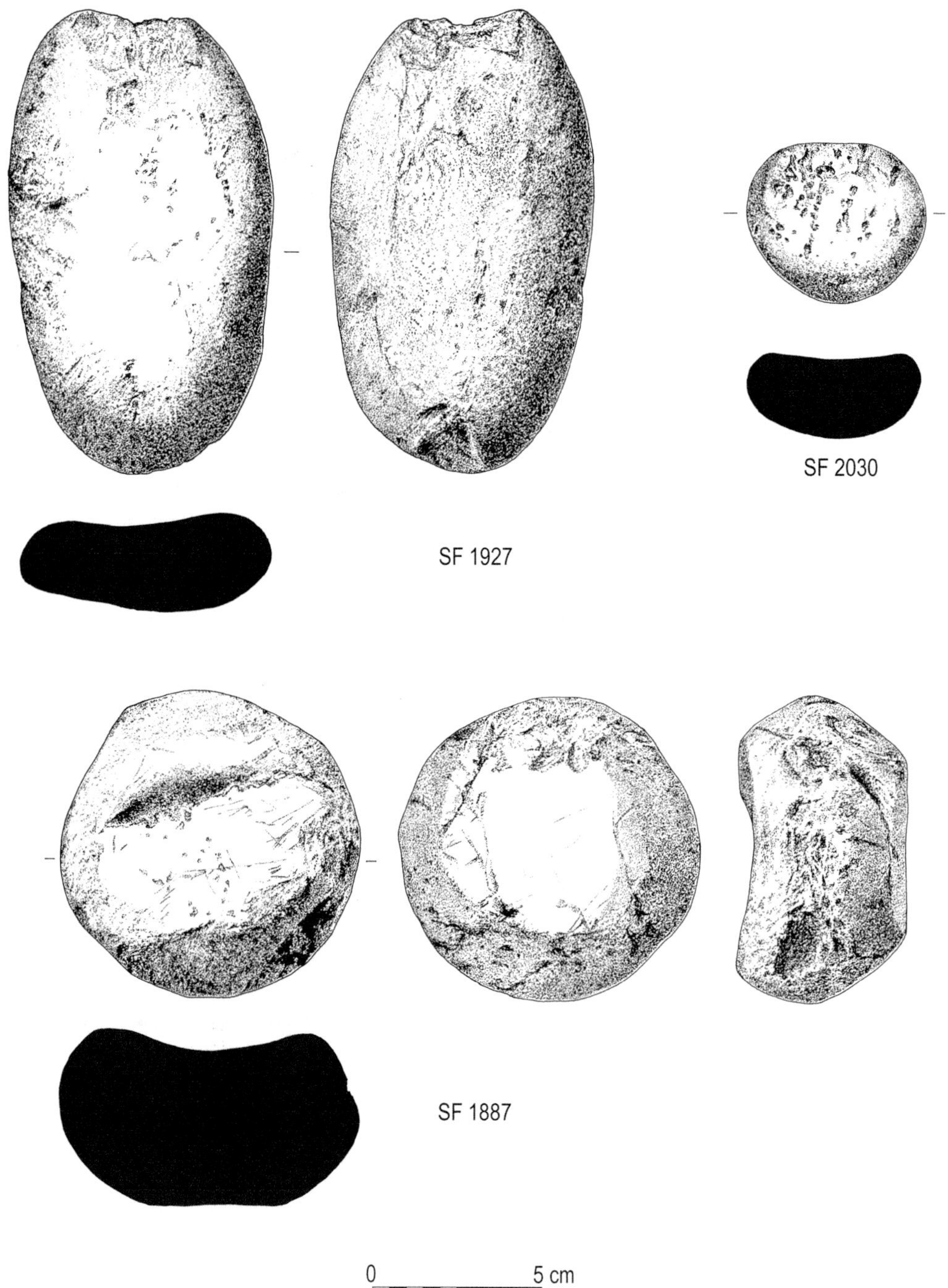

Figure 6.7 Smoother re-used as a hammerstone (SF 1927), polisher (SF 2030) and pounder/grinder with worn facets (SF 1887) from phases 2B and 2C, in and around yard 5

eight quartz hammerstones, most have one main working end and several have been used in a pragmatic manner, where all points and ridges found occasional use.

Cobble tools that bear worn facets

The pounder/grinders (three in total) are made from cobbles of fine-grained meta-igneous rocks. Two of them are sub-circular in shape and bear broad, ridged facets around most of the tool (SF 1372, Fig. 6.10) or the entire perimeter (SF 1887, Fig. 6.7). These have been made by fine pecking and grinding. The faces have also been worn heavily to a flat, polished surface with visible multi-directional striations on SF 1887 and a patch of pecking located centrally on SF 1372. The third piece is a fragment of a larger pounder/grinder (SF 2066) with a rounded, roughly pecked facet made on the surviving end.

The faceted cobbles (three in total) are also made of meta-igneous rocks, but they bear smaller, more undistinguished facets than the pounder/grinders. These facets are formed by rough to fine pecking. The most

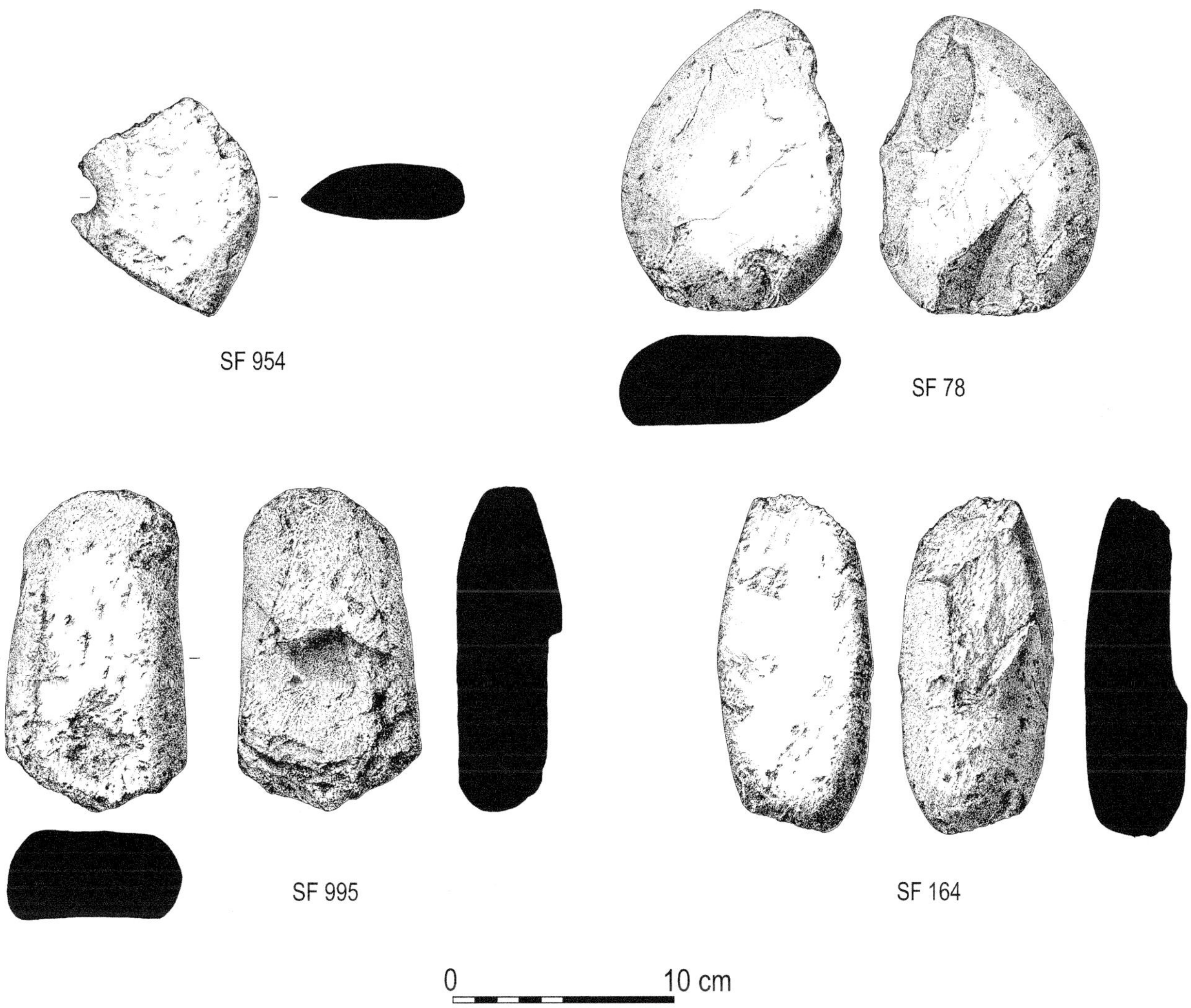

Figure 6.8 Loom weight (SF 954) and hammerstone (SF 995) left among thick midden on the floor of house 1 (phase 6A), and a hammerstone (SF 164) and pounder/grinder later used as smoother and hammerstone (SF 78), both from phase 7C

interesting tool is a flat, circular cobble with a narrow, broken band of faceting that has been pecked and ground around half of the perimeter (SF 1950, Fig. 6.11). This tool and another (SF 2235) also have single faces that have been worn flat and smooth in the manner of the smoothers.

Since pounder/grinders are a common tool form at many Bronze Age and Iron Age sites, they were most likely used to process basic foodstuffs such as grain. However, this is just a guess as no experimental reproduction of wear traces has ever been carried out to assess this. The faceted cobbles, with their smaller worn surfaces, were probably used for more varied processing jobs that did not involve such heavy work.

Anvils

Three anvils were recovered from the excavations. A small anvil (SF 2185) has been made from a tabular schist cobble, which bears circular patches of rough pecking in the centre of both faces, forming slight hollows *c*. 35 mm in diameter. A larger anvil (SF 553) is simply a slabby cobble with a patch of rough pecking in the centre of one face.

The largest piece (SF 597, Fig. 6.12) is an enigmatic stone; the features together resemble a sculpted face and it could be described as a hollowed stone, but it has been grouped with anvils in this report as it was most probably associated with some craft activity. This large schist slab is a naturally squared block with a pointed end. Two oval hollows have been pecked towards the squared end and look like eyes. Hollowed stones of various forms are quite common to some Iron Age contexts and the group is very wide, encompassing squared blocks or rounded cobbles with single bowl-shaped hollows to slabs with pecked depressions (Clarke 2006). At Pool, Sanday the hollowed stones were generally formed of single hollows on a block or cobble. At Mine Howe, Orkney the hollows were more like pecked depressions, as if the block of stone had been used as an anvil or working slab, and these resemble those on SF 597 from Milla Skerra.

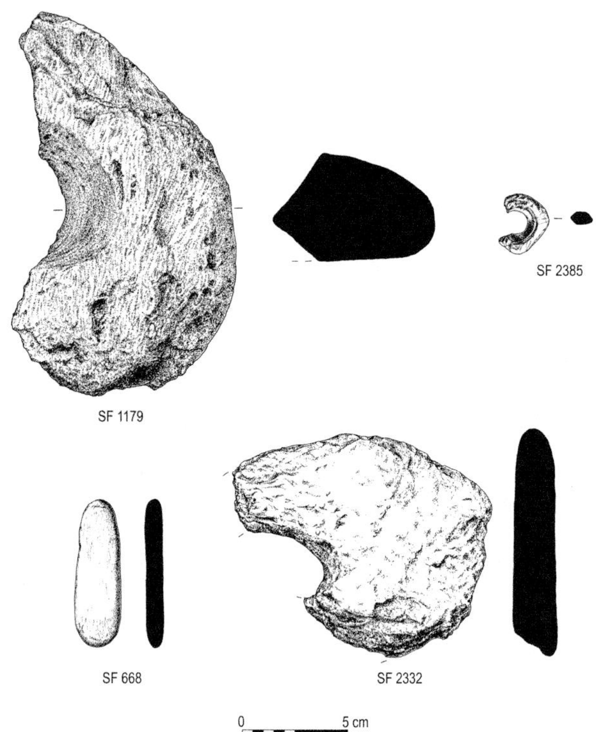

Figure 6.9 Perforated stone (SF 2385, phase 4A), weight (SF 2332, phase 4D), heart-shaped object (SF 1179, phase 5B) and whetstone (SF 668, phase 7B)

This anvil was found in an occupation deposit (54) close to the heap of bog iron (59) in cell 2, and could be associated with the production of metal artefacts. The other two anvils were not directly associated with metal-working activity on site, but the smaller anvil (SF 2185) is very similar in form to a number of anvils found in metal-working contexts at Mine Howe (Clarke 2008).

Perforated stones

Four perforated stones were recovered from the site. There is a small bead made from what appears to be a rounded schist pebble (SF 2380). Breakage has truncated the narrow, straight-sided perforation. The other three pieces are most likely weights, all made from schist cobbles. They vary in shape and size, with the smallest (SF 2385, Fig. 6.9) being a tabular pebble with a wide biconical perforation, apparently drilled into the centre of the piece. An incised circle around the perforation on both faces forms a decorative element.

The other two weights are fragments with traces of biconical perforations pecked into the centre of the cobble (SFs 954, Fig. 6.8 and 2332, Fig. 6.9). Rubbing and polish on the inside of the surviving perforated surface of the smaller weight (SF 954) indicates that it had been suspended.

The weights are so varied in size that it is unlikely that they were used for the same purposes. The weight fragment (SF 954) found in the initial post-abandonment midden in house 1 (122) may have had a domestic use such as a loom weight. The incised decoration around the perforation of the smallest weight (SF 2385) suggests that it also functioned in the domestic sphere, but was used with lighter materials.

Ard points

Both of the ard points were made from metamorphosed, fine-grained, grey micaceous sandstone. The complete ard point (SF 2236, Fig. 6.10) has been very nicely made, with a squared butt end and a fine tapering working end. It has been pecked over most of its surface to shape and strengthen it. Some flake damage on this pointed end indicates that it was used as a tilling tool. The other ard point (SF 1967) is just a fragment from the tip of a very well-worn ard point, and it most likely broke off on impact in the soil.

Heart-shaped object

This is a just a fragment a flat cobble of schist which has been broken around the edges and the perforation (SF 1179, Fig. 6.9). The perforation appears typical of the bean-shaped holes characteristic of heart-shaped implements (Clarke 2006). The only measurable dimension is the thickness, which at 28 mm is rather thicker than those heart-shaped objects from Bayanne, which are made from schist and phyllite (average 18 mm thick) (Clarke 2014), but it is likely that these flatter tabular rocks were less readily available on Unst. These heart-shaped objects have a quite specific period of use, and at larger sites it appears that they are closely linked to keeping animals inside byres (Clarke 2006) (see discussion below).

Saddle quern

This is a fine example of a shallow saddle quern (SF 1304, Fig. 6.13). It is made from an elongated slab of coarse-grained meta-sediment and the upper face has been worn by grinding to a gentle concave cross-section. This working surface is worn right out to the edges in a manner typical of Early Iron Age querns. It was re-used in paving (124) in house 1.

Grinding slab

This is a large cobble of fine-grained meta-igneous rock, which has been used on one face as a grinder (SF 1814). The worked face has been worn to a shallow concave cross-section by rubbing or grinding; it has a very smooth and slightly shiny finish. One end has been heavily bashed and flaked, as if from use as a heavy hammer. This was found together with a smoother (also SF 1814), suggesting that perhaps that the smoothers were used on stone slabs such as this.

Pivot stone

This large water-worn boulder (SF 1272) has a regular round-based hollow ground into the centre of one face. It was most likely a pivot stone, but is unfortunately

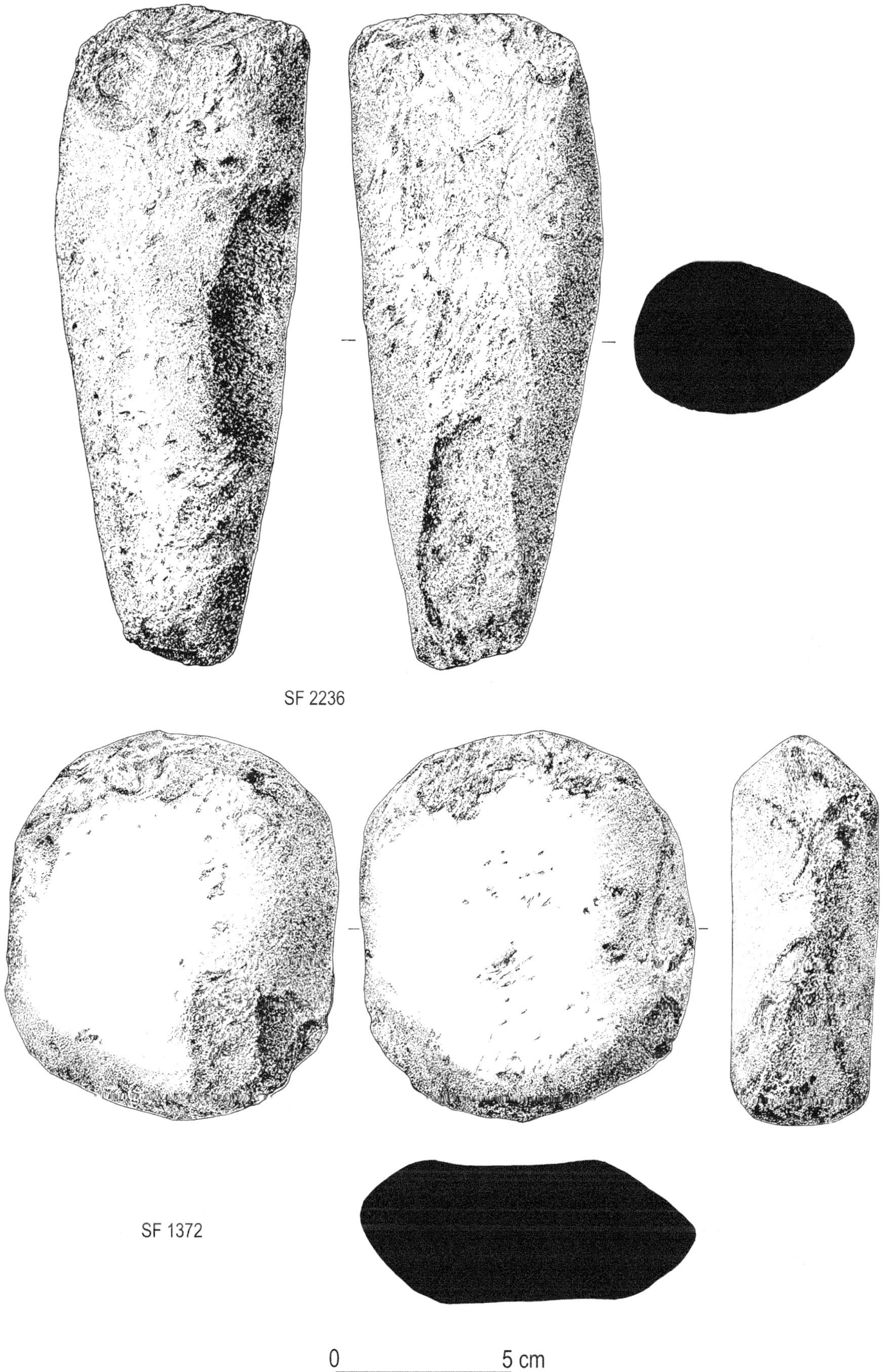

Figure 6.10 Ard point (SF 2236) and pounder/grinder (SF 1372), both from phase 4A

Figure 6.11 Smoother, pecked and ground around the edges (SF 1950), from a phase 4A ploughed midden outside the structures

Figure 6.12 Anvil SF 597 from cell 2 (phase 7A)

unstratified so it is not known with which structure it was associated.

Natural stone 'trough'

This was found in the paved floor of yard 5 and at first sight resembles a fragment of a trough quern (SF 2216). Closer examination indicates that the shaping is a consequence of weathering to the natural bedding formations of the meta-sediment, creating the appearance of a rim and bowl. Whether the shape was important to the occupants is not known. It sat in the paving with the weathered surface facing up.

Architectural fragment

This is a small fragment of a mottled grey and white metamorphic rock, which may have been imported from elsewhere (SF 3). It is an angular block that has most likely been dressed to shape and appears to have been part of a larger stone piece.

Contexts of deposition

The stone artefacts were scattered throughout the various phases of occupation at Milla Skerra. Table 6.5 shows their distribution according to phase and area.

A significant number of stone tools were also found outside of the structures in successive ground surfaces, and this external assemblage has some interesting contrasts in composition to the tools more closely associated with the structures (see *Discussion* below). Exterior middens (contexts 75, 40) that built up and were probably ploughed during phase 4 contained a faceted cobble (SF 1950, Fig. 6.11), a perforated stone (SF 2385, Fig. 6.9) and an ard point (SF 2236, Fig. 6.10). Later ground surfaces (contexts 53, 72) contained four smoothers, a plain hammerstone, a polisher, a faceted cobble and a heart-shaped object (SF 1179, Fig. 6.9). The ground surface (context 25) in use during the latest phase of the settlement (phase 7B) contained two smoothers.

Discussion

This is an interesting assemblage of stone tools because it indicates at least two different periods of activity at the site: late Bronze Age or early Iron Age, and Iron Age. The small earlier assemblage is identified by comparison with other well-dated assemblages in the region and there is some contextual evidence that it was deposited earlier (see below). However, there is some overlap with possibly later tool types, particularly in the external contexts, so the exact mechanism for redeposition is not clear. There are several assemblages from recently excavated sites in the Northern Isles which can help date the use of Milla Skerra:

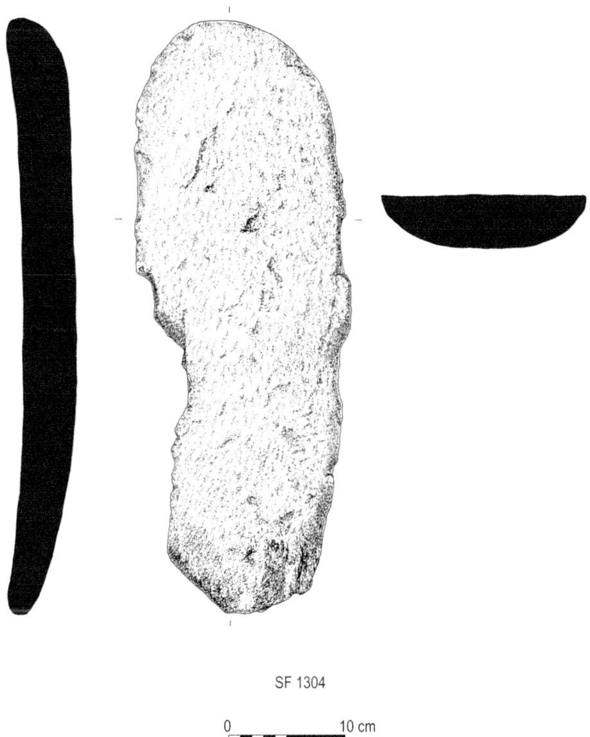

Figure 6.13 Saddle quern SF 1304, re-used for paving in house 1 during phase 4B

Bayanne on Yell; Sumburgh at Dunrossness on mainland Shetland, and Mine Howe on Orkney.

The small late Bronze Age to early Iron Age assemblage at Milla Skerra comprises the two ard points (SFs 2236 and 1967), the heart-shaped object (SF 1179) and possibly the pounder/grinders and faceted cobbles (for example, SFs 1372 and 1887), though these two types of cobble tool were also in common use during the Iron Age of the Northern Isles. At Milla Skerra, most of these stone artefacts were found in midden that built up probably from the 6th century BC or in external ground surfaces that had been ploughed and mixed. A pounder/grinder (SF 2066) was found in an occupation deposit in yard 5 and another (SF 1372) in midden outside the yard; a faceted cobble (SF 596) was also re-used in the rubble base for a partition between yard 3 and cell 2. Thus most of the typologically earlier tools either came from early contexts or were in redeposited contexts. The saddle quern (SF 1304) likewise is of early Iron Age date, and it was re-used as a paving slab in house 1.

The heart-shaped object (SF 1179) finds parallels at Sumburgh and Bayanne (and also Jarlshof), where these artefacts are associated with late Bronze Age structures that were altered in the early Iron Age; the use of these objects appears to span this period, suggesting that the use of the buildings remained the same despite structural alterations (Clarke 2006). The structure at Sumburgh has been interpreted as a byre (Downes and Lamb 2000) and it is likely that the perforated heart-shaped objects were somehow linked to the tethering of animals, perhaps protecting their hides from the rubbing of the tethering rope (Clarke 2006). At Bayanne, these objects also had a very discrete association with one particular structure. The similar heart-shaped object at Milla Skerra came from an external deposit (72) that formed relatively late in the sequence, probably during the construction of cell 2. It may have been redeposited there, perhaps having been taken from a nearby building that was robbed for stone to construct it.

Ard points were in use in Shetland from the Neolithic (at Scord of Brouster) right through the Bronze Age to some point in the early Iron Age (Clarke 2006). At Bayanne, where occupation continued well into the 1st millennium AD, the use or at least the deposition of stone ard points appeared to cease with the construction of structure 1 in the Iron Age (Clarke 2014). Though ard points are cultivation tools, they were often redeposited in structural contexts and thus are common finds on settlement sites up to the early Iron Age. The ard point (SF 1967) found in the external midden (224) associated with yard 5 may have been deposited as early as the 8th century BC, as indicated by radiocarbon dates from the middens, but probably in the 6th century (see Chapter 2). The other ard point (SF 2236), from an external ground surface (75), may have been lost during ploughing of the midden-rich soil.

Pounder/grinders and faceted cobbles are found in many prehistoric contexts and are documented well into the Iron Age, so it may be an error to assign these to the group of LBA/EIA artefacts. However, these tools do appear to have been spatially separate from the other tool types that were found in the various occupation deposits of the structures and one of the most likely explanatio ns for this is related to the use of these areas, as discussed below.

In the dominance of smoothers (some of which were also used as heavy hammers) and polishers together with the presence of plain and large flaked hammerstones, the Milla Skerra assemblage is very similar to that from the structure at Mine Howe, Orkney which has been identified as a workshop specialising in the production of metalwork and other artefacts, with several different phases of use (Clarke 2008). At Mine Howe, particular stone tools were related to the use of the structure as a workshop: large *in situ* anvils, sharpening stones and perforated slabs as well as smoothers and polished pebbles. Stone finds from the bank that formed around the outside of the workshop included whetstones and polishers, tool types that were notably absent from the interior. This suggested that either there were episodes in clearing out the workshop of particular tool types or else that there were spatially separate areas for various steps in the production of metal objects.

Milla Skerra did not produce the same wide range of tool types as the workshop at Mine Howe, and the assemblage is much smaller. However, there are anvils (the smaller one is very similar to a number found at Mine Howe), smoothers, polishers and polished pebbles, and these tools

Table 6.5 Distribution of stone tools by phase and area, in and around the structures

Phase	*Area*	*Tools and SF numbers*
2A	Pre-yard 5 ogs 234	Polisher (SF 2223)
		Polished pebble (SF 2151)
		Plain hammerstone (SF 2222)
2A	Yard 5 paving 220	Pounder/grinder (SF 2066)
		Trough (SF 2216)
2B	Yard 5 occupation deposits	Smoother (SF 1927, Illus 6.6)
		Polisher (SF 2030)
2B	Middens outside yard 5	Smoothers (SFs 1886, 2215)
		Cobble tool (SF 1887, Illus 6.6)
		Plain hammerstones (SFs 1726, 2149)
		Polished pebble (SF 1978)
		Ard point (SF 1967)
		Anvil (SF 2185)
3A	Shell-rich midden outside yard 5	Smoother and grinding slab (SF 1814)
3A	Midden heaped over yard 5	Hammerstones (SFs 996, 997, 1763, 1914)
		Flaked hammerstones (SF 977)
		Pounder/grinder (SF 1372)
		Smoothers (SFs 1359, 1393)
		Polished pebble (SF 217)
4A	Stony midden heaped over yard 5	Hammerstone (SF 1263)
		Flaked hammerstone (SF 1199)
4B	Walls of yards 3 & 4	Anvil (SF 553)
		Flaked hammerstone (SF 2298)
4B	House 1 paving & wall	Plain hammerstones (SF 631, 2261)
		Saddle quern (SF 1304, Illus 6.7)
		Smoother (SF 1094)
4C	First clay floor in yard 3	Smoother (SF 1073)
4D	Rubble floor in remodelled yard 3	Smoother (SF 873)
		Large perforated weight (SF 2332, Illus 6.11)
5A	House 1 occupation	Smoother (SF 136)
5B	Cell 2 construction	Faceted cobble (SF 596)
6A	Midden over house 1 floor	Perforated weight (SF 954, Illus 6.12)
6B	Latest floor in yard 3	Smoother (SF 429)
6B	Post-collapse midden in house 1	Plain hammerstone (SF 784)
		Polisher (SF 2282)
7A	Latest use of cell 2	Large anvil with pecked hollows (SF 597, Illus 6.10)
		Smoother (SF 438)
7B	Yard 6 wall	Flaked hammerstone (SF 2270)
7C	Post-abandonment sandy middens	Smoothers (SFs 19, 89, 285, 93, 111, 163, 164)
		Polished pebble (SF 56)
		Quartz pebble (SF 2352)
10	Temporary occupation in 5th–6th C	Bead (SF 2380)
		Angular masonry fragment (SF 3)

were more often found in occupation deposits associated with the structures than in redeposited contexts. They also appeared throughout the external deposits, but there was no pattern of structured deposition to indicate how they may have been used. There is just a hint of functional differentiation, with the presence of polishers and polished pebbles found in, around and over yard 5, but the numbers here are too small to support a significant difference in the use of this area.

The evidence from the stone tools points to uses other than the typically domestic. Domestic occupation would typically result in a broader range of stone artefacts, such as pounder/grinders, stone discs, spindle whorls, lamps, querns and so on. Comparison with the site at Mine Howe would suggest that some industrial or craft activity was being carried out in the yards.

The radiocarbon dates from Milla Skerra (see Chapter 2) indicate that by AD 90–240, the structures had been abandoned, although settlement continued in the near vicinity until the site was inundated with sand before AD 150–390, the date of death of the person buried next to it. Burials at Mine Howe from *c.* 60 BC–AD 130 (Card and Downes 2007) marked a hiatus in the use of the workshop rather than abandonment. It is possible then that the use of yards 3 and 4 and house 1 at Milla Skerra, during the 2nd and 1st centuries BC, were contemporary with Mine Howe. The varying types and deposition of the stone tools from Mine Howe indicate a broad range of craft activities based in and around the workshop and with several different phases of use.

In contrast, just one or two types dominate the stone tools at Milla Skerra and this would imply a narrower range of activities that employed the tools. Leather-working is the most obvious guess, but this would have to be supported by some experimental replication of wear traces on smoothers and polishers before we can know for sure.

Struck quartz

Torben Bjarke Ballin

A substantial assemblage of chipped quartz was recovered during the excavations at Milla Skerra, numbering 3593 pieces. This report characterizes the lithic artefacts with special reference to raw materials, typological composition and technology, and attempts to date the finds and discuss their affinities. The evaluation of the lithic material is based upon a detailed catalogue of all the lithic finds from Milla Skerra, and the artefacts are referred to by their number (CAT no.) in this catalogue, which is included with the project archive (deposited with Shetland Museum and Archives).

In total, 97% of the assemblage is debitage, while 1% is cores and 2% is tools. Numerous natural pieces were discarded during initial assessment and 151 pieces were discarded during the final examination and characterization of the material. The definitions of the main lithic categories are as follows:

- Blades and microblades: Flakes where $L \geq 2W$ (L = length; W = width). In the case of blades $W > 8$ mm, in the case of microblades $W \leq 8$ mm.
- Cores: Artefacts with only dorsal (negative or concave) surfaces – if three or more flakes have been detached, the piece is a core; if fewer than three flakes have been detached, the piece is a split or flaked pebble.
- Tools: Artefacts with secondary retouch (modification).
- Chips: Usually defined as all flakes and indeterminate pieces, the greatest dimension (GD) of which is ≤ 10 mm. Due to constraints on time, chips from Milla Skerra were defined as pieces smaller than 14 mm.
- Flakes: All lithic artefacts with one identifiable ventral (positive or convex) surface, $GD > 10$ mm and $L < 2W$.
- Indeterminate pieces: Lithic artefacts which cannot be unequivocally identified as either flakes or cores. Generally the problem of identification is due to irregular breaks, frost-shattering or fire-crazing. Chunks are larger indeterminate pieces and, in the case of quartz, the problem of identification usually originates from a piece flaking along natural planes of weakness rather than flaking in the usual conchoidal way.

Raw materials – types, sources and condition

The Milla Skerra lithic assemblage is made up entirely of quartz, in common with the assemblages from Burland on Trondra and Bayanne on Yell (Ballin 2014a; 2014b). Alternative lithic materials are almost non-existent on Shetland, with only jasper having been exploited sporadically in the southern part of the island group (for example, at Sumburgh and Burland); pitchstone appears never to have reached northernmost Scotland (Ballin 2008). The great majority of the quartz artefacts from Milla Skerra are in homogeneous white milky quartz, but a small proportion is in saccharoidal quartz. However, most of the grainier quartz forms may be burnt pieces in various stages of disintegration (see below). Some pieces contain impurities of mainly mica, in many cases forming intersecting layers, and some are characterized by sheets of micro-crystals. Most of the material appears to have been collected from the local beach.

A large proportion of the assemblage is affected by fire (19% of all pieces >chips). As explained in Ballin (2008), it is difficult to identify burnt quartz but, in general, the pieces tend to lose weight when burnt, develop notable cracks or micro-pitting and sometimes change colour to paler white or rusty brown.

Debitage

In total, 3477 pieces of debitage (waste from artefact production) were recovered from the site. The quartz debitage includes 2277 chips (66%), 670 flakes (19%),

Table 6.6 Reduction sequence in the quartz assemblage

	Quantity	*%*
Primary	99	15
Secondary	432	64
Tertiary	139	21
TOTAL	670	100

Table 6.7 Applied percussion techniques and definable unmodified blanks

	Quantity	*%*
Hard percussion	79	17
Bipolar technique	380	82
Platform collapse	4	1
TOTAL	463	100

13 blades (<1%) and microblades (<1%), and 517 indeterminate pieces (15%). No preparation flakes (crested pieces or core tablets) were recovered. The chip ratio is extremely high due to the sieving of selected contexts. As demonstrated in Ballin (1999b), the chip ratio of wet-sieved flint-dominated assemblages usually varies between *c.* 30% and 55%. Most likely, the high ratio is a product of the specific properties of quartz, which tends to flake in an intricate manner, thus producing more waste per finished tool than the same process would on other lithic materials.

Although the chip ratio varies considerably from context to context (*c.* 20–90%), this is probably due to sampling bias. An accurate picture of the variation between the site's sub-assemblages is best provided by the larger artefacts (>chips), which were recovered by traditional excavation.

The nine blades and four microblades are generally elongated bipolar flakes, and they do not represent specialised production. Almost 80% of the debitage is corticated (cortex-covered, with an abraded outer natural surface) (see Table 6.6). This percentage reflects the use of beach pebbles and cobbles rather than vein quartz and the application of an unsophisticated technological approach producing relatively few, usually thick inner flakes. The many primary pieces (15%) indicate that raw nodules were opened and/or quartered on the site.

The blanks were generally manufactured in bipolar technique (82%), although a number of hard percussion flakes (17%) were also identified (Table 6.7). However, it should be borne in mind that, when a corticated surface is struck directly, rather than a prepared platform (which was commonly done at Milla Skerra), the cortex may act as a cushion which softens the percussion indicators slightly. On occasion, this may make blanks produced in hard percussion appear as soft percussion flakes, and bipolar flakes may appear as hard percussion platform flakes. Most likely, the dominance at Milla Skerra of the bipolar technique was more marked than indicated by Table 6.6.

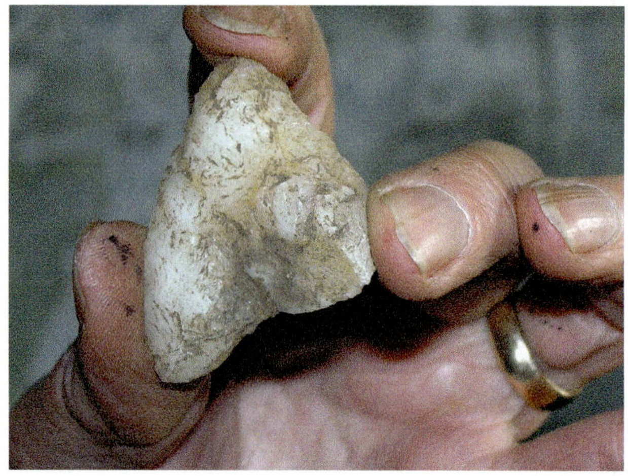

Figure 6.14 Base of a leaf-shaped arrowhead worked in quartz (CAT 1003)

Cores

In total, 45 cores were recovered from the site: 15 split pebbles (early-stage bipolar cores), 18 bipolar cores, five single-platform cores, six irregular (or multi-platform/multi-directional) cores, and one core fragment. The percentage distribution bipolar cores : platform cores is 73:27, which is a somewhat smaller bipolar ratio than that suggested by the blanks (82:17). The reason may be that, frequently, nodules worked in bipolar technique disintegrate into a series (4–6) of so-called orange-segment flakes without leaving any recognisable bipolar cores, and resulting in the general under-representation of such cores (cf. Ballin 1999a). A total of 28 orange-segment flakes were recovered from Milla Skerra (approximately 5% of all flakes).

Tools

A total of 71 tools were recovered during the excavations. The 33 scrapers dominate the assemblage, and the 20 simple edge-retouched pieces comprise another significant category. The tool assemblage also includes one arrowhead, three knives, one piercer and five notched or denticulated pieces. The technologically definable tool blanks include eight hard-hammer flakes and 17 bipolar flakes. The 71 tools make up 2% of the entire assemblage, which corresponds well to the ratio expected from a sieved assemblage (Ballin 1999b).

Arrowhead

The terminal (base or tip) fragment of a leaf-shaped arrowhead (CAT 1003, Fig. 6.14) was recovered from a cultivated soil (40) to the south of the structures. The surviving half of this rather large specimen measures 40 35 8 mm, with a probable original length of approximately 80 mm (Clark's Type 1B; Green 1980, 69). The rounded character of the pointed terminal suggests that it may be the base of a double-pointed piece.

Knives

Two of these are scale-flaked knives (CAT 3481, 3537) and one is an obliquely truncated piece (CAT 3468). The two scale-flaked pieces are of roughly the same size (average dimensions: 39 30 10 mm). CAT 3481 has dorsal scale-flaking along its right lateral cutting-edge, with the left lateral side having been blunted by cruder retouch. CAT 3537 has ventral scale-flaking along its left lateral cutting edge, with the opposed edge having been blunted by sporadic retouch. Both working edges are approximately straight. CAT 3468 is an obliquely truncated knife (35 19 7 mm), with the right lateral side forming a straight cutting-edge, whereas the left lateral side is blunted by abraded cortex.

Scrapers

The 33 scrapers are mainly short end-scrapers, but one blade-scraper, two double-scrapers, one side-scraper, and one concave scraper were also retrieved. The short end-scrapers form a heterogeneous category (average dimensions: 34 30 16 mm), mainly comprising fragments. However, it is possible to define a number of different sub-categories on the basis of general size, thickness, level of execution, and scraper-edge morphology. One category immediately stands out, namely seven almost intact, well-executed pieces (CAT 917, 1769, 1851, 2099, 2778, 3372, 3554). These are generally flake-based, are of medium to large size, and they have regularly convex, relatively acute to steep working-edges. Two thick pieces (CAT 918, 1850) are based on chunks and have convex, steep, denticulated working edges. CAT 965 is a relatively large piece (51 36 23 mm) with a thick handle-end and a narrow, convex, steep scraper edge at the distal end. The remainder includes very small pieces (for example, CAT 2570: 24 15 13 mm), as well as highly expedient pieces (for example, CAT 2444).

The site's solitary blade-scraper (CAT 325) is based on a fairly long but somewhat irregular and thick piece with a convex, slightly denticulated, steep scraper-edge at the distal end. Two double-scrapers form a small heterogeneous group, one of which is based on a regular, thin flake (CAT 919), whereas the other is based on an irregular, thick flake (CAT 438). Both are defined by their opposed, regularly convex, steep scraper-edges (one at the proximal end and one at the distal). CAT 919 is a well-executed piece with additional regular blunting along either lateral side. CAT 2862 is a small expedient side-scraper on a raw pebble with a crude, steep working edge along one side. The concave scraper (CAT 436) is an equally expedient piece on a thick flake, with concavities at either end transformed into concave scraper-edges by sporadic retouch.

Piercer

One small piercer was retrieved (CAT 30). It is a very small, thin flake with a distal tip, and the working end was formed by merging two retouched lateral sides. The tip is clearly abraded and rounded by use.

Notches and denticulates

Three notched (CAT 280, 924, 1050) and two denticulated pieces (CAT 2758, 3438) were found. They are all flake-based, and most are fragmented. The notched pieces have one lateral notch each, generally formed by a single large removal, and sporadic retouch (probably blunting) along various edges. A pointed end may have broken off CAT 1050, and the position of the notch and lateral retouch on either side of the break indicates that this piece may be a piercer which lost its working part.

One of the denticulated pieces (CAT 2758) is the small fragment of a thin flake with three small notches along one lateral side. The other denticulate is a much larger and thicker piece with three more substantial notches along one lateral side and shallow concavities along other edges. In general, the notches of the denticulated pieces are single-removal notches.

Pieces with edge-retouch: This category comprises 20 pieces. They differ considerably in shape and size and probably also function.

Technology

The lithic industry of Milla Skerra focused entirely on the production of slightly elongated flakes in quartz, with proper parallel-sided blades being absent, using both hard percussion and bipolar technique. The raw quartz was procured almost exclusively from the local beach walls, as evidenced by the abraded surfaces of the artefacts. The bipolar technique dominates the finds, with 82% of all definable unmodified blanks being bipolar flakes and 73% of the cores having been reduced using the technique.

No crested pieces or platform rejuvenation flakes were identified, but this may partly be due to difficulties associated with recognising delicate attributes on quartz (Ballin 2008), such as retouch or trimming. However, it is thought that the initial preparation of the platform cores may have been relatively simple, involving the preparation of a plain platform by striking a core, limited or no decortication and limited trimming of the platform edges. Of the five single-platform cores, only one displays platform-edge trimming and the flakes do not typically exhibit trimming.

The fact that several single-platform and irregular cores display crushed apexes or protuberances suggests that, when platform technology was employed at Milla Skerra, the method was thus: basic preparation of plain single-platform cores, followed by the manufacture of elongated flakes from the cores, probably by supporting them on anvils. Single-platform cores were probably rejuvenated by adding one additional platform (as witnessed at other quartz-using sites in the north and west of Scotland; Ballin 2008). Dual-platform cores were then transformed into irregular cores (with three or more platforms), and irregular cores were exhausted entirely by using bipolar technique. Thus, the bipolar technique was used to deplete the raw material of the platform, resulting in the production of many small bipolar flakes.

Table 6.8 Schema of the most important distributional trends in the quartz assemblage

	Yard 5	House 1	Yard 3	Yard 4	Cell 2	NW exterior	W exterior	SW exterior	S exterior	SE exterior
Burnt pieces	■		■	■			■			
Many primary flakes						■	■	■	■	■
Many flakes	■	■			■				■	■
Many chunks			■	■		■	■	■		
Many cores			■	■				■	■	■
Many tools				■			■	■	■	
Hammerstones			■	■		■		■		

The approach was also employed as an entirely separate way of reducing lithic material, allowing the production of much larger blanks. Although here blanks were usually modified using plain edge-retouch, a few tools were made using invasive retouch. This is most clearly demonstrated by CAT 1003, the leaf-shaped arrowhead. This piece is a fairly accomplished implement, shaped by full invasive retouch of both faces. Although the retouch of the two scale-flaked knives is much more difficult to define, their cutting edges were sharpened by the limited use of invasive retouch (scale-flaking).

Distribution

It is possible to provide a basic picture of the activities taking place at prehistoric Milla Skerra – as well as their spatial configuration – by examining a number of key artefact categories. Chips have not been included in the distribution analysis due to sampling bias, and the debitage was not weighed due to funding constraints. The analysis (see Table 6.8) focuses on the general artefact categories; burnt pieces; primary flakes; the flake : chunk ratio; cores and tools.

Although some of the quartz artefacts are undoubtedly residual from earlier activity at the site, the recovery of quartz debitage, cores and tools throughout the stratigraphic sequence and across the site suggests that much of it is contemporary with the settlement's occupation. Activity areas may not have been devoted to particular functions such as living, work, storage and waste disposal; the spatial analyses of the quartz-bearing sites Bayanne on Yell, Scord of Brouster in the Walls peninsula and Dalmore on Lewis (Ballin 2002b; 2005; 2014a) indicate that knapping could take place in dwellings as well as on middens.

The distribution indicates that quartz was being knapped in yards 3, 4 and 5 as well as outside the structures. The fact that primary flakes were found almost exclusively outside the structures probably shows that it was more strictly organised, with different forms of knapping taking place in different areas. The cruder functions of bipolar knapping were conducted outside the yards; this is supported by a measurable difference between hard-hammer and bipolar flakes in terms of find location, with three-quarters of all bipolar flakes being recovered outside the structures, whereas only two-thirds of the hard-percussion flakes were found outside. From a common-sense perspective, it would make sense to carry out the more polluting forms of knapping away from the main living areas.

The retrieval of many flakes in house 1 and cell 2, but few or no primary flakes, chunks, cores and tools, may suggest they were either areas for the use of flakes (unmodified tools) or the storage of usable tool blanks. The recovery of higher than average numbers of tools in yard 4 and several external areas may pinpoint either areas for tool use (yard 4, external areas) or areas of final deposition (external areas).

Dating

Only one strictly diagnostic tool was recovered during the excavations at Milla Skerra – the fragment of a large leaf-shaped point (CAT 1003). This piece indisputably dates to the early Neolithic period. The two scale-flaked pieces (CAT 3481, 3537) are only datable to the broader Neolithic to early Bronze Age. In Britain, invasive retouch like these pieces display was introduced at the beginning of the early Neolithic (Butler 2005, 119), and it does not form part of the technical repertoire of industries post-dating the early Bronze Age (Clark 1936, 47). The scrapers include several well-executed pieces (for example, CAT 919, 1769, 1851, 2099, 2778), which suggests a date prior to the Bronze Age / Iron Age transition. The assemblage from later Bronze Age Bayanne includes a large number of well-formed scrapers, whereas that from early Iron Age Burland only includes more expedient, informal pieces (Ballin 2014b; 2014c).

This was clearly a flake industry, but due to the generally poorer flaking properties of quartz, compared to for example flint, quartz assemblages usually include very low numbers of blades (Ballin 2008). However, even flake industries may be more or less sophisticated. In comparison with other quartz assemblages from Shetland (ibid), the quartz artefacts from Milla Skerra are reasonably well executed, despite the fact that they were produced mainly using bipolar technique.

It has been suggested (Ballin 2002a) that, in peripheral parts of Scotland, systematic lithic production continued into later prehistoric periods long after it had been overtaken by metal technology in the south. This suggestion is supported by the recovery of several very late and fairly large quartz assemblages from Shetland, such as those of Bayanne and Burland (Ballin 2014b; 2014c).

The Milla Skerra material is technologically more closely related to the finds from Burland than to those from Bayanne in terms of technology, with the hard percussion technique dominating the Bayanne assemblage and the bipolar technique dominating the Milla Skerra and Burland assemblages. However, this is more likely to reflect the character of the procured raw material than chronology (Ballin 2008); vein quartz is more conducive to the platform technique, with its somewhat wasteful core preparation, while rounded quartz cobbles and pebbles may be more easily worked in bipolar technique. The reduction process employed at Milla Skerra appears more systematic and the resulting artefacts more standardised than at Burland, whereas the reduction process employed at Burland appears more unschematic and haphazard and the artefacts more expedient.

Conclusion

The typo-technological character of the quartz assemblage would suggest that these finds represent activity on the site during the period from the early Neolithic to the early Bronze Age (5th to 2nd millennium BC), although the dated stratigraphic sequence in fact built up during the mid 1st millennium BC to the early 1st millennium AD. Quartz artefacts were recovered throughout the site, from top to bottom, as well as inside and outside the structures. Due to the complexity of the site, it has not been possible to produce an unequivocal plan of the activities taking place at Milla Skerra, but it appears that quartz artefacts were being made and used throughout the settlement's history, although some spatial separation of activities may have occurred.

It may be possible to distinguish between several levels of quartz-related activities at the site. Crude reduction/quartering took place outside the buildings and on the middens; mainstream reduction/production of blanks took place in the yards and outside the buildings; quartz tools were used throughout the site, but especially in cell 2 and house 1, and rejected blanks and cores, as well as spent implements, were deposited in middens.

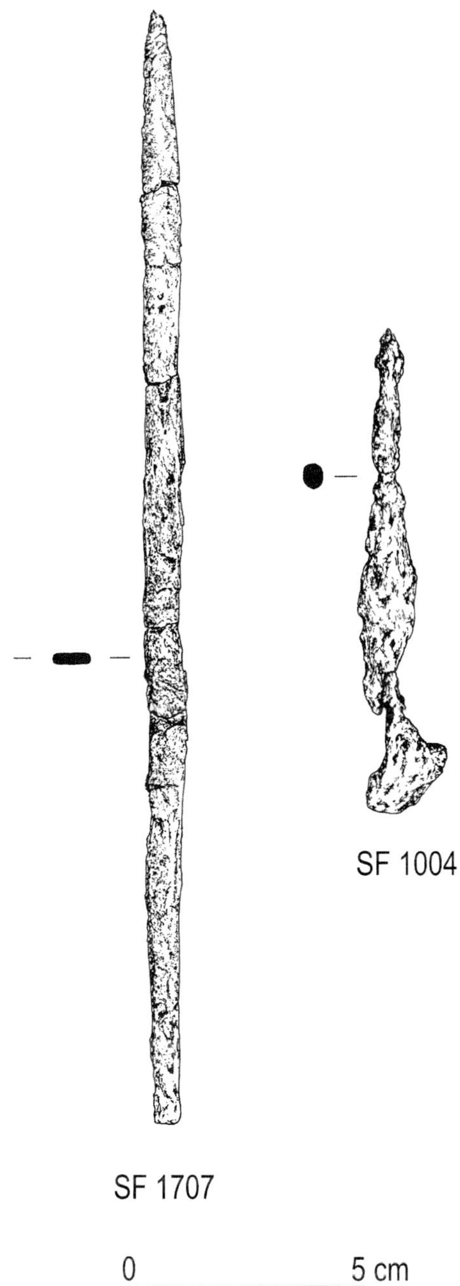

Figure 6.15 Iron file (SF 1707, phase 4A) and fitting (SF 1004, phase 4B)

Objects made of iron and bone

Martin Goldberg and Fraser Hunter

Among the few iron objects found at Milla Skerra is a fine file (SF 1707, Fig. 6.15) that would have been suitable for metal- or bone-working. What might at first seem a much more prosaic item, the deposit of bog ore (59) from cell 2, is paradoxically an unusual find, even though it represents a resource that would have been widely exploited and integral to the ferrous metal technologies of Iron Age Scotland (see McLaren, this chapter).

The small assemblage of bone artefacts includes a few examples of common types (points, spatulate objects and antler rings). Four perforated phalanges (SFs 2183, 2212, 2232; Fig. 6.17) are more enigmatic. They were probably distributors or fasteners with the well-defined axial wear around the perforations indicating fixed points of tension applied from two directions; they perhaps acted as distributors for cordage strung through them. Their occurrence together in a midden (238) is paralleled elsewhere, suggesting the deposition of a composite organic object such as a leather bag or a net. The unfinished bone needle and the bone point could be related to clothing manufacture.

The closest comparanda for the phase 2B perforated phalanges are from the souterrain attached to Dwelling IVc

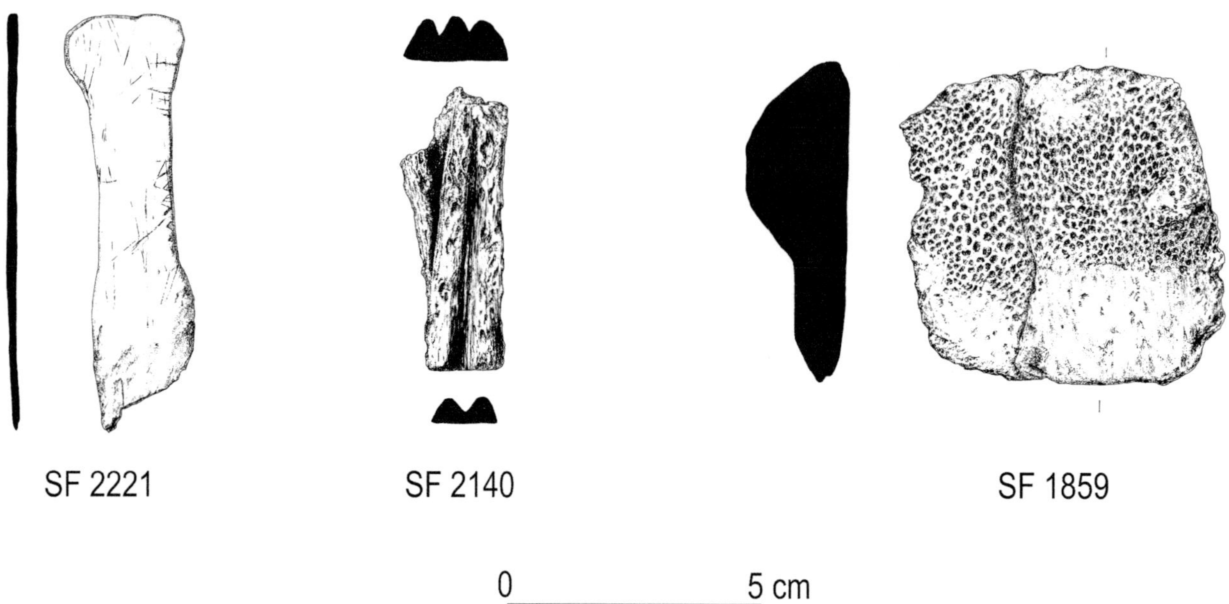

Figure 6.16 Worked bone objects from phases 2A (SF 2221), 2B (SF 2140) and 3A (SF 1859)

at Jarlshof and the thick-walled simple Atlantic roundhouse at Bu (Hamilton 1956, 33; Hedges 1987, 99, fig 1.15 nos 29–30). The same context (238) produced the long-handled comb rough-out, providing valuable confirmation of the type's early Iron Age origins in Atlantic Scotland; again, Bu provides parallels (*ibid.*, 43, fig 1.14 no. 2).

Iron objects

SF 1707 Fine file, exterior ground surface (75), phase 4 (Fig. 6.15)
Narrow rectangular-sectioned tapering bar, the blade tip a rounded point, the tang squared and slightly burred. The bar is bent and broken where the handle probably finished, although there is no shoulder to demarcate the tang; the break has corroded and no longer joins. One narrow edge of the tip is serrated with evenly spaced transverse teeth for 60 mm, spaced at about 10 per centimetre; a well-preserved surface beyond this indicates the serration did not extend further. The faces are less well-preserved; no teeth survive, but this is typical for files, and the identification is plausible given the object's form. Such a delicate file would be well-adapted for fine metal-working or bone-working, the teeth on the edge as well as the face allowing greater control in tight spots; the teeth are too fine for wood-working. Overall L 233 mm, W 9mm, T 4mm, m 12.9 g

SF 1004 Fitting?, dump of hearth waste (131) in house 1, phase 4B (Fig. 6.15)
Circular-sectioned rod with an asymmetrical T-shaped head and a sharp tip. One arm of the head is damaged and angled markedly downwards. The object's function is unclear; the effort to make a round shaft indicates it is not a nail, and it may be a clamp for inserting in timber. Currently in four refitting fragments. Head 21 11 mm, L 104 mm, shank D 7 mm, m 13.7 g

SF 767 Numerous small fragments of thin iron plate, laid clay floor (58) in yard 3, phase 4C
Approx. 20 fragments of thin sheet iron; original edges, where preserved, are straight, suggesting a thin plate. No sign of holes or fittings. Largest piece 11 8 2 mm; total m 12 g

Bone implements

SF 2221 Handle from broken spatulate object, ground surface (234) pre-dating the construction of yard 5, phase 2A (Fig. 6.16)
Handle of bone spatulate object, broken where the tip begins to curve round, expanding to a squared fish-tail terminal. Thin and relatively flat, the natural bone shape giving a lower slightly convex surface and an upper concave one. Shallow parallel cut marks are visible on one edge of the lower side and criss-cross scratches on the lower side of the handle. The upper surface is well worn. L 75 mm, W 14.5 mm W of spatula 21 mm, T 2.5 mm, m 5.6g

SF 2140 Long-handled comb rough-out, midden (238) that was piled up outside yard 5, phase 2B (Fig. 6.16)
Sub-rectangular fragment of cetacean bone, broken while being worked, probably into a long-handled comb. One side is worked smooth and polished; the other has two parallel, longitudinal, V-shaped cuts into the softer cancellous material (7–8 mm apart). One end is broken while the other has been cut and filed smooth. The V-shaped grooves are deepest towards the surviving tip, tapering away towards where the handle would have been. The rough-out appears to have broken while the grooves were being cut through to the harder outer surface to form the teeth of the comb. Its incomplete nature makes the identification slightly tentative, but it is consistent with the observed features, and no other identification suggests itself. The early Iron

Age context would put it among the earliest such combs known from Scotland. The piece was later burnt. L 54 mm, W 16–21 mm, H 6–10 mm, m 7.4 g

SF 1859 Fragmentary cetacean blade tool rough-out, silty midden (217) overlying tumbled wall of yard 5, phase 3A (Fig. 6.16)
Longitudinally-cut cetacean long bone or rib, roughly square as it survives, broken at one end, in two conjoining fragments. Rounded parallel edges and a wedge-shaped profile, tapering to a bevelled working edge; flaking along this edge probably represents the process of thinning it to the desired finish, while irregularities in the thickness of the cancellous tissue imply the shaping of this was also incomplete. The form is reminiscent of notched implements from wheelhouse sites of the Western Isles (Hallén 1994, 200–03), and flat blades of cetacean bone with similar working ends have been found at Howmae, North Ronaldsay (NMS GO 69; Hallén 1994, 202), but the small size of this fragment makes identification difficult. 61 59 mm, T 6–20 mm, m 37.4 g

SF 2183 Perforated phalange – toggle/fastener, midden (238) that was piled up outside yard 5, phase 2B (Fig. 6.17)
Cattle phalange perforated vertically near the distal end, exposing the interior cavity. The knife-cut holes are oval, the long axis of the upper being parallel to the bone, the lower transverse; this difference may arise from wear patterns. The margins of the holes are rounded from use; the surface is generally slightly eroded, but with no other trace of handling polish. The double perforation with evidence of wear indicates the form is deliberate rather than, for instance, the accidental by-product of marrow extraction, which would require only a single hole. It is probably a fastener or toggle, with string or thread causing wear around the hole. There is a close parallel from Jarlshof, where five such perforated phalanges (NMS HSA 3105–9) were found together in an early Iron Age souterrain (Hamilton 1956, 37). The four Milla Skerra examples (see below) were also found close together, suggesting these are the surviving fasteners or distributors from composite organic objects, perhaps bags or nets. Perforated bones have been suggested as play-things when mounted on a piece of twisted string and spun, but this would be awkward with phalanges, and is more common for metapodials (MacGregor 1985, 102–3); the wear on the Milla Skerra examples indicates relatively fixed rather than mobile fittings. 49 23 26 mm; perforations 13.5 10 mm, 11 9 mm; m 13.6 g

Figure 6.17 Perforated phalanges from a phase 2B midden outside yard 5

SF 2212 Perforated phalange, midden (238) that was piled up outside yard 5, phase 2B (Fig. 6.17)
Perforated cattle phalange with cut-marks from skinning at the proximal articulation. Near-central oval perforation, larger than SF 2183 and more irregular, possibly due to limited use – the margins are quite sharp and irregular, with only slight polish and flaking damage in one area. 56 29.5 25 mm; perforations 17 10 mm, 17.5 12 mm; m 12.9 g
SF 2232 Two perforated phalanges – toggles/fasteners, midden (238) that was piled up outside yard 5, phase 2B (Fig. 6.17)
Two cattle phalanges perforated vertically near the distal end, exposing the interior cavity. Both are very similar to SF 2183 with oval knife-cut holes, their margins rounded from use, but the wear patterns are subtly different on each example. On the larger phalange, the long axis of the upper hole is transverse to the bone while that of the lower hole is parallel to the bone; this is the opposite configuration to SF 2183. On the smaller phalange the long axis of the upper hole is parallel to the bone, but with an additional sharply defined wear groove perpendicular to the axis making the perforation larger; the lower hole is transverse, but with the wear groove on one side of the perforation running at an oblique angle. On both phalanges the surface is generally slightly eroded, but with no other trace of handling polish. The varying alignments imply these acted as fixed distributors for cords or fine ropes, probably as a set given their occurrence together in the midden.

> Larger phalange: 57 29 34 mm, upper transverse perforation 12 9 mm, lower parallel perforation 13 8 mm, m 18.7g
> Smaller phalange: 51 28 29 mm, upper parallel perforation 13 10 mm, lower transverse perforation 11 8 mm, m 14.7 g

SF 2194 Cetacean vertebra rough-out, occupation deposit (226) in yard 5, phase 2B
Cetacean vertebra with outer processes and part of the natural surface cut off and smoothed, working the natural

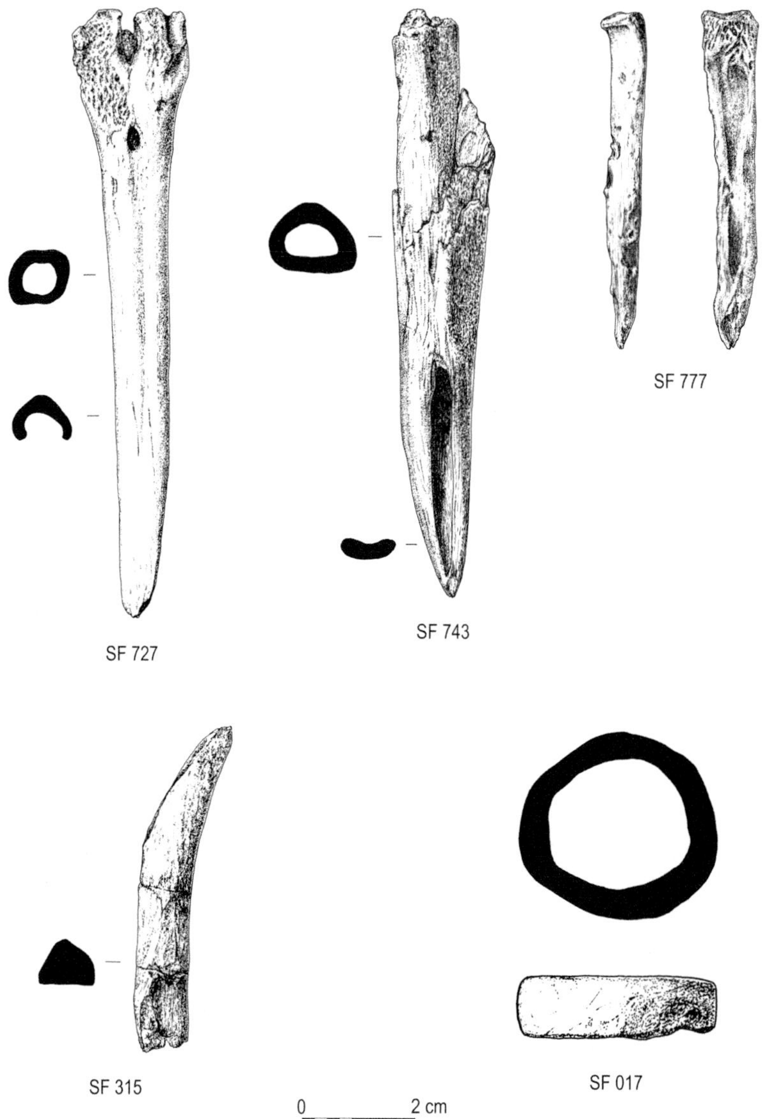

Figure 6.18 Worked bone and antler from phases 7B (SFs 727, 743, 777), 7C (SF 315) and 9 (SF 17)

rounded shape into a more sub-rectangular form. Vertebrae were often used as working surfaces due to their natural strength under pressure, but the purpose of this fragment being worked against its natural shape is unknown. 97 65 mm, H 78 mm, m 146g

SF 727 Bone spatula, exterior ground surface (25), phase 7 (Fig. 6.18)
Worked sheep metatarsal, with modern breaks in three places. Shallow angled cut across the shaft, exposing the central hollow along a third of the length, to create a tapering blunt rounded tip. There are file-marks from manufacture on the tip and faint use-polish extending back from the tip, plus damage on the handling end. The plane of the tip is slightly angled to that of the articular surface, which is unusual. L 105 mm, W 12 mm, H 9 mm, m 5.1 g

SF 743 Heavy bone point, exterior ground surface (25), phase 7 (Fig. 6.18)
Made from the tibia of a pig or sheep, the proximal end damaged. A shallow angled cut created a tapering point, exposing the central hollow of the bone, with the point then shaped by abrasion. There is use-polish on the tip and handling polish at the proximal end. A common type on Iron Age sites (Hallén 1994, 215; MacGregor 1974, 79). L 103 mm, W 17 mm, H 20 mm, m 7.4 g

SF 777 Small bone point, midden deposited in yard 6 over house 1 (33), phase 7B (Fig. 6.18)
Sheep/goat long bone split longitudinally, exposing the medullary cavity over the whole length; extensive surface damage obscures any wear traces. Another common type on Iron Age sites (Hallén 1994, 215; MacGregor 1974, 79). L 58 mm, W 7 mm, H 5 mm, m 1.6 g

SF 135 Unidentified cetacean object, post-abandonment midden (7), phase 7C
Piece of cetacean bone, split and shaped to a blunt rounded tip at one end. Sub-oval in form, surviving in three conjoining fragments, but heavily eroded down to cancellous material on most surfaces, making identification uncertain. L 84 mm, W 32 mm, H 13 mm, m 14.4 g

SF 315 Broken pin/point rough-out, post-abandonment midden (7), phase 7C (Fig. 6.18)
A larger piece of bone (probably a scapula) split on one side and trimmed along the other to create a slightly curved, parallel-sided sliver of bone, sub-rectangular in section, with an angled cut across one end to create a point. Modern damage to the other end. Probably a rough-out for a pin or point; the use of a scapula ridge rather than a mammalian long bone is unusual (Hallén 1994, 215). L 58 mm, W 10 mm, H 8 mm, m 2.9 g

SF 17 Unfinished antler cylinders, windblown sand (8) that sealed the settlement, phase 9 (Fig. 6.18)
The complete ring is a short sawn cylinder, the ends unsmoothed, the exterior surface smoothed and the middle hollowed; D-shaped section; extensive knife-cut facets imply it is unfinished, though polishing was in progress. There are fragments of at least two further unfinished rings, of the same technology and diameter, but varying in height (one about 10 mm H, one 11–13 mm). Such rings could have a range of uses in composite objects such as handles (Hallén 1994, 221). Dimensions of complete ring: D 32–35 mm, H 10–11 mm, W 4.6–7.3 mm, m 5.1 g

Discussion

Among this small group of objects is evidence for a range of manufacturing activities. The bog ore and very small slag assemblage (see MacLaren, above) and residues from metalworking (see Derham, Chapter 3) together indicate some iron-working took place in or near the settlement. This is attested on a number of Shetland Iron Age sites, but is by no means commonplace. In contrast, bone- and antler-working, represented by the long-handled comb and antler rings (SFs 17, 2140), is evident on many sites. The iron file (SF 1707) is a valuable example of what must have been a widespread object, which often left its tooth marks on bone items but is very rarely discovered itself.

Chapter 7

Technologies of the self: painted pebbles, ornaments and the burial

Martin Goldberg and Fraser Hunter

with contributions by Paul Duffy, Katharina Dulias, Ceiridwen J. Edwards and Amanda Forster

The Milla Skerra assemblage of painted pebbles, polished stone disc and ornaments made of shale, glass and marine ivory, from both the settlement and the later burial, contains much material familiar from Iron Age contexts in the Northern Isles, but also some distinctive and unique elements. Much of it, as we discuss at the close of this chapter, relates to appearance, clothing and ornamentation – what might be called technologies of the self.

Painted pebbles

SF 1119 Painted pebble fragment, stony midden (102) deposited before construction of yards 3 and 4, below western wall of yards, phase 4A (Fig. 7.1)
Approximately half of an irregular rounded water-worn opaque white quartzite pebble. Faint traces of dark pigment form irregular meandering lines *c.* 1.5 mm W. There are two slightly darker oval dots at one end and faint traces of a further large dot on the adjacent broken face, apparently overlain by a line. Colour and design differences suggest three phases of painting: the faint dot, the lines, and finally the darker dots. 44 × 38 × 24 mm, m 54.1 g

SF 1048 Painted pebble, laid clay floor (96) in cell 2, below stone block (142), phase 4C (Fig. 7.1)
Sub-oval water-worn opaque white quartzite pebble. An irregular series of lines and loops (typically W 1–1.5 mm), some intersecting, have been painted in a dark pigment in no obvious pattern (see Ritchie 1998, 176, fig.114 for a similarly decorated pebble from Scalloway). The pebble has been damaged, probably deliberately, with two adjacent flakes removed at one end, leaving a sharp edge between them. A white residue overlies one flaked edge and parts of the design. 27 × 23 × 21 mm, m 16.3 g
SF 1538 Painted pebble fragment, exterior old ground surface (53) south of house 1, phase 4 (Fig. 7.1)
Sub-oval, water-worn opaque white quartzite pebble fragment. The surviving design (in dark pigment) comprises an oval dot and a series of broad lines *c.* 4 mm wide. Any pattern is impossible to discern, with less than 30% of the original stone remaining. The well-formed curved fracture facets suggest deliberate breakage. 20 × 29 × 15.5 mm, m 10.7 g

Ornaments in shale, glass and marine ivory

SF 2002 Blue bead, midden (224) that was piled up outside yard 5, phase 2B (Fig. 7.2)
Mid-blue translucent globular bead of Guido (1978) group 7(iv); very bubbly, slightly tapered in section and with a slightly iridescent surface. A long-lived and widely distributed type. D 7.5 mm, perforation D 1.6 mm, T 4.8–5.8 mm, m 0.39 g

SF 1898 Disc bead, midden (171) spread over the former yard 5, phase 3A (Fig. 7.2)
Fine broken bead with off-centre perforation and triangular section tapered to a fine edge. The material appears to be marine ivory. D 12 mm, perforation D 6 mm, T 1–1.3 mm, m 0.08 g

SF 1702 Fragment of reworked shale bangle, exterior ground surface (75), phase 4 (Fig. 7.2)
Little of the original bangle form survives, although the rounded outer face was well-polished and worn, while the inner bears faint knife facets from manufacture. After breakage the faces were split horizontally and abraded smooth, giving a narrow sub-rectangular section. The ends were carved into tenons, one stepped (the other may have been stepped and subsequently broke); these tenons are set at the original inner face and follow the original curve. This secondary reworking and reshaping

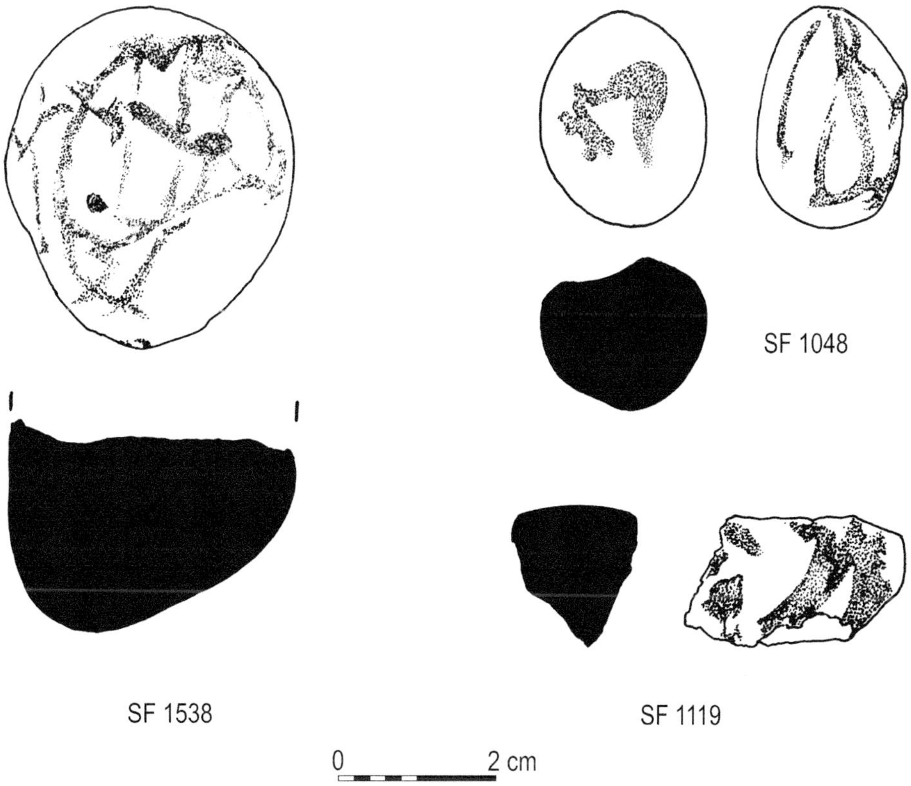

Figure 7.1 Painted pebbles from phase 4A (SF 1119), 4B (SF 1538) and 4C (SF 1048)

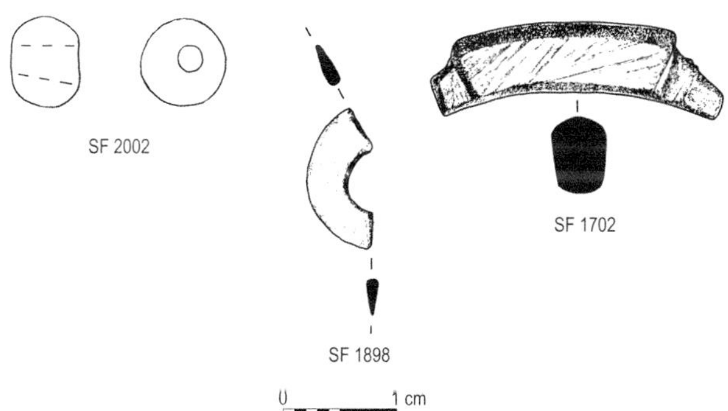

Figure 7.2 A blue glass bead (SF 2002) from a phase 2B midden, part of a bead carved from marine ivory (SF 1898) from a phase 3 midden and a piece of shale bangle (SF 1702) from a phase 4 ploughed midden

implies it was re-used as an element in a composite ornament rather than simply repairing the broken bangle by collaring and binding the ends, as is more common. The nature of this secondary ornament is unclear, although the tenon positioning suggests a circular or curved form. The material is a medium-dark brown organic-rich stone with a granular texture and laminar splitting, suggesting it is an oil shale. The raw material is unknown on Shetland and must have been imported (cf Hunter 2008, fig 1); the efforts put into repair indicate it was valued. L 25.8 mm, W 6.4 mm, H 4.7 mm, m 0.6 g. Original diameter 65–70 mm; 15% survives

The burial

Paul Duffy

In the 2nd or 3rd century AD, a grave was cut through the thick sand that had covered the settlement. The body (Skeleton 1) was laid supine with the head towards the SSW and facing north-west towards a polished stone disc (SF 222), which was just beside and partly under the mouth (Figs 7.3 and 7.4). A ring of beads (SF 221) was positioned between the left humerus and left scapula. In the lowermost fill was a large steatite bead, apparently placed in the grave during backfilling (SF 87). A rib bone from the burial was dated to cal AD 150–390 (SUERC-10745, calibrated to 95.4% probability).

The analysis and subsequent reporting of Skeleton 1 followed current discipline standards and guidelines, as outlined by English Heritage (Mays *et al.* 2002), British Association of Biological Anthropologists and Osteologists/Institute of Field Archaeologists (Brickley and McKinley 2004) and Historic Environment Scotland (Historic Scotland 1997). The study employed standard methods for determining age at death (Bass 1995; Brooks and Suchey 1990; Buikstra and Ubelaker 1994; Işcan *et al.* 1984; Lovejoy *et al.* 1985; White and Folkens 2000), pathology (Aufderheide and Rodriguez-Martin (1998) and sex and stature (Brickley and McKinley 2004).

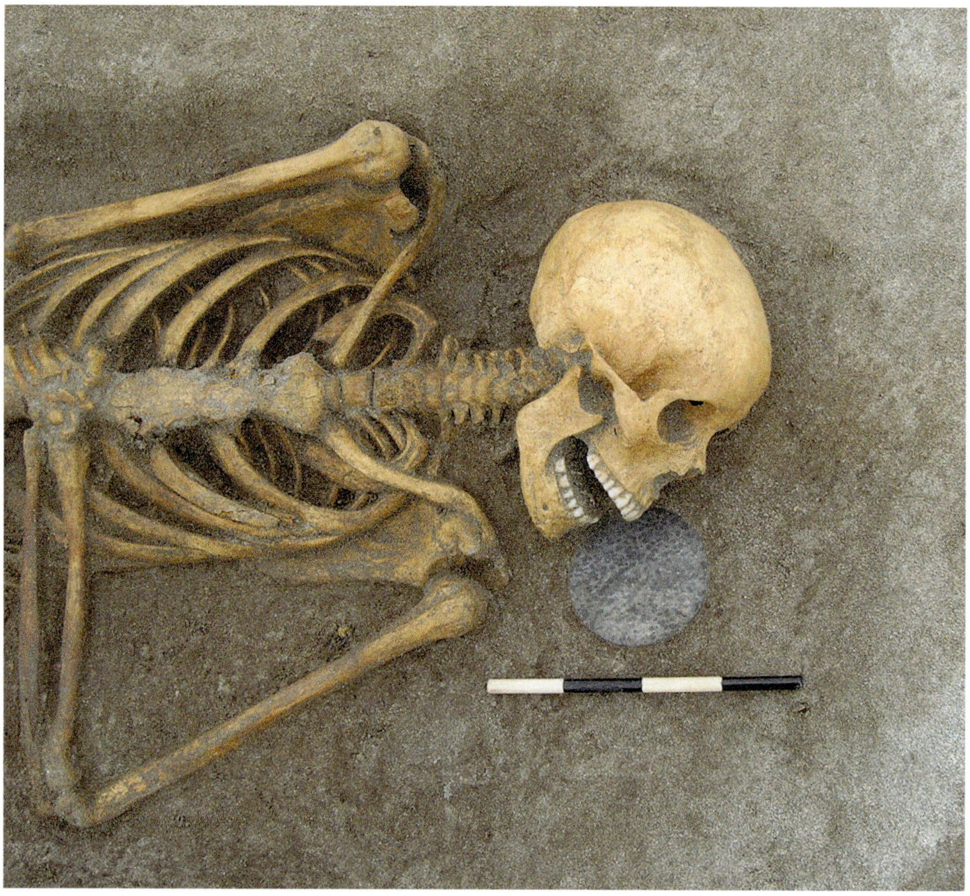

Figure 7.3 Detailed view of the burial

The preservation of Skeleton 1 was good. The entire skeleton was available for study, and only a small proportion of the material was fragmented. The surface erosion present on the bone was slight, although discrete areas of post-mortem cortical erosion were observed across most of the elements of the skeleton.

Indications of significant disease processes were largely absent from the skeletal remains observed. The individual was, however, noted to have evidence of periodontal disease of the maxillary alveolar process. Several lesions, attributed as Schmorls nodes, were also observed on the spine, in particular on the superior aspects of T11, L2 and L3. Minor changes to the malleolar fossa of both fibula and the right rib facet of T2 indicated slight degenerative joint disease. The insertion of pectonius on the medial aspects of both femurs was observed to be roughened and visibly enlarged.

The individual was observed to have the following non-metric traits:

- Bilateral supraorbital notch
- Lambdoid ossicle on the right side of the suture line
- Accessory transverse foramen on the right side of C4 and 6 and the left side of C4, 5 and 6
- Tibial squatting facets

The burial from Milla Skerra was identified as an older male, probably aged between 50 and 60 years at death. He was gracile in build and not particularly tall by modern standards, measuring between 1.64 and 1.71 m in height (5' 4" and 5' 7"). He suffered some degree of gum disease, probably as a result of continuous formation of plaque on the teeth, but had suffered no caries or abscesses, suggesting a diet low in starchy carbohydrate and sticky foods. Tooth wear was also slight, suggesting a diet that was not particularly rich in coarse foods.

Several small lesions were noted on the spine, particularly in the lower back. These were attributed to inter-vertebral herniations resulting in skeletal lesions known as Schmorls nodes. Such lesions are not uncommon in older individuals, and recent research (Faccia and Williams 2008) indicates that the location of the lesion would be unlikely to have caused the individual much pain. Small areas of age-related degenerative joint disease were also noted, but again these are unlikely to have had significant impact on everyday life for the individual, beyond perhaps the familiar aches of ageing. Several non-metric traits were also recorded. Without a wider reference population, these observations must remain only as unelucidated skeletal variations.

Genetic analysis

Katharina Dulias and Ceiridwen J. Edwards

Genetic analysis was conducted of the individual buried at Milla Skerra in hope of shedding light on population

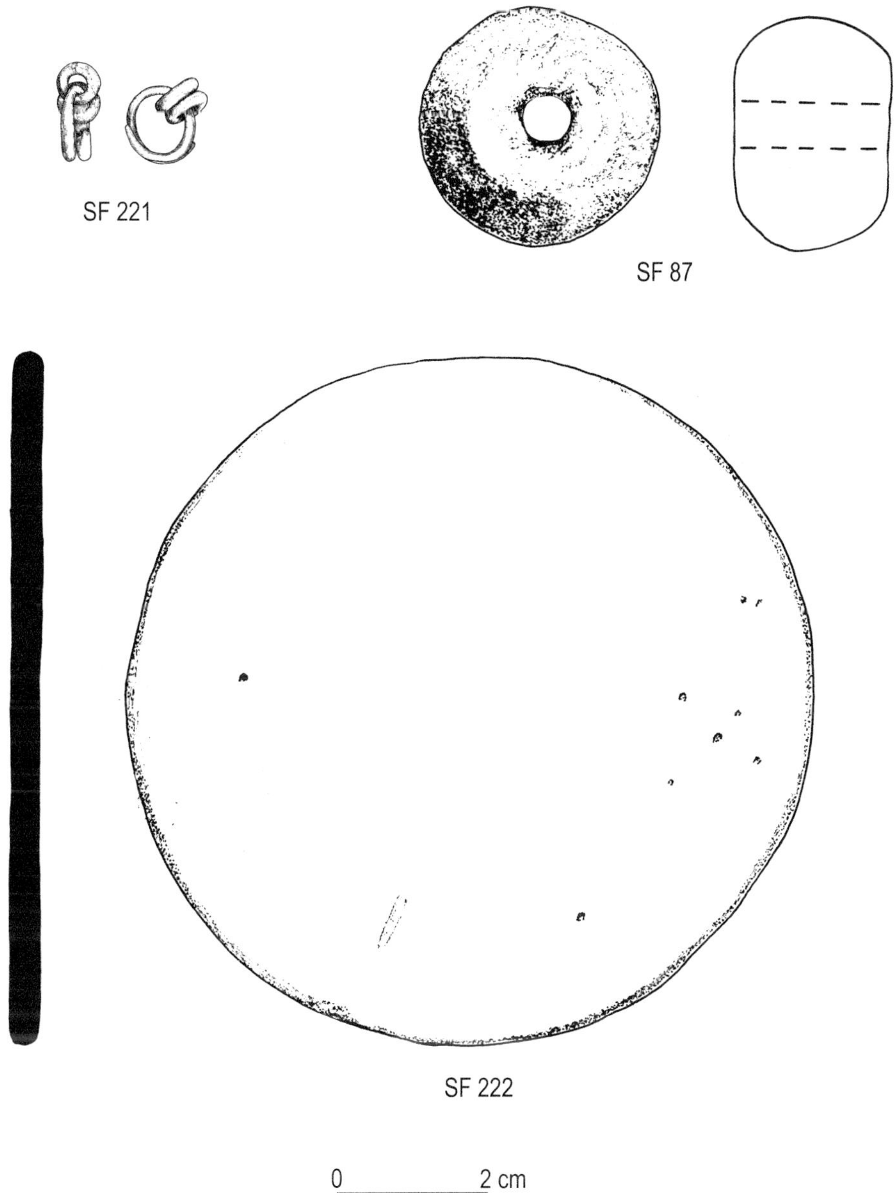

Figure 7.4 Objects placed with the burial

movements in Shetland during the first millenium AD. A small portion of the petrous bone was sampled for DNA extraction, following the protocols by Yang *et al.* (1998) with modifications by MacHugh *et al.* (2000). The Next-generation sequencing library was constructed for 100 bp, paired-end sequencing on a HiSeq4000 using the method by Meyer and Kircher (2010) with modifications outlined in Gamba *et al.* (2014) and Martiniano *et al.* (2014). Principal Component Analysis and admixture analysis will be undertaken to compare the Milla Skerra individual with other Iron Age individuals from the British Isles and to make inferences on possible population replacements in Shetland using modern data in comparison (Dulias *et al.* in prep).

The overall sample quality was not promising, with only 6.76% endogenous content. After shot-gun sequencing, the analysis retrieved 0.0131× whole genome coverage and 3.14× mitochondrial genome coverage. This allowed the individual to be assigned with confidence to the haplogroup J1b1a1. Haplogroup J1b1a is a European subclade of the predominantly Near Eastern haplogroup J1b. It is a trace of major expansions from the Near East to Europe in the Late Glacial period. J1b1 appears to have arrived in Europe by ~ 14,000 years ago, spreading beyond the Mediterranean not before ~ 8,000 years ago (Pala *et al.* 2012).

Objects placed with the burial

with observations on the steatite bead by Amanda Forster

SF 222 Stone disc, context (22), fill of grave (24), phase 9 (Figs 7.3 and 7.4)
Cordierite talc schist, chipped to shape with the edges then ground into a near-perfect circular shape; the edges

are slightly rounded. A near-central curvilinear dull area on one surface (L 45 mm, W 11 mm) may represent wear; it is pitted where pyrite inclusions have dropped out. The disc was a grave good with an inhumation burial. The type is widespread in northern Scotland, with similar talc schist discs from other Iron Age sites in Shetland, and polished discs from other funerary contexts in northern Scotland (see Discussion). Occasional linear marks on the surface (L 6–8 mm, W <1 mm) are elongated albite needle inclusions, characteristic of talc schists rather than micaceous schist. D 90.7–93.7 mm (appears circular to the naked eye), T 4.5–5 mm, m 82.6

SF 221 Beads mounted on a ring, context (22), fill of grave (24) between the left humerus and left scapula of the skeleton (23) buried in phase 9 (Fig. 7.4)
Two yellow beads threaded onto a copper alloy D-sectioned spiral ring (H 2.1 mm, T 1 mm) of 1.5 turns; the tip of one terminal is lost, the other (damaged) tapering to a rounded tip. The two identical dull yellow, small opaque annular beads are of Guido (1978) class 8; D-shaped section with flattened edge. See MacKie (2000, 386–7, fig. 24, nos 45, 51) for a similar composite of bronze spiral ring and red glass bead from Dun Ardtreck, Skye. Ring outer D 10.2 mm, inner D 7.8 mm, maximum H 4.6 mm. Beads D 6.6 mm, perforation D 2 mm, H 2 mm. Total mass 0.66 g

SF 87, context 22 (Fig. 7.4)
Small rounded bead/whorl weighing 33 g and with a diameter of 33 mm. The object is 22 mm thick with a bi-conical perforation of 5 mm. It is well-worn and appears well-used. The original working is no longer visible, but faint facets suggest it was filed into shape. The size of perforation is suitable for holding a spindle rod and the weight is also comparable to other whorls. The profile of the object is oval, but flattened on both upper and lower surfaces; this would be a profile 'B' using Walton Rogers' typology of whorl profiles (1997, 1736). The find was well-sealed in the sterile sand fill of the burial; it may have been placed there during backfilling of the grave, but it could also have been introduced later, for example by animal burrowing. While plain items such as this are difficult to date, at both Clickhimin and Jarlshof, beads of varying shapes and sizes were recovered from contexts associated with the Iron Age deposits (see Hamilton 1968, 84, 113, 141; 1956, 36ff.). This type of whorl was a common find from Iron Age deposits at Old Scatness broch and, while whorls of this size were particularly associated with either the earlier Iron Age (but pre-Pictish) or Viking period, the form of the Milla Skerra example is much akin to the Iron Age examples (Forster 2015).

Discussion of the burial assemblage

The Milla Skerra burial contains some of the most unusual material culture from this assemblage, while the inhumation itself is a relatively rare find for Iron Age Scotland. It has become a trope of the literature on Iron Age Britain that there was no distinct burial rite (Whimster 1981), with sporadic regional traditions often short-lived or indicative of rapid social change immediately prior to the Roman conquest (Hingley 1992, 38; Harding 2004, 79–81). While this general picture holds true, increasing numbers of Iron Age burials in Scotland have been found over the last 20 years, suggesting that the burial record was more complex and varied than previously thought.

Typological distinctions within the burial record of the early 1st millennium AD are blurred by considerable variation created from a common pool of component elements: single or multiple inhumation, cremation, cists, different coloured sand and stones, quartz, cobbles, round or rectangular cairns, barrows, ditches, low kerbs or orthostatic kerbs (Ashmore 1980; Close-Brooks 1984). The kerbed cairns on the foreshore at Sandwick, excavated by Bigelow (1984), and the inhumation burial in close proximity considered here demonstrate something of the unity and diversity of first millennium AD burial traditions in northern Scotland. Even in this diverse picture, the Milla Skerra burial provides links to poorly known but recurrent habits, notably burial accompanied by a stone disc.

The polished stone disc

Polished stone discs have seen little discussion since the work of Stevenson (1966, 28). They are relatively common on northern broch sites, but there are examples from elsewhere in Atlantic Scotland, north-east Scotland, southern Scotland and even as far afield as Yorkshire caves (*ibid*., 41 n.68). The circular form is focused on here, but they must be related to carefully manufactured quadrangular palettes (for example, at Clickhimmin; Hamilton 1968, 79–80, 83, pl XXIIa).

The material commonly used for such discs has frequently been referred to as mica schist or, for Shetland examples, garnetiferous schist (Hamilton 1968, 79). Garnetiferous implies a robust crystalline garnet inclusion within the schist, which is not a feature of the Milla Skerra disc and would have interfered with the smooth finished surface. It has been identified as cordierite talc schist (Fiona McGibbon, pers comm). The mottled silver-grey lustre appears dappled according to brightness and angle of light, with the darker, less-lustrous areas of the surface being rich in cordierite, the dominant mineral allowing differentiation from other talc schists. The striated bedding planes of the schist can be seen on the polished edges of the disc and slight foliation in the rock adds to the rippled effect of the surface. Future work could usefully study the various rock types employed for such discs throughout Scotland, to see whether local or exotic sources were used.

Polished examples can be differentiated from other stone discs by the material, often lustrous or otherwise distinctive, and the effort in manufacturing the finely polished surface and carefully ground edges. Less-sophisticated stone discs are generally designated as pot-lids, with larger, rougher types for cooking and smaller discs for storage, but the shaping and selection of an attractive raw material for polished ones suggests a less-prosaic function (Clarke 1998b, 145–6).

Clues to the manufacturing process lie in assemblages such as Scalloway, with several examples of unfinished polished discs that were damaged and abandoned during the grinding and polishing stages, or of damaged finished pieces, some altered and re-modelled after breakage. Re-examination of this material shows that every removal of an edge fragment ran the risk of laminating the flattened surface. With grinding and polishing of the edge, a gradual thinning of the flat surface could be accomplished through controlled lamination. It is likely that little polishing of cordierite talc schist discs would have been necessary, as the natural cleavage planes provide a naturally lustrous surface if carefully flaked. Grinding the edge into a smooth, circular form would have been the most difficult aspect of manufacture, and apparently led to some being abandoned during production; they were possibly re-used as pot-lids or else re-worked to smaller diameters.

Contextualising polished stone discs

Anderson's (1874) first notice of these polished stone discs speculated that they may have been used as mirrors by dipping them in water, although a superior reflecting surface would be provided by a basin of water itself. The surface of the stone discs may still have been polished for reflection, but valued as a portable reflective surface for light rather than for the direct reflection of images.

Stevenson (1966, 28) suggested their use as palettes. The time and effort put into manufacture might support such specialised use. This creates different technological inferences – the higher arts of cosmetics, cookery and medicine and their use for preparing pigments, prized ingredients for food, or narcotics. Distinctive wear patterns on the polished surfaces are rare, but examples of fine cut marks on a polished cordierite talc schist disc from Yell, Shetland (Shetland Museum ARC 1992.652) and slightly concave or dished surfaces on several others would indicate fine grinding and cutting on the discs. However, supporting evidence of residues or chemical analysis has not so far been obtained. Unfortunately analysis of the white residue under the Milla Skerra disc has so far proved inconclusive (see Jones, Chapter 6).

The possibility of polished stone discs being finely worked versions of storage lids is rendered irrelevant by the Milla Skerra burial, where the disc was definitely not associated with a pottery vessel. Jar stoppers or pot-lids seem in any case an unlikely role for such finely made objects, while the occasional traces of use-wear indicate the polished surfaces had a function in their own right.

The Milla Skerra disc was clearly a valued item chosen by the burial party as a suitable accompaniment for the deceased. Its role as a palette, perhaps still carrying valued substances, would be plausible and its location by the mouth suggesting it was intended for ingestion or inhaling. The motivations behind the inclusion of such an object would have relied on personal, symbolic or metaphorical associations as much as functional. The lustre of the material and its dappled appearance and circular shape could even evoke an association with the moon.

The Milla Skerra burial provides a welcome modern addition to a pattern of funerary associations that is vaguely discernible in antiquarian records and casual finds from the northern mainland and the Northern Isles. Four other examples are relevant.

A polished stone disc from a burial on Westray (NMS AV 1) is an old find from the Links of Trenabie, in an area which also contained Viking burials (Graham-Campbell 2004, 213–14). Pennant (1794, xxxvi) records a range of finds, including 'small flat circular pieces of marble', but Low, his source and a more reliable recorder, notes only one 'round flat piece of marble about 2½ inches in diameter' (Low 1778, quoted in Cuthbert 1995, 119). The same cemetery produced a Roman glass cup of late 2nd- to early 3rd-century date (Davidson and Anderson 1886, 138–9), but the association suggested in the donation record (*Proceedings of the Society of Antiquaries of Scotland* 8 (1868–70), 390–1) is not repeated in earlier sources and cannot be trusted. Another funerary context is the fragmentary inhumation accompanied by a polished stone disc discovered in ploughing at Portgower, Helmsdale, Sutherland (Pennie 1960; *Proceedings of the Society of Antiquaries of Scotland* 94, 1960–61, 327; NMS AV 17). Another stone disc from Gorn, Shapinsay, Orkney, (NMS AV 18) was originally recorded as from a cist; the orthostatic stone structure described by the finder, at 4 3 m too large to be a cist, could represent the type of low rectangular kerbed cairn recorded at Ackergill, Caithness (Edwards 1927). Ackergill provides another, less-direct funerary association, for the material donated to NMS from Edwards' excavations includes a polished stone disc from the surface of the cairn (NMS AV 11); it is not mentioned in the publication, but can plausibly be seen as a funerary offering, although not directly connected to a burial. The Portgower and Ackergill discs are both siltstones with micaceous or muscovite particles, providing less natural lustre than talc schist but more readily available in Caithness. The Milla Skerra disc brings the total to five burials, a noteworthy regional pattern of associations given the relatively limited Scottish Iron Age burial contexts.

Glass beads

The Milla Skerra burial provides an all-too-rare fixed point for the dating of Guido class 8 beads, but more importantly illustrates a rarely attested use for such beads. The bronze spiral on which they are mounted suggests this was not simply a necklace. The wire was intended either as a piercing ornament worn directly on the body or attached to clothing; the former finds parallel among ear-rings (Allason-Jones 1989). The decay of the body makes identification tricky;

its position in the grave suggests it was in the chest region (a nipple-ring or costume ornament?) rather than the ear, as it was found between the left shoulder blade and humerus.

Technologies of the self

Overview of the assemblage

Although small, the assemblage of painted pebbles, polished stone disc and ornaments made of shale, glass and marine ivory from the settlement and burial represents a distinctive range of objects. Although it lacks the dramatic drystone architecture of a broch, the more ephemeral structural remains belie the rich range of artefacts present in this small assemblage.

A rare and delicate ivory disc bead (SF 1898) highlights the role of scarce cetacean ivory for ornamental material, while another rare item, a bangle of imported shale (SF 1702), was sufficiently valued to be reused after breakage. Painted pebbles (SFs 1048, 1119, 1538) are found on other Northern Isles and northern Scottish Iron Age sites, but these examples add usefully to the dating evidence and distribution, and allow further speculations about their uses (see below). The secure dating of their contexts of deposition supports the growing appreciation that the origins of these painted pebbles lie in the pre-Roman Iron Age.

Painted pebbles

Ritchie (1998, 176–8, 218–19) provides a valuable summary of painted pebbles, with the Milla Skerra ones fitting readily among existing examples. Another is known from Unst, a stray find from Balta Isle (*ibid.*, 219, no. 26; *DES* 1997, 68). Ritchie suggests a floruit from AD 200 to the 8th century AD (Ritchie 1972, 298–9), although it seems that finds from Old Scatness are earlier than this (Dockrill *et al.* 2015). An early dating is supported by the painted pebble fragment from Milla Skerra (SF 1119); animal bone from this context (102) was dated to 200–50 cal BC (SUERC-26138 at 95.4% probability). It sits securely within the stratigraphic sequence at the top of midden deposited in phase 4A, although its position beneath the wall of yard 3 would suggest it was put there just before the wall was built in phase 4B. The other two, also from phase 4B, should similarly be 2nd to early 1st century cal BC.

Folklore analogy suggests their use as charm stones, which finds some support from accounts of St Columba blessing a pebble used in healing, although no mention is made of it being painted (Ritchie 1972, 299; Sharpe 1995, II.33,181). It seems clear that these pebbles were handled; evidence of multiple phases of painting (as on SF 1119) indicates the patterns became worn, a feature noted on other examples (Ritchie 1998, 176–7). The biography of these pebbles was clearly extended. Two of the Milla Skerra pebbles also show fracture patterns which may represent deliberate damage – perhaps the deliberate destruction of the powerful stone. A more complex sequence is evident in Scalloway find 4017, where a pebble was repainted after fracture, with the pigment running over the fractured edge (Ritchie 1998, fig. 114 no 1). The deposition of two of the Milla Skerra ones was purposeful, with SF 1119 coming from the top of the levelling deposit under the south-west wall of yard 3 and SF 1048 from the laid clay floor in the same yard, an otherwise sterile layer. Both could readily be interpreted as foundation offerings.

Manufacturing and contacts

Two unusual finds indicate the use of scarce resources to make objects. One is the small cetacean ivory disc bead (SF 1898), very thin, light and well-crafted, from a context (171) dated to 390–210 cal BC (SUERC-26135 at 95.4% probability). The teeth of sea mammals were a rare commodity, and mostly used for restricted and decorative items such as beads, pin heads, gaming pieces and sword fittings (for example, at Midhowe and Mine Howe, Orkney and High Pasture Cave, Skye; Callander and Grant 1934, 490; unpublished work in NMS). The raw material could have become available on Shetland when animals were stranded on beaches.

More definitely exotic is the oil shale bangle fragment (SF 1702), as the raw material is unknown on the islands, the nearest source being in Sutherland (Hunter 2008, fig. 1). Iron Age jewellery in such black, organic-rich stones is rare on Shetland, occurring on only a handful of sites. There is a finger ring from Underhoull (Small 1966, fig. 9), a bangle from Kebister (Clarke 1999, fig. 149 no 7) and a bead and pendant from Clickhimmin (Hamilton 1968, 115, fig 47.6; unpub, Shetland Museum CLN 76135). The evidence of repair indicates the value placed on the Milla Skerra piece, and this is also evident on the three other Shetland finds. From Mavis Grind comes one bangle with evidence of repair and another which was being reworked into a bead after breakage, while the (Bronze Age) bangle from Bayanne also showed evidence of repair (Cracknell and Smith 1983, fig. 8 no 11, fig. 9 no 28; Hunter 2014).

Conclusions

One theme that emerges from much of this material – the objects placed with the burial, the painted pebbles and the ornaments, as well as an unfinished bone comb (SF 2140) (discussed in Chapter 6) – relates to technologies of the self: appearance, clothing and ornamentation.

The polished stone disc from the burial, if it was a palette for preparing pigments, body paint or another cosmetic application, has clear bodily associations. The oil shale bracelet was of obvious value as a personal ornament, and the scarcity of this material in Shetland meant that it was worth reworking into another form of composite ornament. The tiny discoid bead may represent ivory from marine resources available locally, but still rarely utilised in northern Scotland.

Evidence for paint and pigment so rarely survives in the archaeological record, but paint was undoubtedly being applied to quartzite pebbles, and indeed one role of the stone discs may have been preparing the pigments for such pebbles – or even for use on human bodies. Much of that inference hinges on the interpretation of polished stone discs as palettes for preparing pigments or other cosmetic applications, and this still remains uncertain. Milla Skerra strengthens the association of these discs as personal, valued items, and wear patterns on a few examples are consistent with grinding or cutting, but whether for colours, culinary treats or narcotics remains elusive.

The personal nature evident from this material is not always apparent on later prehistoric Scottish sites. It allows us the opportunity to see the past in a more colourful way – through the lustrous, dappled, silver-grey polished disc, but also through the contrasts between the pearlescent ivory bead and the organic brown of oil shale, the dull grey strength of iron and the delicate bronze spiral ring, opaque yellow and translucent blue glass, white quartzite and dark pigment.

Chapter 8

Rhythms of life at Milla Skerra

Olivia Lelong

Over the course of several hundred years, from the 6th century BC to the 2nd century AD, successive generations of a community made their home at Milla Skerra on the eastern shore of Unst. The excavated evidence illuminates long-held practices and individual moments, incidental accumulations and careful acts, and how the character of the settlement changed throughout its lifetime. It sheds light on what took place in the relatively small, intensively used area that was excavated and beyond, in the parts that were lost to the sea or that may still lie buried on the foreshore. It also opens windows onto people's links across land and sea, to other communities and wider trends.

The built environment of Milla Skerra – the house and successive yards discovered through excavation, along with others that once stood nearby – formed the hub of domestic life. However, far from containing the inhabitants' lives, the settlement was simply a nodal point in a wider taskscape – 'an array of related activities' (Ingold 1993) that occurred at different rhythms across the areas of land, littoral and sea where they herded, fished and hunted animals, gathered fuel and materials for building and craft work, cultivated crops, and traded and socialised with neighbours.

People's activities in this socially constructed, dynamic space generated much of the excavated material. The rhythms of activity varied in nature and intensity according to the seasons, as they addressed needs for shelter, warmth, food, clothing, community and spiritual comfort. There is some evidence for change over the generations, but also for considerable cultural inheritance and an awareness of the residues and structures of previous generations.

Building and rebuilding

Although people were present at least sporadically along the foreshore from the 5th millennium BC, the excavations found direct evidence for sustained occupation from the 6th century cal BC (see Chapter 2). In the alkaline, Aeolian environment of the Shetland coast, the residues of these hundreds of years built up like a miniature tell. The shell sand that accumulated on and around the settlement preserved materials like bone, shell, pottery and peat ash (but not iron) and helped form thick layers of occupation debris that covered old floors and stabilised upstanding walls. The settlement's eventual inundation with windblown sand preserved good evidence for the sequence of construction in the area that survived coastal erosion (see Chapter 2 and Fig. 2.1).

This was part of a larger settlement which extended farther towards the sea, its ghost lingering in the ashes from cooking fires and metalworking hearths and other residues of daily life. The narrative for its establishment, occupation and abandonment has been organised here into phases (Table 2.3), but the evidence actually conveys impressions of a more messy, organic development. At certain times there were carefully constructed buildings and clearly defined spaces for living, cooking, crafts and animal husbandry. At other times, mounds of organic waste and discarded objects were piled up over former working areas and living spaces, spilling over tumbled walls or contained by new ones.

Gathering building materials would have involved finding suitable stones for walls, collecting driftwood or bones from beached whales for roof structures, cutting heather and straw to make roof and floor coverings, and digging up the coarse yellow clay that was used to bond walls and form floors and hearths. Some of the building techniques (such as part-corbelling) and materials (such as yellow clay) were similar to those used at contemporary settlements elsewhere in Shetland – for example, in Structure 1 at Bayanne on Yell (Moore and Wilson 2014, 105–7) and at Old Scatness (Dockrill 2003; Dockrill *et al.* 2015) (see Fig. 8.10).

Figure 8.1 Yard 5 with its paved floor to the left and robbed-out wall to the right, with massive upright stones left in place from the later yard 3 wall (centre background), taken from the north

Figure 8.2 Yard 5 covered with ash-midden and rubble wall 144 (phase 3), from the south

Figure 8.3 House 1 during excavation, from the east. The worn slab that may have served as a seat lies to the left of the white bucket; the wall slab against which its occupant may have leaned has tipped out of line. The excavated wall trench (155), sealed by hearth rake-out, is visible to the left; in the foreground, orthostats (111) from the southern arc of the wall, disturbed by robbing and erosion, pitch against its side. The pair of white sandbags supporting the fireback (78) occupy the site of the now-excavated ash-midden heap behind it

Yard 5, the earliest excavated structure, was an unroofed space where, over the course of several generations, people made tools from stone and bone and swept the ashes from cooking fires, eventually covering the paved floor (Fig. 8.1). A high wall that was built in the 4th century BC across its south-east end may have radiated from an adjacent house or other structure; during this period (phase 2C), a hearth was built in the yard and used to roast shellfish. The yard eventually lost definition as its original perimeter was robbed for stone and thick layers of midden built up over and around it (phase 3A). Later (phase 3B), the space was subdivided with a rough wall as it continued to be used as a midden heap and animal pen or latrine (see contributions by Ellis and McKenzie, Chapter 3) (Fig. 8.2).

In the 2nd to early 1st century BC (phase 4), a fresh burst of building created two adjoining yards (3 and 4) and a house (1) with at least one radial internal division. Hauling the massive boulders into position for the yard walls would have taken careful planning, engineering and teamwork (as became clear to the excavation team, when we hauled all but the two largest onto the spoil heap and then back again using ropes, planks and muscles, but with considerably less finesse than the original operation probably employed). Low phosphate levels and the absence of food waste in the yards suggest they were used mainly for craft work rather than for penning animals or domestic activities (McKenzie, Chapter 3). The house originally extended farther towards the sea, beyond the surviving semi-circular bay with its successive hearths, paved floor and well-worn seat tucked into a nook in an internal partition (Fig. 8.3). The adjacent, largely truncated bay was also paved with large slabs that included a well-used saddle quern (SF 1304; Fig. 6.13), and ashes from the hearth were swept into it and heaped up behind the partition wall. The lack of wear on the paving slabs suggests they were covered, perhaps with straw that was regularly refreshed, as the evidence from Iron Age buildings at Old Scatness indicates was regular practice there (Dockrill *et al.* 2015, 470).

House 1 may have belonged to a tradition of roundhouse construction that commenced in the mid- to late 1st millennium BC in the Northern Isles, in which rooms or bays were defined by radial partitions and arranged around a central hearth. An alternative interpretation is that it was a smaller, cellular building of the type widespread in Shetland during the early Bronze Age to early Iron Age (Downes and Lamb 2000, 119–22); it has been suggested that traditions of cellular architecture continued in Shetland even as monumental roundhouses like brochs were beginning to be constructed (Hingley 1992, 17). If it was a roundhouse, it may have been comparable to

Structure 1 at Bayanne on Yell, which was likewise built in the late 1st millennium BC (Moore and Wilson 2014, 119–20; see Fig. 8.10). The excavators of Bayanne suggest that the individual bays in Structure 1 were separately roofed with stone, with several large, flat slabs found among the rubble infill representing collapsed roofing stone. In Milla Skerra's house 1, massive slabs forming part of the rubble collapse were similarly interpreted as the remains of a part-corbelled wall or roof; the inward-curving profile of the surviving wall also supports this interpretation.

Roundhouses with radial partitions were built at Old Scatness (Structures 12 and 14) in the last two centuries BC (Dockrill *et al.* 2010, 11; Dockrill *et al.* 2015), and at Jarlshof (Hamilton 1956, 48–58, 200–3) and Mavis Grind (Structure A, Phase II; Cracknell and Smith 1983) during the Iron Age (see Fig. 8.10). At Old Scatness and Jarlshof, the roundhouses were built after the brochs and in close association with them; those at Mavis Grind and Bayanne stood in isolation, in settlements without brochs. The introduction of this new architectural form at Bayanne, a long-established settlement, may have been a local initiative that drew on wider trends but employed construction techniques that had long been in use (Moore and Wilson 2014, 120). Bayanne's Structure 1 stood in relation to earlier buildings (Moore and Wilson 2014, 120) rather than as a free-standing, monumental, highly visible dwelling, as Armit (1990, 195) proposes for Atlantic roundhouses more generally. In a similar way, house 1 at Milla Skerra was built into a mound that had accumulated through generations of inhabitation, its north-west side supported by the much older wall (context 83) that closed off the south-east end of yard 5 in phase 2C.

The excavated part of Milla Skerra developed in a more piecemeal way during the 1st centuries BC/AD (phase 5). In the house, a new hearth was built on top of the first one and then a third hearth on top of that, as ash-midden continued to pile up behind the internal partition and later around the hearth itself. Yard 3 was remodelled and enlarged to subsume its north-western neighbour (yard 4) and its south-eastern end was dismantled and rebuilt to create a tiny cell (2) against the upstanding yard 5 wall (83), which by now was several hundred years old (Fig. 8.4).

Figure 8.4 Cell 2 from the north, with the old yard 5 wall (83) to the left, the possible anvil (142) at the rear and the partition slot in the foreground, cut through the yellow clay floor (phase 5)

Figure 8.5 Midden and hearth waste lying over rubble collapse in house 1, with the rough yard 6 wall (28) lying parallel to the rear ranging rod (phase 7B), from the north-west

Then, abruptly in the 1st century cal AD, house 1 ceased to be a home (phase 6). Midden brought from elsewhere in the settlement – other houses, cooking fires, a metalworking hearth – was left over the floor and against the walls, with discrete concentrations of material as if basketfuls were turned upside down here and there. Next, its part-corbelled wall collapsed inward and rubble covered the loose midden. This deliberate midden deposition, coupled with the abandonment of so much good-quality building stone, hints that these acts had symbolic significance, representing the closure of a former home. Within the community's system of beliefs and values, they may have been seen as necessary to bring about some spiritual or metaphorical outcome – perhaps in response to an event or condition that affected the occupants. They could also indicate that the settlement was beginning to contract.

Certainly by the late 1st to 2nd century AD (phase 7), people appear to have been using the excavated area in a rather desultory way, but they clearly continued to live close by, presumably in areas since lost to erosion. As they carried on leaving midden over the ruins of house 1 (Fig. 8.5), they robbed stones from its south-east wall and pulled them into place to create a yard (6) that contained the midden. Later, after more midden had built up, they recreated the house's half-buried internal partition by setting large stones upright along its still-visible line. Use of the older yard (3) and adjacent cell (2) continued in ways that formed trampled, midden-rich floor layers. After a large heap of bog iron ore was placed in the cell, activity there appears to have been minimal: the ore lay undisturbed, never smelted (Fig. 8.6).

Figure 8.6 The heap of bog ore in cell 2 (phase 7) towards the top of the frame, with peat ash and midden overlapping it, from the north

Figure 8.7 The tumbled structures (phase 7), from the south

As conditions along the coast grew windier, the remaining buildings were allowed to tumble while domestic waste mixed with windblown sand piled up over and around them (Fig. 8.7). The constituents of the sandy midden indicate that some other parts of the settlement were still occupied, but the sense of general neglect suggests the community was in the process of contracting; perhaps some older members chose to remain in their homes while younger ones were moving inland to a more sheltered location. In the 2nd or early 3rd century cal AD, life in the settlement became unviable after winds blew thick layers of sand onto the foreshore. This may have happened suddenly, during the course of a season or even a single catastrophic storm. Doorways would have been blocked and yards choked, infield rendered infertile and grazing land lost. It must have forced any remaining inhabitants to move out. They may not have gone far, resettling a safe distance inland and continuing to use the foreshore, evident in the abundance of butchered bones of sea birds in the layers of clean, windblown sand that sealed the tumbled walls (Smith, Chapter 4).

Rhythms of food production and craft work

Discarded tools, broken pots and the residues of fires and meals make it possible to sketch many of the routines and seasonal rhythms of the settlement's life. However, given how intensively the space was used and the degree to which some deposits were reworked and moved around, it can be difficult to distinguish how these changed over the course of centuries.

The main fuel for domestic fires consisted of peat and turf, along with some animal dung, seaweed and heather (see Ellis, Chapter 3; Miller and Ramsay, Chapter 4). Maintaining a steady supply of fuel would have been a priority and at times a challenge in the largely treeless landscape of Unst. Driftwood made valuable building material, although the occasional charcoal fragment shows that wood – perhaps from old buildings or locally gathered willow and hazel – was sometimes burnt in fires (see Miller and Ramsay, Chapter 4). When timber was burnt, it may have been reserved for industrial processes, which required higher temperatures.

Seaweed and driftwood could have been gathered throughout the year from beaches. Peat and turf would have been cut and dried during summer, from the areas of blanket mire that covered much of Unst and from heathland and grassland, and stockpiled for use during the rest of the year. Sometimes it was still damp when it was burnt, as evident in a particular dump of peat ash left in a midden heap in phase 3 (Ellis, Chapter 3). Heather was likewise cut from heathland habitats for use as fuel, or perhaps used first to soften beds, make brooms, cover floors or roof buildings and later burned when it had become worn or dirty.

The foods that people ate and the ways they grew, reared, caught and gathered them remained fairly consistent over the centuries of occupation. Fish made up a significant part of the community's diet during all phases of the settlement. Although fish bones that were identifiable macroscopically (with the naked eye) were most plentiful in the earlier phases (Cerón-Carrasco, Chapter 4), the layers of ash midden swept out of the house 1 hearth (phases 4B-5) contained abundant microscopic fragments of burnt fish bone (Ellis, Chapter 3). It may be that, after fish were eaten, the bones were routinely thrown back on to the fire. The species represented indicate that people were catching fish in a range of environments, from rock pools to shallow, inshore waters. They also fished in deeper water using boats and hooked lines, hauling in very large ling and cod over 1.5 m long (Cerón-Carrasco, Chapter 4). A fish of that size would have provided many meals and indeed might have been dried or salted for winter consumption. Deep-sea fishing would have been a summer pursuit, but inshore and rock-pool fishing for salmon and young saithe and cod could have been done year-round. People also gathered limpets, periwinkles and mussels from exposed, rocky shores; oysters from shallow waters; and bivalves like clams and cockles from inter-tidal sand. Someone roasted mussels and limpets on the outdoor hearth in yard 5 (phase 2) and, generations later, the inhabitants of house

1 dined on crab claws and sea urchin (phase 5) (Cerón-Carrasco, Chapter 4). Meals like these were also evident in the layers of burnt shells that piled up outside yard 5 (phase 2), were dumped against the wall of house 1 (phase 6), and lay in the entrance to yard 6 (phase 7).

People were catching and eating seabirds from phase 2 onward, including little auk, gannet, cormorant, shag, goose, duck species, razorbill, guillemot, the flightless great auk and – at least once in phase 2B – sea eagle (Smith, Chapter 4). They probably also gathered sea birds' eggs, those potent packages of protein. Birds could have been caught and eggs gathered from colonies on cliffs and rocky locations around the coast of Unst in the summer breeding season, perhaps using heather ropes and nets.

Domestic cattle, sheep/goats and pigs were being reared and butchered from as early as the 6th century cal BC, from just before the construction of yard 5 all the way through to the 2nd century cal AD (Smith, Chapter 4). They provided meat, milk, cheese and butterfat for the community as well as raw materials for tools and textiles. The cattle and sheep/goat were diminutive, of a size consistent with contemporary herds in the Northern Isles. The withers (the ridge between the shoulder blades) of one cow or bull, for example, would have reached to just above the hip (101.4 cm) of the man (164–171 cm tall) who was buried on the foreshore in phase 9; the withers of a sheep would have come to about his knee (53.4 cm) (*ibid.*).

In autumn the community killed and butchered many of the younger cattle and sheep/goat, especially males, in order to bring down the number of animals that had to be stabled and fed during the long, stormy Shetland winters (Smith, Chapter 4). Animals would have been kept under shelter over winter, perhaps in dedicated bays in the houses, with heart-shaped stones such as SF 1179 (Fig. 6.9) used to keep the tethering ropes from rubbing against their hides (Clarke, Chapter 3). People would have used hafted iron or quartz tools to butcher livestock and other creatures such as seal pups caught at summer breeding grounds. Animal and bird bones bear cut marks from sharp implements, like the one used to extract the brain from a pig's skull in phase 2C (Smith, Chapter 4). Meat and fish may have been dried in the salty air or hung to cure in the smoke from cooking fires, providing valuable sources of protein in winter.

Cereal crops – mainly six-row barley with some hulled barley and perhaps a little wheat – provided staple starches in the form of bread and porridge (Miller and Ramsay, Chapter 4). The harvest would have been gently dried over a low heat, such as that yielded by smouldering turf, so it could be stored over winter. Some charred grain slipped into the fire during drying, but relatively little of it was found, suggesting that most of the cereal was dried in a different part of the settlement (Miller and Ramsay, Chapter 4). The dried, hoarded grain would have been ground into flour using saddle querns like the one re-used for paving in house 1 (SF 1304, Fig. 6.13; Clarke, Chapter 3), pounder/grinders and slabs, or perhaps in later phases using rotary querns (although none was found). Other foods that might have formed part of their diet, such as nuts, berries or kelp, have left no archaeological trace.

The inedible parts of animals would have been put to many uses, only some of which are visible archaeologically. Animal and cetacean bones were shaped with knives and smoothed with sea-borne pumice, gathered from the shoreline, to create implements like combs, awls and toggles. Stone smoothers (for example, SF 1927, Fig. 6.7) hint that animal hides were processed to make bags, bellows, strings, clothing and shoes. Feathers may have been used to make blankets, clothing and ornaments. Loom weights (such as SF 954, Fig. 6.8) indicate that people were weaving cloth at the settlement, presumably using wool spun from the fleeces of sheep or goats, and sewing it into garments and blankets using bone points like SFs 315 and 777 (Fig. 6.18). Sheep fat was boiled down in pottery vessels to make tallow for light or soap, residues of which were trapped in the fabric (Derham, Chapter 4). Larger bones scavenged from beached whales may have been put to use in buildings or as work surfaces, while smaller ones were made into tools or chopped up to extract the oil to use for lighting.

From the amount of broken pottery found piled in middens and scattered through deposits from all phases, the making and breaking of pots must have provided a steady, underlying beat to daily and seasonal life at Milla Skerra. This cycle had its own rhythmic sequence of practices. Potters would have known where to dig for suitable clay on Unst or neighbouring islands, and the quarried clay may have had to be puddled, sorted and mixed with temper to make it more workable. They may have travelled north along the coast to Clibberswick to find the steatite that outcrops there, which they ground up and mixed into clay to increase the thermal resistance of cooking pots. However, unlike their contemporaries at settlements like Bayanne (Forster 2014; Forster 2015), they chose not to fashion vessels and lamps from the soft stone.

The pottery assemblage shows a high degree of continuity, as well as an awareness of the trends and techniques in use more widely across Shetland at settlements of varying scales. Steatite was the preferred temper at Milla Skerra (phases 2–7), as it was at Old Scatness and Bayanne, but thinner-walled vessels tempered with quartz were being made by the Middle Iron Age (phase 10) (Lelong and Ballin Smith, Chapter 5; Murray 2016, 139, 159; MacSween 2014). Unlike at most contemporary settlements, however, hardly any of the pots were decorated. There are also some marked changes evident in the kinds of pottery made, such as the fairly abrupt abandonment of the well-made Sparkly Cooking Wares so ubiquitous in phase 2. Perhaps specialist potters in the community routinely passed on their skills to younger generations, who sometimes continued to work with traditional forms and fabrics and at other times chose to develop new ones.

Certain consistently used forms and fabrics evoke particular practices and scenes (Lelong and Ballin Smith, Chapter 5). Shallow dishes or platters (phases 2, 4 and 6) may have held food that was shared among a group during communal meals. The small jars termed Burnished Mugs, just the right size for gripping between the hands, may have held warming drinks on cold days (Lelong and Ballin Smith, Chapter 5). Cooking pots often eventually broke on the fire, like the large globular pot that cracked and was thrown (in disgust at the loss of a meal?) almost whole onto a midden heap (phase 3). Heavy, durable Grey-Buff Coarse Ware jars would have kept valuable stores of dried grain safe from rodents and insects.

The fires that generated much of the peat ash found in middens had burnt at relatively low temperatures (around 400°C), hot enough to smoke or grill food or bring liquids to the boil (Ellis, Chapter 3). Much higher temperatures (around 800°C) are usually needed for industrial work. Different strands of evidence indicate that ore was being smelted and metal smithed somewhere at the settlement. The assemblage of stone anvils (for example, SF 597 (Fig. 6.12), smoothers, polishers and polished pebbles from Milla Skerra is similar, although much smaller and narrower in range, to that from a specialised metal workshop dating to the 2nd–1st century BC at Mine Howe in Orkney (Clarke, Chapter 6; Clarke 2008). The block tuyère (SF 942, Figs 2.16 and 6.1) left in house 1 would have protected a bellows made of leather and wood from the heat of a metalworking hearth (Forster, Chapter 6). Other vestiges include slag spheres, unsmelted bog iron ore (SF 305) and residues of manganese, copper and zinc in midden deposits (see Derham, Chapter 3 and contributions by MacLaren, Clarke and Forster, Chapter 6). It may have been a craft practised intermittently when new tools were needed or old ones had to be repaired – everyday iron implements such as a fine file (SF 1707, Fig. 6.15), a thin, corroded plate (SF 767) found on yard 3's clay floor and the knives that left cut-marks on animal bones. No metalworking hearths or highly combusted ash were found in the excavations, and it is likely that the process with its toxic fumes was kept away from the settlement's densely built core.

People made numerous implements from stones collected on beaches or dug out of the ground. They also chipped quartz pebbles to make knives, scrapers, piercers and other tools. The first stage of knapping quartz to remove primary flakes was largely done away from the buildings, presumably so that large, sharp flakes did not fall underfoot in heavily used areas, while the finer work to shape implements took place in the yards (Ballin, Chapter 6). Heavy stone tools made of finer-grained, softer rock like serpentine were used for smoothing hides or metal objects, while elongated schist cobbles were selected for their toughness and shape to use as hammerstones (Clarke, Chapter 6). Stones employed as smoothers and pounders/grinders (for grinding steatite to use as temper, for example) may likewise have been chosen because their size and shape made them easy to grasp. Pebbles such as SF 668 may have been used to burnish leather-hard pots before firing. Some of the tools show evidence of long use, such as one dark green serpentine cobble (SF 1887, Fig. 6.7) found in a midden outside yard 5. Its pecked facets, smoothed sides and flake scars show it was used first as a pounder/grinder, then as a smoother and finally as a hammerstone. A beautiful, glossy object that fits perfectly in the hand, it may have been the favourite, well-used tool of a crafts-person living in Middle Iron Age Milla Skerra.

The evidence of all these processes, objects and materials can evoke other, sensory aspects of everyday life. The smell of smouldering peat and turf from cooking fires and pottery kilns would have hung over the houses and yards on calm days, mingling with the ripe smell of decaying midden. The fishy tang of the sea would have been ever-present, with onshore winds carrying the taste of salt. The sounds of conversation and craft work – stone pounding steatite, flaking quartz or grinding grain – would have punctuated the air above the steady, rhythmic crashing of waves on the beach.

Middens and the significance of stuff

At Milla Skerra, people lived on and among the residues of daily life – their own and those of previous generations. They piled up ashes, food waste and broken objects outside yard 5 (phase 2) and then over it (phases 3 and 4A), but kept yards 3 and 4 very clean. They ploughed and cultivated midden deposits immediately outside the buildings. They spread midden over the paved floor of house 1 after it was abandoned and then later over its ruins. At least some of these acts represented the deliberate deposition (rather than incidental disposal) of material perhaps seen as charged with meaning, power and potential fertility. Particular objects that may have held special significance were sometimes incorporated into the walls and floors of buildings. These included the broken, highly burnished cooking pot (V 745), tucked into the wall at the south-eastern end of yard 3 (phase 4); the anvil (SF 553) built into the joint yard 3/4 south wall; the hammerstone and saddle quern (SFs 2261 and 1304) that formed part of the paved floor in house 1, and the large, silvery pot sherds used to make the house's second hearth (Fig. 8.8).

Polished and painted pebbles may have carried particular kinds of symbolism. Two of the three painted quartzite pebbles found in the excavations were placed as what might be considered foundation deposits in areas devoted to craft work (phases 4 and 5). One pebble (SF 1119, Fig. 7.1), which had been painted three times with wavy lines and dots, was set beneath the edge of the yard 3/4 south wall. Another (SF 1048, Fig. 7.1), painted with irregular lines and loops, lay in the clay floor beneath the edge of the large anvil in cell 2. Of the nearly 60 painted pebbles so far found in Scotland, about 60% are from Shetland (Arthur and Murray 2014); it has been suggested that

Figure 8.8 A rim sherd from a large, burnished vessel (V 25) set into the yellow clay of the second hearth in house 1

they were charm stones (Ritchie 1972, 299) or shamanic equipment (Ritchie forthcoming). The association here with an area of craft production resonates with another recent interpretation, that they were made and used in conjunction with metalworking – a process that generated intense heat and peat tar, both of which may have been used to paint the stones (Arthur and Murray 2014, 7). Experimental work has also found that chimney soot, mixed with cod-liver oil and painted onto pre-heated quartzite pebbles, produces indelible marks like those on painted pebbles (Bashford 2015).

The residues, objects and midden spreads that people generated and deployed at Milla Skerra seem to have been saturated with meaning. This perceived potency would have lain in their associations with other practices and their places within complex contemporary narratives. These in turn were woven through social relations and incorporated the memories, stories, myths and beliefs that constituted people's views of the world. Alongside the examples of deliberate, structured deposition observed during the excavations, there must have been many more that left no archaeological traces or – in the absence of access to the belief systems that governed deposition – were not observed. Among later prehistoric communities around Atlantic Europe, a growing body of evidence indicates how thoroughly enmeshed were belief systems with everyday existence and how frequently practical acts carried symbolic weight (see, for example, Bowden and McOmish 1987; Needham and Spence 1996; Lelong and MacGregor 2007, 263).

Seasonal rhythms

Summers on Unst see long hours of daylight interspersed with a prolonged twilight, known in the Shetland dialect as the 'simmer dim'. The poet Jen Hadfield has spoken about the effects of this quality and quantity of light – how the simmer dim compels one to intense, mainly outdoor activity and productivity which changes, as winter descends, to a slower pace of life that is based mainly indoors.

The rhythms of life on Iron Age Unst would have also varied according to the seasons. During the summer, people may have spent much of their time outdoors – tending livestock; growing and harvesting crops; catching seabirds and collecting eggs; fishing from rocks; cutting and stacking peat; gathering materials to build and repair houses, yards and boats; digging up clay and ore; firing pottery, and making new tools from stone, bone and iron. If summers were periods of intensive outdoor work, there must have also been times when people paused to take in the sight of gannets diving for fish in the bay or watch otters chase each other across the beach (as the excavation team sometimes did). There were days when sunlight made the shallows look like liquid blue-green glass, and maybe they splashed into the water to relieve the unfamiliar heat. Some took to the sea in boats to fish for ling and cod in deep water and perhaps to visit other settlements on Unst and neighbouring islands. The long, light days and periods of calmer weather may have also drawn boats to Sandwick from other places, bringing things to trade such as the shale bangle (SF 1702, Fig. 7.2) and blue glass bead (SF 2002, Fig. 7.2).

Autumn would have seen some activities increase in pace to prepare for winter: butchering younger cattle, sheep/goats and pigs; salting or smoking meat; drying grain to preserve it against dampness; checking buildings were in good repair. During the dark, storm-lashed winters, when Unst sees only about six hours of light each day, people would have spent a great deal of time indoors around hearths like the one that warmed house 1. Whale oil burning in stone lamps may have illuminated the interior; although no lamps were found here, they are common on contemporary sites in Shetland (Forster, Chapter 6). Highly burnished, steatite-tempered pots like those used to build the second hearth would have glowed like freshly caught mackerel in the firelight.

Winters may have been times for repetitive indoor work like spinning wool, making fishing nets, grinding steatite or smoothing hides, and for sharing stories and songs. People could still have fished for young saithe from the rocks at either end of the beach on calm days (Cerón-Carrasco, Chapter 4), although when gales blew and waves pounded the shore they may have stayed indoors and eaten preserved food instead. During stormy spells they may have let the ashes pile up behind the hearth (Fig. 8.9); when the weather settled, they would have ventured out to gather driftwood that waves had thrown up on the shores of Unst.

As days lengthened into spring, their focus would have begun to shift outdoors again. They would have carried weak livestock outside to nibble on new grass. They would have inspected roofs and walls for damage and begun gathering materials to repair them or build new structures. They would have shovelled out middens and ash heaps that had built up over winter, ploughed some

Figure 8.9 The ash-midden heap behind the hearth in house 1 (phase 5) under excavation (from the north-west), with large pottery sherds visible

of the nutrient-rich material into the ground – a practice in evidence at contemporary settlements in the Northern Isles (Guttmann *et al.* 2004; Guttmann 2005) and sowed carefully hoarded seeds for that year's cereal crop.

The community's social relations would have been woven through all of these daily and seasonal practices. The well-worn seat close to the hearth in house 1 may have been reserved for elders or particularly respected members of the community. Certain people may have had responsibility for (and special skills in) making pottery, for example, or smelting iron or catching seabirds and would have passed on their knowledge to younger members. They would have held not only technical knowledge of craft production but also geographical familiarity with the best places to find nesting seabirds, dig up iron ore and so on – the kinds of knowledge that had developed over generations. Such roles may have been defined by gender, age, social status or a combination of factors that are invisible archaeologically.

The character of the settlement

As it grew upward and outward over the centuries, the settlement would have come to look like a low, broad mound sprouting a huddle of conjoined buildings, yards and midden heaps. Anecdotal evidence based on local knowledge indicates the foreshore has eroded considerably since the mid-20th century (Margaret Hunter, pers comm). The part of the settlement that extended further towards the sea, beyond the excavated portion, would have occupied a promontory founded on the bedrock dykes which are visible at low tide on the beach. It may also have extended along the bay to the west, where erosion has encroached further inland, and to the south-east where a building apparently similar to house 1 is eroding out of the foreshore (Canmore ID 340671).

How extensive was the settlement, and did it include a broch? There are certainly accounts of a broch on the shore at Sandwick (Canmore ID 114). In 1863, the architect and Yell native James Thomas Irvine included it in a list of brochs on Unst and described it as lying two-thirds of the way towards the eastern end of the beach (Irvine nd), a location that corresponds approximately to Milla Skerra. It had been first observed by the schoolmaster at Uyeasound after north-easterly gales removed some of the sand that completely covered it. Irvine was an experienced observer, who knew a broch when he saw one. That said, only a small part of the structure was visible when he recorded it, and geophysical survey conducted for this project found no evidence for outerworks (see Chapter 1, Fig. 1.6). The Shetland Historic Environment Record (site 204) also contains an account of a 'ruined chapel' at Milla Skerra, which was partially destroyed by the encroaching sea in 1905; this apparently stood on top of a much older structure. Into the mid 20th century, some locals recalled seeing a high wall containing a window, which was eventually washed away by storms, on this spot (Margaret Hunter, pers comm).

If there was a broch at Sandwick, it might have been built during phase 4 or 5 by comparison to other dated sites such as Old Scatness (Dockrill *et al.* 2015) (Fig. 8.10). Sandwick certainly fits the criteria that Fojut (1983, 50) identified for broch territories on Shetland: it provided access to the shore, abundant grazing and some cultivable land. If there was not a broch at Sandwick, it seems there should have been one. Fojut's (*ibid.*, fig 5) model of Iron Age territories on Shetland includes the seven confirmed brochs on Unst, although not the seven other possible examples in the National Record of the Historic Environment, several of which were recorded in antiquity but have since been lost to erosion. These include Irving's broch at Sandwick and another at Brough Taing at the north-east edge of the bay, where in 1878 the Ordnance Survey recorded local traditions of structural remains and rubble; the site is now wave-eroded bedrock (Fig. 8.11; Canmore ID 116). If the seven possible examples are discounted, there is a striking absence of brochs along the eastern side of Unst, with only one confirmed example on Balta Island at the mouth of Baltasound, and most of them clustered around the southern end (see Fojut 1983, fig 5).

Although (understandably, given their complexity and monumentality) brochs have tended to dominate studies of the Iron Age in the Northern Isles, settlements that co-existed with and complemented brochs also made up a significant part of the later prehistoric social fabric. Settlements like Kebister in east Mainland (Owen and Lowe 1999) and Bayanne on Yell (Moore and Wilson 2014) – built on good agricultural land and occupied throughout the Iron Age – are proof that not every Shetland community incorporated a broch. In discussing Kebister, Owen and Lowe (1999) suggest that, in the period before people began building brochs (in the 4th to 3rd century BC; Dockrill *et al.* 2015, 18, 44–5), the Shetland population was dispersed more widely to maximise agricultural potential at a time when

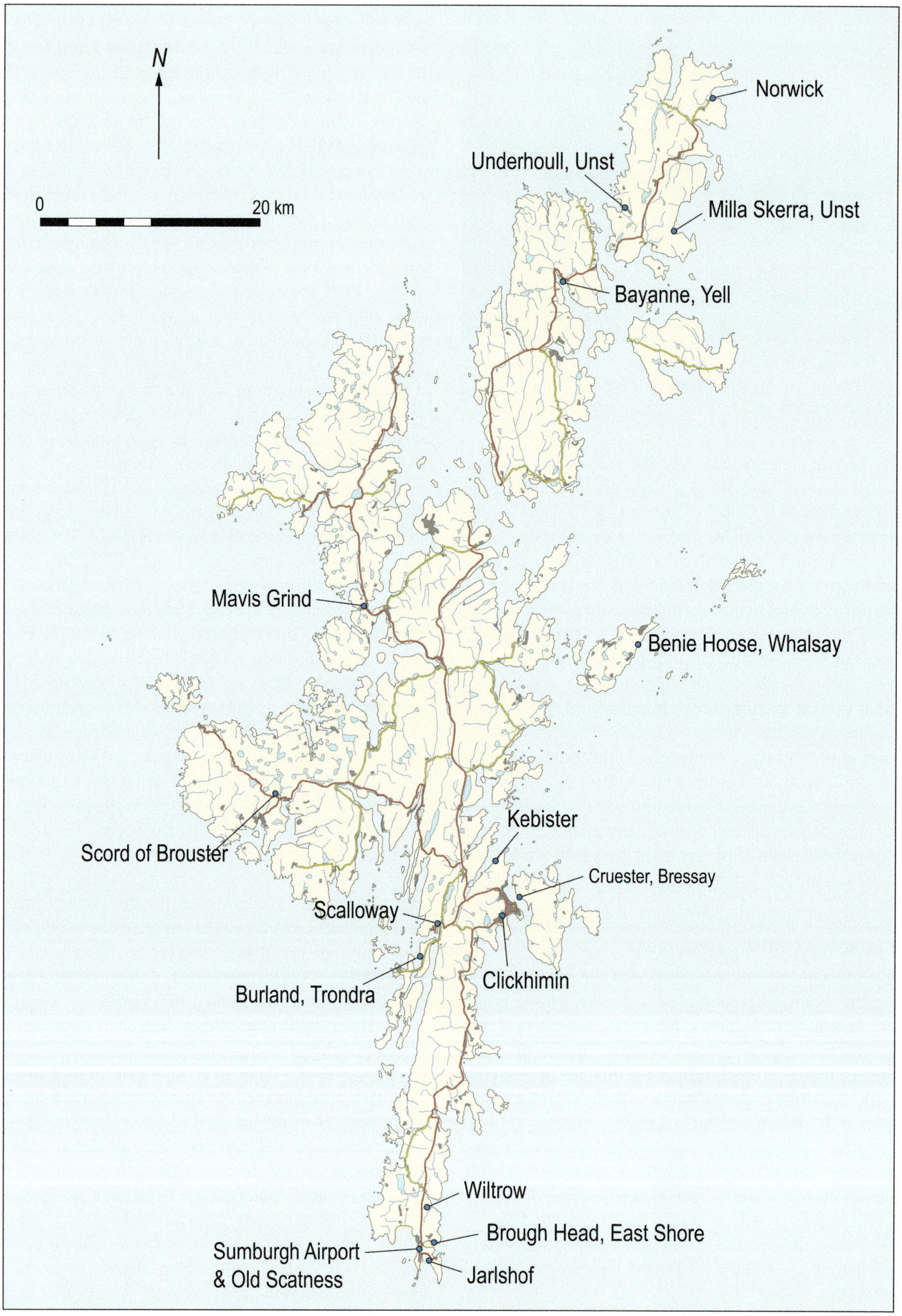

Figure 8.10 Some key prehistoric settlements on Shetland

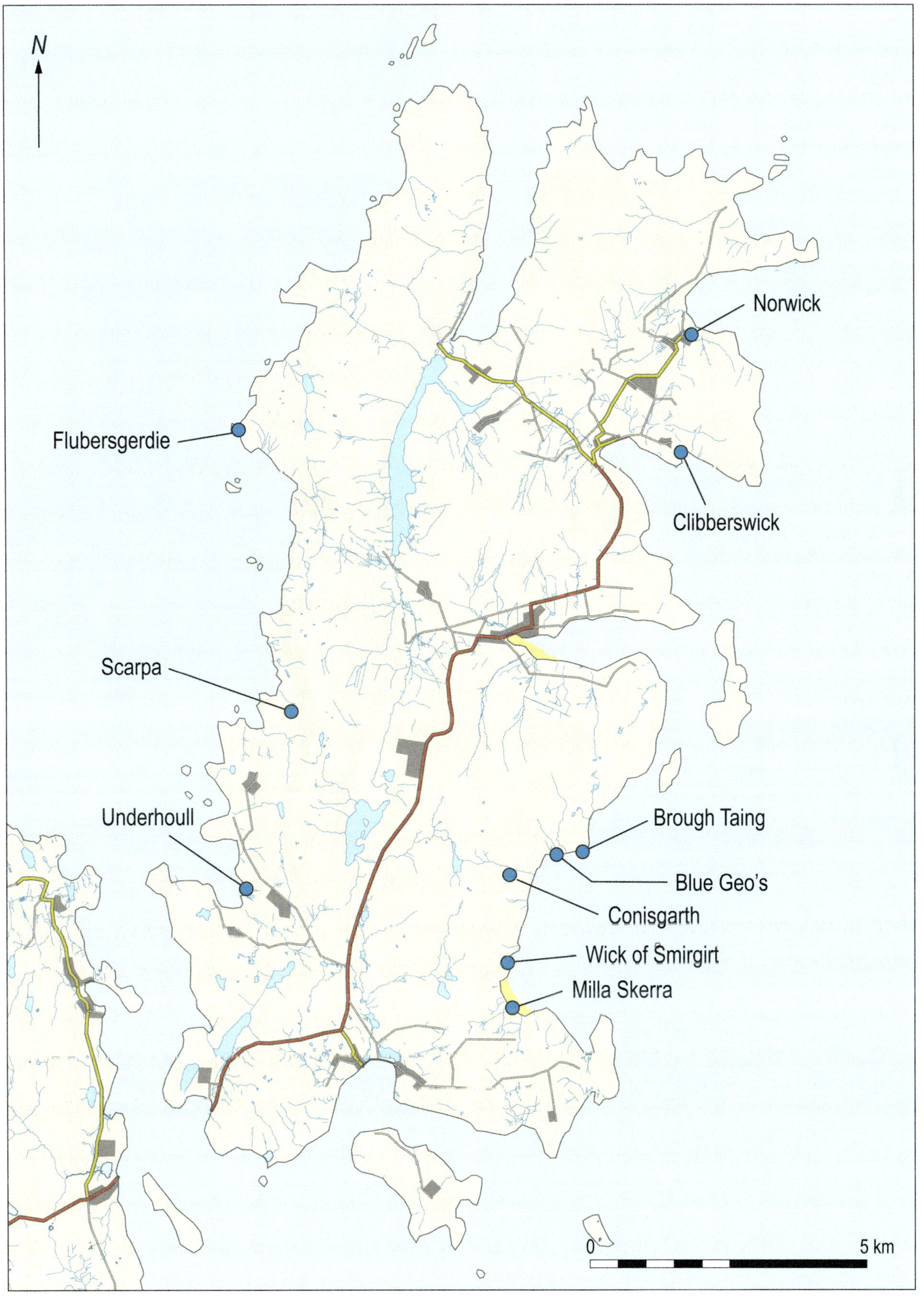

Figure 8.11 Excavated later prehistoric settlements on Unst

the climate was worsening and crop yields were declining. 'With the advent of the brochs and the changes in social organization that they imply, it may be that not all of these settlement units could or elected to "support" a broch' (Owen and Lowe 1999, 287). Two other probable Iron Age settlements not directly associated with brochs are known around Sandwick – at Blue Geos and Wick of Smirgirt (Canmore IDs 121 and 124 respectively) – and elsewhere on Unst, for example at Skaw in the north-east (Small 1965) (see Fig. 8.11). At times of external threat, these communities might have found refuge and solidarity with others who had built brochs (Fojut 1983, 43). The broch at Old Scatness was the centre of a complex, hierarchical settlement and economy, indicated by (among other things) evidence for large-scale grain storage and meat that was sourced from local producers (Dockrill *et al.* 2015, 463). At Milla Skerra, the evidence points to a smaller-scale if diverse economy. If a broch did once stand by the shore at Sandwick, it does not appear to have left traces in the excavated evidence.

In any case, the generations of Milla Skerra's community sailed to a large extent in Shetland's cultural mainstream. They participated socially, economically and culturally in a world made up of other communities of various scales who were linked by land and sea; shared architectural conventions and farming, fishing and craft practices; trading relationships; personal and family histories, kinship and beliefs. Given their facility with boats, evident in the bones of large fish caught in deep water, people would have seen the sea as a medium that linked them to other places rather than as a barrier. The characteristics of certain stretches of water may have influenced the strength of connections between communities. A voyage to Underhoull (Fig. 8.11) on the western shore of Unst would have meant navigating the treacherous currents of Bluemull Sound between Unst and Yell. Milla Skerra may have had closer links to communities living on the eastern shores of Unst, Yell and mainland Shetland than to their contemporaries on the western seaboard.

Life after death

At some point after Milla Skerra was inundated with sand, the body of a man was buried near the abandoned buildings. He was in his 50s when he died (Duffy, Chapter 7), elderly for contemporary life spans, sometime in cal AD 150-390 (95.4% probability), or probably cal AD 240-330 (68.2% probability; SUERC-10745). His grave was dug through windblown sand until it just clipped an old cultivated soil; was this intentional, an effort to reach physically back through the sand to an archaeological horizon with which he had some connection? Possibly he was a descendant of someone who had been driven out by the inundation, an elder member of a family that still identified the buried settlement as its ancestral home. Although genetic analysis has not been able to identify his origins beyond a general European context, future work may refine our

Figure 8.12 Photograph taken in 1953 of a burial excavated on the beach west of Milla Skerra (© Rudi Saunders)

understanding of his family ties (see Dulias and Edwards, Chapter 7; Dulias *et al.* in prep).

He wore a delicate glass and bronze ornament on his clothing or body, and next to his mouth someone set a dappled, silver-grey stone disc, finely made and polished (SFs 221 and 222, Figs 7.3 and 7.4). One of only a handful of polished stone discs so far found with burials in the Northern Isles and north mainland of Scotland, this must have been a special object with particular significance to those conducting the burial. The sticky white substance under the disc may have been intended for consumption, inhalation or application in the afterlife. His burial close to the abandoned settlement echoes other late Iron Age instances in which articulated bodies were placed into and around the rubble of collapsed buildings (Maldonado 2011) – for example, at Howe (Ballin Smith 1994) and Knowe of Skea (Moore and Wilson 2006), both in Orkney. The many variations on this practice suggest it expressed broadly shared ideas about connections between the dead and buildings that had died (Maldonaldo 2011, 84–7). Only certain people were selected for this treatment, which must have been designed to achieve a particular outcome; placing their bodies at abandoned ancestral homes may have been a way of formally joining them to their lineages (*ibid.*).

Around the time of the burial, a tiny cairn of schist stones and some quartzite pebbles was built above the sand-covered ruins and some half-finished carved antler rings were left nearby (Figs 8.13 and 6.18). The choice of stones for the cairn resonates with the later use of white quartzite pebbles to build two rectangular cairns on the foreshore (see below).

People continued to bury the dead at least occasionally in the vicinity. There are vague records of human remains in short cists having been found at Easting (Canmore ID 135). These probably include one found on the beach in 1953, which was reported to Shetland Museum. Although it was not recorded archaeologically, photographs taken at the time appear to show an inhumation lying supine in the cist with the knees raised and bent (Fig 8.12). The cranium lies at a peculiar angle (perhaps replaced in this position by the excavator) and the knees appear to be disfigured by bony growths (P Duffy, archive report). Dr Rudi Saunders, who used to visit his family at nearby Hannigarth during childhood summers, related seeing the skeleton when it was uncovered and supplied photographs of it. He confirmed that it was left in place and the cist was backfilled with beach sand (Rudi Saunders, pers comm).

Figure 8.13 The tiny cairn that was built on the stable dune covering the settlement in phase 9

Other acts of burial and commemoration took place after this, when two rectangular, kerbed cairns of white quartzite pebbles were built beside the shore to the north-west of Milla Skerra; one contained the skeleton of someone who died in cal AD 420–640 (GU-1291 at 95.4% probability; Bigelow 1984). The cairns' character points to broader awareness of funerary rites and materials in use across northern Scotland at the time (discussed in Maldonaldo 2011, 84–9; also see Ashmore 1980). The calibrated date range for this burial overlaps with that for the brief phase of activity on the fixed dune which by this time covered the settlement (phase 10). It involved the construction of what may have been a light fence or

Figure 8.14 Members of the Unst Archaeology Group and excavation team with stonemasons at the newly reconstructed settlement, 2007

windbreak, with large stones dragged into place to support it. People lit cooking fires and left behind ashes, a few pot sherds and the remains of domestic animals, seabirds, fish and shellfish they had eaten. This might have been a temporary camp, although the presence of domestic animals suggests that a farming settlement lay fairly close by. A possible interpretation is that, in the 5th to 6th centuries AD, Sandwick was a place where people came specifically to conduct burial rites and other ceremonies that also involved gathering around fires and food. It may have been known more widely as the former home of an ancestral community, a spot suitable for rites that would connect the living community with its roots and traditions. In this light, it is worth considering the tradition of a chapel that sealed an older structure at Milla Skerra.

It is possible that, with the spread of Christianity around Shetland from the mid 8th century, the ancient significance of the site was enveloped by new beliefs and formalised with the construction of a chapel, as happened for example on St Ninian's Isle (Barrowman 2011). Given the lack of any more concrete evidence for early Christian activity at Sandwick, this is pure speculation.

The concrete evidence from the excavations, meanwhile, forms a robust basis for this narrative about rhythms of life on Iron Age Unst. With the discovery of the eroding site by members of the Unst Archaeology Group, its subsequent excavation and the community-led reinstatement of the structures (Fig. 8.14), Milla Skerra has re-emerged into the island's landscape. It has found a place in archaeological narratives on Shetland's prehistoric past and also in the consciousness of people who come to Sandwick, whether they live on Unst or are visiting the island. It stands now as a monument – to the community that inhabited the Iron Age taskscape and to the interests and values of Unst's community today. It will stand as such for as long as waves and weather allow.

Bibliography

Adderley, P., Simpson, I. and Davidson, D. 2006 'Historic landscape management: A validation of quantitative soil thin-section analysis', *Journal of Archaeological Science* 33(3), 320–34.

Allason-Jones, L. 1989 *Ear-rings in Roman Britain*. Oxford: British Archaeological Report 201.

Alldritt, D. M. 2003 Economy and Environment in the First Millennium AD in Northern Scotland and the Northern Isles. Unpublished PhD Thesis, University of Glasgow.

Anderson, J. A. 1874 'Notes on some polished stone discs of unknown use, in the Museum', *Proceedings of the Society of Antiquaries of Scotland* 10, 717–19.

Armit, I. 1990 'Epilogue: The Atlantic Scottish Iron Age', in I. Armit (ed.), *Beyond the Brochs: Changing perspectives on the Atlantic Scottish Iron Age*. Edinburgh: Edinburgh University Press, 194–210.

Armit, I. (ed.) 2006 *Anatomy of an Iron Age Roundhouse: The Cnip Wheelhouse excavations, Lewis*. Edinburgh: Society of Antiquaries of Scotland.

Arthur, R. and Murray, J. 2014 *Painting the stones black: Solving the mystery of painted quartz pebbles*. Archaeology Reports Online 12. http://www.archaeologyreportsonline.com/PDF/ARO12_Painted_Pebbles.pdf

Ashmore, P. J. 1980 'Low cairns, long cists and symbol stones', *Proceedings of the Society of Antiquaries of Scotland* 110, 346–55.

Ashmore, P. J. and Griffiths, D. 2011 'Introduction: Aeolian archaeology' in Griffiths and Ashmore (eds) 2011, 1–7.

Aufderheide, A. C. and Rodriguez-Martin, C. 1998 *The Cambridge Encyclopaedia of Human Palaeopathology*. Cambridge: Cambridge University Press.

Ballin, T. B. 1999a 'Bipolar cores in southern Norway; Classification, chronology and geography', *Lithics* 20, 13–22.

Ballin, T. B. 1999b Kronologiske og Regionale Forhold i Sydnorsk Stenalder. En Analyse med Udgangspunkt i Bopladserne ved Lundevågen (Farsundprosjektet). Unpublished PhD thesis, Institute of Prehistoric Archaeology, Aarhus University.

Ballin, T. B. 2002a 'Later Bronze Age flint technology: A presentation and discussion of post-barrow debitage from monuments in the Raunds area, Northamptonshire', *Lithics* 23, 3–28.

Ballin, T. B. 2002b The Quartz Assemblage from Dalmore, Lewis, Western Isles. Unpublished report, Lithic Research.

Ballin, T. B. 2005 *Re-Examination of the Quartz Artefacts from Scord of Brouster: A lithic assemblage from Shetland and its Neolithic context*. Scottish Archaeological Internet Report 17. http://archaeologydataservice.ac.uk/archives/view/sair/volumes.cfm

Ballin, T. B. 2008 *Quartz Technology in Scottish Prehistory*. Scottish Archaeological Internet Report 26. http://archaeologydataservice.ac.uk/archives/view/sair/volumes.cfm

Ballin, T. B. 2014a 'The lithic assemblage', in Moore and Wilson 2014, Section 2: Excavations at Cruester Burnt Mound, Bressay, Shetland, 80–3.

Ballin, T. B. 2014b 'The quartz assemblage', in Moore and Wilson 2014, Section 3: Excavations at Bayanne, Yell, Shetland, 138–44.

Ballin, T. B. 2014c 'The quartz assemblage', in Moore and Wilson 2014, Section 4: Excavations at Burland, Trondra, Shetland', 307–12.

Ballin Smith, B. (ed.) 1994 *Howe: Four Millennia of Orkney Prehistory Excavations 1978–82*. Edinburgh: Society of Antiquaries of Scotland Monograph 9.

Barrett, J. H., Nicholson, R. A. and Cerón-Carrasco, R. 1999 'Archaeo-icthyological Evidence for Long-Term Economic Trends in Northern Scotland: 3500 BC to 1500 AD', *Journal of Archaeological Science* 26(4), 353–88.

Barrowman, C. 2000 'The Pumice', in Downes and Lamb 2000, 109–111.

Barrowman, R. C. 2011 *The Chapel and Burial Ground on St Ninian's Isle, Shetland: Excavations past and present*. London: Society for Medieval Archaeology Monograph 32.

Bashford, D.J. 2015 'Coarse stone', in Dockrill *et al.* 2015, 341-64

Bass, W. M. 1995 *Human Osteology: A Laboratory and Field Manual*, 4th edition. Missouri: Missouri Archaeological Society.

Baxter, J. M. 1982 'Population dynamics of *Patella vulgata* in Orkney', *Netherlands Journal of Sea Research* 16, 94–104.

Beatty, J. 1992 *Sula: The Seabird-hunters of Lewis*. London: Michael Joseph.

Beijerinck, W. 1947 *Zadenatlas der Nederlandsche Flora*. Wageningen: Veenman and Zonen.

Bennett, K. D., Bunting, M. J. and Fossitt, J. A. 1997 'Long-term vegetation change in the Western and Northern Isles, Scotland', *Botanical Journal of Scotland* 49(2), 127–40.

Bigelow, G. F. 1978 'Unst, Norse-Medieval settlement', *Discovery and Excavation Scotland*, 18.

Bigelow, G. F. 1979 'Unst, late Norse settlement', *Discovery and Excavation Scotland*, 27.

Bigelow, G. F. 1980 'Sandwick, late-Norse settlement, pre-Norse burials', *Discovery and Excavation Scotland*, 26–7.

Bigelow, G. F. 1984 'Two kerbed cairns from Milla Skerra, Unst, Shetland' in J. G. P. Friell and W. G. Watson (eds), *Pictish Studies: Settlement, burial and art in Dark Age northern Britain*. Oxford: British Archaeological Report 125, 115–30.

Binns, R. E. 1972 'Composition and derivation of pumice on post-glaciation strandlines in northern Europe and western Arctic', *Geological Society of America Bulletin* 83(8), 2303–24.

Bowden, M. and McOmish, D. 1987 'The required barrier', *Scottish Archaeological Review* 4(2), 76–84.

Braids, O. C. and Miller, R. H. 1975 'Fats, waxes and resins in soils' in J. E. Gieseking (ed.), *Soil Components, Volume 1: Organic Components*. New York: Springer, 343–68.

Bramwell, D. 1983 'Appendix 5: Bird bones from Knap of Howar, Orkney', in Ritchie 1983, 100–3.

Bramwell, D. and Ballin Smith, B. 1994 'The bird remains' in B. Ballin Smith (ed.), *Howe: Four Millennia of Orkney Prehistory*. Edinburgh: Society of Antiquaries of Scotland Monograph 9, 153–7.

Brickley, M. and McKinley, J. 2004 *Institute of Field Archaeologists Technical Paper No 7: Guidelines to the Standards for Recording Human Remains*. Reading: Institute of Field Archaeologists/Southampton: British Association for Biological Anthropology and Osteoarchaeology.

Brooks, S. and Suchey, J. M. 1990 'Skeletal age determination based on the os pubis: A comparison of the Acsádi-Nemeskéri and Suchey-Brooks methods', *Human Evolution* 5(3), 227–38.

Brown, L. D. 2014a 'Painted quartz pebbles', in Dockrill *et. al.* 2015, 377-84.

Brown, L. D. 2014b 'Prehistory pottery', in Dockrill *et al.* 2015, 313-40.

Buck, C. E., Cavanagh, W. G., and Litton, C. D. 1996 *The Bayesian Approach to Interpreting Archaeological Data*. Chichester: Wiley.

Buikstra, J. E. and Ubelaker, D. H. (eds) 1994 *Standards for Data Collection from Human Skeletal Remains*. Arkansas: Arkansas Archaeological Survey Research Series 44.

Bullock, P., Fedoroff, N., Jongerius, A., Stoops, G., Tursina, T. and Babel, U. 1985 *Handbook for Soil Thin Section Description*. Wolverhampton: Waine Research.

Bunting, M. J., Tipping, R. and Downes, J. 2001 '"Anthropogenic" pollen assemblages from a Bronze Age cemetery at Linga Fiold, West Mainland, Orkney', *Journal of Archaeological Science* 28, 487–500.

Butler, C. 2005 *Prehistoric Flintwork*. Stroud: Tempus.

Calder, C. S. T. 1963 'Excavations in Whalsay, Shetland', *Proceedings of the Society of Antiquaries of Scotland* 94 (1960–61), 28–38.

Callander, J. G. and Grant, W. G. 1934 'The broch of Midhowe, Rousay, Orkney', *Proceedings of the Society of Antiquaries of Scotland* 68, 444–516.

Campbell, E. 1998 'Metalworking debris', in Sharples 1998, 160–4.

Campbell, A. C. and Nicholls, J. 1989 *Seashores and Shallow Seas of Britain and Europe*. London: Hamlyn Guides.

Cappers, R. T. J., Bekker, R. M. and Jans, J. E. A. 2006 *Digital Seed Atlas of the Netherlands*, Groningen Archaeological Studies 4. Eelde, Netherlands: Barkhuis.

Card, N. and Downes, J. 2003 'Mine Howe – the significance of space and place in the Iron Age' in Downes and Ritchie (eds) 2003, 11–19.

Card, N. and Downes, J. 2007 Radiocarbon dates from Mine Howe. Unpublished report, ORCA.

Carter, S. and Fraser, D. 1996 'The Sands of Breckon, Yell, Shetland: archaeological survey and excavation in an area of eroding windblown sand', *Proceedings of the Society of Antiquaries of Scotland* 126 (1996) 271–301.

Cerón-Carrasco, R. 1994 'Investigation of the fish remains from an Orkney farm mound', in W. Van Neer (ed.), 'Fish exploitation in the past', *Sciences Zoologiques* 274, 122–55.

Cerón-Carrasco, R. 1998a 'The fish bone assemblage from St. Boniface, Papa Westray, Orkney', in C. Lowe (ed.), *St. Boniface Church, Orkney: Coastal Erosion and Archaeological Assessment*. Edinburgh: Sutton Publications and Historic Scotland, 149–55.

Cerón-Carrasco, R. 1998b 'Fishing: evidence for seasonality and processing of fish for preservation in the Northern Isles of Scotland during the Iron Age and Norse times', *Environmental Archaeology* 3, 73–80.

Cerón-Carrasco, R. 1998c 'Fish', in Sharples 1998, 112–15.

Cerón-Carrasco, R. 2006 'The sieved fish remains' and 'The marine molluscs with notes on the Echinoidea remains and the terrestrial snails', in Armit 2006, 173–82.

Clark, J. G. D. 1936 'Report on a Late Bronze Age Site in Mildenhall Fen, West Suffolk', *Antiquaries Journal* 16, 29–50.

Clarke, A. 1998 'The pumice', in Sharples 1998, 119, 149–50.

Clarke, A. 1998 'Miscellaneous stone tools', in Sharples 1998, 144–9.

Clarke, A. 1999 'The pumice', in Owen and Lowe 1999, 151–64.

Clarke, A. 2005 'The pumice from Barnhouse', in C. Richards (ed.), *Dwelling Among the Monuments: The Neolithic village of Barnhouse, Maeshowe passage grave and surrounding monuments at Stennes, Orkney*. Cambridge: MacDonald Institute Monograph, 335–8.

Clarke, A. 2006 *Stone Tools and the Prehistory of the Northern Isles*. Oxford: British Archaeological Report 406.

Clarke, A. 2008 Mine Howe, Tankerness, Orkney: Coarse Stone Assemblage. Final report, January 2008. Unpublished report, ORCA.

Clarke, A. 2014 'The pumice', in Moore and Wilson 2014, Section 3: Excavations at Bayanne, Yell, Shetland, 181–3.

Close-Brooks, J. 1984 'Pictish and other burials', in J. G. P. Friell and W. G. Watson (eds), *Pictish Studies: Settlement, burial and art in Dark Age northern Britain*. Oxford: British Archaeological Report 125, 87–114.

Courty, M. A., Goldberg, P. and Macphail, R. 1989 *Soils and Micromorphology in Archaeology*. Cambridge: Cambridge University Press.

Cracknell, S. and Smith, B. 1983 'Archaeological Investigations at Mavis Grind, Shetland', *Glasgow Archaeological Journal* (10), 13–39, fig. 18.

Crawford, B. E. and Ballin Smith, B. 1999 *The Biggings, Papa Stour, Shetland: The history and archaeology of a royal Norwegian farm*. Edinburgh: Society of Antiquaries of Scotland Monograph Series 13.

Curle, A. O. 1936 'Account of the excavation of an iron smeltery and of an associated dwelling and tumuli at Wiltrow in the parish of Dunrossness, Shetland', *Proceedings of the Society of Antiquaries of Scotland* 70 (1935–36), 153–67.

Cuthbert, O. D. 1995 *The Life and Letters of an Orkney Naturalist: Reverend George Low, 1747–95*. Kirkwall: Orkney Press.

Davidson, J. and Anderson, J. 1886 'Notice of a small cup-shaped glass vessel, found in a stone cist at the public school, Airlie, and now presented to the museum by the School Board of Airlie', *Proceedings of the Society of Antiquaries of Scotland* 20, 136–41.

Davis, S. J. M. 1996 'Measurement of a group of adult female Shetland sheep skeletons from a single flock: a baseline for zooarchaeologists', *Journal of Archaeological Science* 23, 593–612.

Dawod, V. and FitzPatrick, E. A. 1992 'Some population sizes and effects of the Enchytraeidae (Oligochaeta) on soil structure in a selection of Scottish soils', *Geoderma* 56, 173–8.

Dawson, T., Lelong, O. and Shearer, I. 2011 'Local community groups and aeolian archaeology: Shorewatch and the experience of the Shetland Community Archaeology Project', in Griffiths and Ashmore 2011, 87–105.

Dickson, C. A. 1983 'Macroscopic plant remains from Knap of Howar, Orkney', in Ritchie 1983, 114–15.

Dickson, C. A. 1994 'Plant remains', in Ballin Smith 1994, 125–39.

Dickson, C. A. 1998 'Past uses of turf in the Northern Isles', in C. M. Milles and G. Coles (eds), *Life on the Edge: Human settlement and marginality*. Oxford: Oxbow Books, 105–9.

Dickson, C. 1999 'The plant remains', in Crawford and Ballin Smith 1999, 104–18.

Dickson, C. A. and Dickson, J. H. 2000 *Plants and People in Ancient Scotland*. Stroud: Tempus.

Dickson, J. H. 1992 'North American driftwood, especially *Picea* (spruce) from archaeological sites in the Hebrides and Northern Isles of Scotland', *Review of Palaeobotany and Palynology* 73, 49–56.

Dockrill, S. J. 2003 'Broch, wheelhouse, and cell: redefining the Iron Age in Shetland', in Downes and Ritchie (eds) 2003, 82–94.

Dockrill, S. J., Bond, J. M., Turner, V. E., Brown, L. D., Bashford, D. J, Cussans, J. E. and Nicholson, R. A. 2010 *Excavations at Old Scatness, Shetland, Volume 1: The Pictish village and Viking settlement*. Lerwick: Shetland Heritage Publications.

Dockrill, S. J., Bond, J. M., Turner, V. E., Brown, L. D., Bashford, D. J, Cussans, J. E. and Nicholson, R. A. 2015 *Excavations at Old Scatness, Shetland, Volume 2: The broch and Iron Age village*. Lerwick: Shetland Heritage Publications.

Downes, J. 2000 'Site sequence and chronology', in Downes and Lamb 2000, 35–76.

Downes, J. and Lamb, R. 2000 *Prehistoric Houses at Sumburgh, Shetland: Excavations at Sumburgh Airport 1967–74*. Oxford: Oxbow Books.

Downes, J. and Ritchie, A. (eds) 2003 *Sea Change: Orkney and Northern Europe in the later Iron Age AD*. Balgavies: Pinkfoot Press.

Dugmore, A. J. and Newton, A. J. 1999 'The pumice: Origins of the material', in Owen and Lowe 1999, 167–8.

Edwards, A. J. H. 1927 'Excavations of graves at Ackergill', *Proceedings of the Society of Antiquaries of Scotland* 61, 196–200.

Edwards, R. 1997 'Norse settlement', in S. Buteux (ed.), *Settlements at Skaill, Deerness, Orkney: Excavations by Peter Gelling of the prehistoric, Pictish, Viking and later periods, 1963–81*. Oxford: British Archaeological Report 260, 70–95.

Faccia, K. J. and Williams, R. C. 2008 'Schmorl's Nodes: Clinical significance and implications for the bioarchaeological record', *International Journal of Osteoarchaeology* 18, 28–44.

Fenton, A. 1978 *The Northern Isles: Orkney and Shetland*. Edinburgh: John Donald.

FitzPatrick, E. A. 1993 *Soil Microscopy and Micromorphology*. Chichester: Wiley.

Fojut, N. 1983 'Towards a geography of Shetland crochs', *Glasgow Archaeological Journal* 9, 38–59.

Fojut, N. 2006 *Prehistoric and Viking Shetland*. Lerwick: Shetland Times.

Food Standards Agency 1998 *McCance and Widdowson – The Composition of Foods*. London: Institute of Food Research.

Forster, A. 2009 'Viking and Norse steatite use in Shetland', in Forster and Turner 2009, 58–69.

Forster, A. 2014 'Steatite', in Moore and Wilson (2014), Section 3: Excavations at Bayanne, Yell, Shetland.

Forster, A. 2015 'The steatite assemblage', in Dockrill *et al.* 2015, 365–74.

Forster, A. and Sharman, P. 2009 'Use in early prehistoric Shetland, from the Neolithic to the early Iron Age', in Forster and Turner 2009, 27–36.

Forster, A. K. and Turner, V. E. (eds) 2009 *Kleber, Shetland's First Industry: The archaeology of steatite in Shetland*. Lerwick: Shetland Amenity Trust.

Goodlad, C. A. 1971 *Shetland Fishing Saga*. Lerwick: Shetland Times.

Graham-Campbell, J. 2004 '"*Danes ...* in this Country": discovering the Vikings in Scotland', *Proceedings of the Society of Antiquaries of Scotland* 134, 210–39.

Grant, A. 1982 'The use of tooth wear as a guide to the age of domestic ungulates' in B. Wilson, C. Grigson and S. Payne (eds), *Ageing and Sexing Animal Bones from Archaeological Sites*. Oxford: British Archaeological Report 109, 55–71.

Gray, M. 1978 *The Fishing Industries of Scotland 1790–1914*. Oxford: Oxford University Press.

Green, H. S. 1980 *The Flint Arrowheads of the British Isles: A detailed study of material from England and Wales with comparanda from Scotland and Ireland*. Oxford: British Archaeological Report 75.

Griffiths, D. and Ashmore, P. J. 2011 *Aeolian Archaeology: The archaeology of sand landscapes in Scotland*. Scottish Archaeological Internet Report 48. http://archaeologydataservice.ac.uk/archives/view/sair/volumes.cfm

Guido, M. 1978 *The Glass Beads of the Prehistoric and Roman Periods in Britain and Ireland*. London: Report of the Research Committee of the Society of Antiquaries of London 35.

Gunstone, F. D., Harwood, J. L. and Padley, F. B. 1994 *The Lipid Handbook*. London: Chapman and Hall.

Guttmann, E. B. A. 2005 'Midden cultivation in prehistoric Britain: arable crops in gardens', *World Archaeology* 37(2), 224–39.

Guttmann, E. B. A., Dockrill, S. J. and Simpson, I. A. 2004 'Arable agriculture in prehistory: new evidence from soils in the Northern Isles', *Proceedings of the Society of Antiquaries of Scotland*, 134, 53–64

Hallén, Y. 1994 'The use of bone and antler at Foshigarry and Bac Mhic Connain, two Iron Age sites on North Uist, Western Isles', *Proceedings of the Society of Antiquaries of Scotland* 124, 189–231.

Hamilton, J. R. 1956 *Excavations at Jarlshof, Shetland*. Edinburgh HMSO: Ministry of Works Archaeological Report 1.

Hamilton, J. R. 1968 *Excavations at Clickhimin, Shetland*. Edinburgh: HMSO Ministry of Works Archaeological Report 6.

Hansen, S. S. 1995 'Sandwick North (Unst parish), Norse farmstead', *Discovery and Excavation Scotland*, 105–6.

Harding, D. W. 2004 *The Iron Age in Northern Britain: Celts and Romans, natives and invaders*. London: Routledge.

Heald, A. and McLaren, D. 2014 'Metalworking at Burland and beyond', in Moore and Wilson 2014, Section 4: Excavations at Burland, Trondra, Shetland, 259–64.

Hedges, J. W. 1987 *Bu, Gurness and the Brochs of Orkney – Part I: Bu*. Oxford: British Archaeological Report 163.

Heron, C., Evershed, R. P. and Goad, L. J. 1991 'Effects of migration of soil lipids on organic residues associated with buried potsherds', *Journal of Archaeological Science* 18(4), 403–14.

Hingley, R. 1992 'Society in Scotland from 700 BC to AD 200', *Proceedings of the Society of Antiquaries of Scotland* 122, 7–53.

Historic Scotland 1997 *The Treatment of Human Remains in Archaeology*. Historic Scotland Operational Policy Paper 5.

Hunter, F. 2008 'Jet and related materials in Viking Scotland', *Medieval Archaeology* 52, 103–18.

Hunter, F. 2014 'The shale bangle', in Moore and Wilson 2014, 189.

Ingold, T. 1993 'The temporality of the landscape', *World Archaeology* 25(2), 152-74.

Işcan, M. Y., Loth, S. R. and Wright, R. K. 1985 'Age estimation from the rib by phase analysis: White females', *Journal of Forensic Sciences* 30, 853–63.

Irving, J. T. nd Miscellaneous literary collections, mainly unclassified. NMS Research Library, Society of Antiquaries of Scotland, Edinburgh.

Jacomet, S. 1987 *Prähistorische Getreidefunde, Eine Anleitung zur Bestimmung Prähistorischer Gersten und Weizen Funde*. Basel: Herausgegeben im Eigenverlag.

Jones, A. M. and Baxter, J. M. 1985 'The use of *Patella vulgata* L in rocky shore surveillance', in P. G. Moore and R. Seed (eds), *The Ecology of Rocky Coasts*. London: Hodder and Stoughton.

Jones, R. E. 2007 Rare earth element analysis of steatite artefacts found at the Time Team site FG02 – on Fetlar, Shetland. Unpublished report, University of Glasgow.

Jones, R. E. 2015 'Rare earth element analysis of steatite artefacts', in Moore and Wilson 2014, 153–4.

Jones, R. E., Olive, V. and Ellam, R. 2006 Chemical (rare earth element) analysis of Viking steatite artefacts from Kaupang: a preliminary report. Museum of Cultural History, University of Oslo unpublished report.

Jones, R. E., Olive, V., Kilikoglou, V., Ellam, R., Bassiakos, Y., Bray, I. and Sanderson, D. 2007 'A new protocol for the chemical characterisation of steatite – Two case studies in Europe: the Shetland Isles and Crete', *Journal of Archaeological Science* 34, 626–41.

Larsen, G., Newton, A. J., Dugmore, A. J. and Vilmundardóttir, E. 2001 'Geochemistry, dispersal, volumes and chronology of Holocene silicic tephra layers from the Katla volcanic system, Iceland', *Journal of Quaternary Science* 16(2), 119–32.

Lelong, O. and MacGregor, G. 2008 *The Lands of Ancient Lothian: Interpreting the archaeology of the A1*. Edinburgh: Society of Antiquaries of Scotland.

Lovejoy, C. O., Meindl, R. S., Mensforth, R. and Barton, T. J. 1985 'Chronological metamorphosis of the auricular surface of the ilium: a new method for the determination of adult skeletal age at death', *American Journal of Physical Anthropology* 68, 15–28.

Low, G. 1813 *Fauna Orcadensis or The Natural History of the Quadruplets, Birds, Reptiles, and Fishes of Orkney and Shetland*. Edinburgh: George Ramsay.

Macartney, E. 1984 'Analysis of faunal remains', in H. Fairhurst (ed.), *Excavations at Crosskirk Broch, Caithness*. Edinburgh: Society of Antiquaries of Scotland Monograph 3, 133–47.

MacGregor, A. 1974 'The Broch of Burrian, North Ronaldsay, Orkney', *Proceedings of the Society of Antiquaries of Scotland* 105, 63–118.

MacGregor, A. 1985 *Bone, Antler, Ivory and Horn: The technology of skeletal materials since the Roman period*. Beckenham: Croom Helm.

McKenzie, J. T. 2006 Deep anthropogenic topsoils in Scotland: A geoarchaeological and historical investigation into distribution, character, and conservation under modern land cover. Unpublished PhD thesis, University of Stirling.

Mackie, E. 2000 'Excavations at Dun Ardtreck, Skye, in 1964 and 1965', *Proceedings of the Society of Antiquaries of Scotland* 130, 301–412.

MacKie, E. W. 2002 *The roundhouses, brochs and wheelhouses of Atlantic Scotland c. 700 BC–AD 500: Architecture and material culture, Part 1 – The Orkney and Shetland Isles*. Oxford: British Archaeological Report 342.

MacSween, A. 2009 'A note on the use of steatite as temper', in Forster and Turner 2009, 37–8.

MacSween, A. 2014 'The pottery', in Moore and Wilson (2014), Section 3: Excavations at Bayanne, Yell, Shetland', 123–37.

Maldonado Ramírez, A. D. 2011 Christianity and Burial in Late Iron Age Scotland, AD 400–650. Unpublished PhD thesis, University of Glasgow.

Mays, S., Brickley, M. and Dodwell, N. 2002 *Human Bones from Archaeological Sites: Guidance for Producing Assessment Documents and Analytical Reports (Centre for Field Archaeology Guidelines)*. Swindon: English Heritage/British Association for Biological Anthropology and Osteoarchaeology.

Moore, H. and Wilson, G. 2006 'Knowe of Skea, Orkney (Westray parish), eroding multi-period funerary complex', *Discovery and Excavation Scotland* 7, 127.

Moore, H. and Wilson, G. 2014 *Ebbing Shores: Survey and Excavation of Coastal Archaeology in Shetland 1995–2008*. Edinburgh: Historic Scotland Archaeology Report 8.

Moreno-Nuño, R. 1994a *Arqueomalacología. Identificación de Moluscos*. Informe no. 1994/18. Laboratorio de Arqueozoologia. Madrid: Universidad Autónoma de Madrid.

Moreno-Nuño, R. 1994b *Arqueomalacología. Cuantificación de Moluscos*. Informe no. 1994/19. Laboratorio de Arqueozoologia. Madrid: Universidad Autónoma de Madrid.

Murray, J. 2017 Late Bronze Age and Iron Age pottery in the Shetland Isles: A synopsis of design, construction methods and typological trends. Unpublished MPhil thesis, University of St Andrews.

Needham, S. and Spence, T. 1996 *Refuse and Disposal at Area 16, East Runnymede*. London: British Museum Press.

Newton, A. J. 1999a Ocean-transported Pumice in the North Atlantic. Unpublished PhD Thesis, University of Edinburgh.

Newton, A. J. 1999b 'Report on the pumice', in Crawford and Ballin Smith 1999, 178.

Newton, A. J. 2001 'The pumice', in S. Mithen (ed.), *Hunter-gatherer Landscape Archaeology: The Southern Hebrides Project 1988–98*. Cambridge: McDonald Institute Monograph, 403–5.

Newton, A. J. 2004 'Pumice', in C. R. Wickham-Jones and K. Hardy, *Camas Daraich: A Mesolithic site at the Point of Sleat, Skye*. Scottish Archaeological Internet Report 12, 47–9. http://archaeologydataservice.ac.uk/archives/view/sair/volumes.cfm

Newton, A. J. 2006 'Pumice', in Armit 2006, 153–4.

Newton, A. J. and Dugmore, A. J. 1995 'The pumice, analytical report', in *Barra: Archaeological Research on Ben Tangaval*. Sheffield: Sheffield Academic Press, 145–8.

Newton, A. J. and Dugmore, A. J. 2003 'Analysis of pumice from Baleshare', in J. Barber (ed.), *Bronze Age Farms and Iron Age Farm Mounds of the Outer Hebrides*. Edinburgh: Society of Antiquaries of Scotland with Historic Scotland and the Council for British Archaeology, 135–8.

Nicolaisen, W. F. H. 1980 'Early Scandinavian naming in the Western and Northern Isles', *Northern Scotland* 3, 110.

Nicholson, J. R. 1990 *Traditional Life in Shetland*. London: Robert Hale.

Nicholson, R.A. 1991 An investigation into variability within archaeologically recovered assemblages of faunal remains: The influence of pre-depositional taphonomic processes. Unpublished D. Phil. thesis, University of York.

Nicholson, R. A., Barber, P. and Bond, J. M. 2005 'New evidence for the date of introduction of the House Mouse, *Mus musculus domesticus* Schwartz and Schwartz, and the Field Mouse, *Apodemus sylvaticus* (L.), to Shetland', *Environmental Archaeology* 10(2), 143–51.

Orton, C., Tyers, P. and Vince, A. 1993 *Pottery in Archaeology*. Cambridge: Cambridge University Press.

Owen, O. E. and Lowe, C. (eds) 1999 *Kebister: The four thousand year old story of one Shetland township*. Edinburgh: Society of Antiquaries of Scotland Monograph Series No 14.

Payne, S. 1973 'Kill-off patterns in sheep and goats – the mandibles from Aşvan Kale', *Journal of Anatolian Studies*, 23, 281–303.

Pennant, T. 1794 *Arctic Zoology, Volume 1*. London: Henry Hughs.

Pennie, I. D. 1960 'Portgower', *Discovery and Excavation Scotland*, 40.

Platt, M. I. 1934 'Report on the animal bones from Jarlshof, Sumburgh, Shetland', in A. O. Curle, 'An account of further excavations at Jarlshof, Sumburgh, Shetland, in 1932 and 1933, on behalf of HM Office of Works', *Proceedings of the Society of Antiquaries of Scotland* 68, 313–19.

Prehistoric Ceramics Research Group (PCRG) 1995 *The Study of Later Prehistoric Pottery: General policies and guidelines for analysis and publication*. PCRG Occasional Papers 1 and 2.

Rice, P. 1987 *Pottery Analysis: A sourcebook*. Chicago: University of Chicago Press.

Ritchie, A. 1972 'Painted pebbles in early Scotland', *Proceedings of the Society of Antiquaries of Scotland* 104, 297–301.

Ritchie, A. 1983 'Excavation of a Neolithic farmstead at Knap of Howar, Papa Westray, Orkney', *Proceedings of the Society of Antiquaries of Scotland* 113, 40–121.

Ritchie, A. 1998 'Painted pebbles', in Sharples 1998, 176–8.

RCAHMS 1946 *The Royal Commission on the Ancient and Historical Monuments of Scotland. Twelfth report with an inventory of the ancient monuments of Orkney and Shetland*. Edinburgh: HMSO, 141, No. 1581.

Schweingruber, F. H. 1990 *Anatomy of European Woods*. Haupt: Berne and Stuttgart.

Senesi, N. and Loffredo, E. 1999 'The chemistry of soil organic matter', in D. L. Sparks (ed.), Soil Physical Chemistry. London: CRC Press, 239–370.

Serjeantson, D. 1988 'Archaeological and ethnographic evidence for seabird exploitation in Scotland', *Archaeozoologia* 2 (1988), 209–24.

Sharman, P. M. 1998 'The Steatite', in Sharples 1998, 119.

Sharman, P. M. 2000 'Steatite and other fine stone objects', in Downes and Lamb 2000, 82–7.

Sharpe, R. (trans.) 1995 *Adomnán Of Iona, Life of Saint Columba*. London: Penguin.

Sharples, N. 1998 *Scalloway: A broch, Late Iron Age settlement and medieval cemetery in Shetland*. Oxford: Oxbow Monograph 82.

Simpson, I. A., Vésteinsson, O., Adderley, W. P. and McGovern, T. H. 2003 'Fuel resource utilization in landscapes of settlement', *Journal of Archaeological Science* 30, 1401–20.

Simpson, I. A., Guttmann, E. B., Cluett, J. and Shepherd, A. 2006 'Characterizing anthropic sediments in north European Neolithic settlements: an assessment from Skara Brae, Orkney', *Geoarchaeology*, 21(3), 221–35.

Small, A. 1965 'Shetland, Skaw, Unst', *Discovery and Excavation in Scotland* 1965, 37.

Small, A. 1966 'Excavations at Underhoull, Unst, Shetland', *Proceedings of the Society of Antiquaries of Scotland* 98, 225–48.

Smith, A. 2007a 'Pumice' in J. Hunter and A. N. Smith, *Investigations in Sanday Orkney, Volume 1: Excavations at Pool, Sanday, a multi-period settlement from Neolithic to Late Norse times*. Kirkwall: The Orcadian, 404–12.

Smith, A. 2007b 'The Pumice', in S. J. Dockrill, *Investigations in Sanday Orkney, Volume 2: Tofts Ness, Sanday, an island landscape through 3000 years of prehistory*. Kirkwall: The Orcadian, 288–92.

Smith, B. 2003 'Not welcome at all: Vikings and the native population in Orkney and Shetland', in Downes and Ritchie (eds) 2003, 145–50.

Smith, C. and Hodgson, G. W. I. 1994 'Animal bone report,' in Ballin Smith 1994, 139–53.

Smith, K. T., Larsen, G., Dugmore, A. J., Newton, A. J. and Knudsen, Ó. forthcoming 'Holocene jökulhlaups from western Mýrdalsjökull, Iceland: a chronology', *Quaternary Science Reviews*.

Stace, C. 1997 *New Flora of the British Isles*. 2nd edition. Cambridge: Cambridge University Press.

Starley, D. 2000 'Metalworking debris', in K. Buxton and C. Howard-Davis (eds), *Bremetenacum: Excavations at Roman*

Ribchester 1980, 1989–1990. Lancaster: Lancaster Imprints Series 9, 337–47.

Stevenson, R. B. K. 1966 'Metalwork and some other objects in Scotland and their cultural affinities', in A. L. F. Rivet (ed.), *The Iron Age in Northern Britain.* Edinburgh: Edinburgh University Press, 17–44.

Stoops, G. 2003 *Guidelines for Analysis and Description of Soil and Regolith Thin Sections.* Madison: Soil Science of America.

Teichert, M. 1975 'Osteometrische Untersuchungen zur Berechnung der Widerristhöhe bei Schafen', in A. T. Clason (ed.), *Archaeozoological Studies*, 51–69.

Ubelaker, D. 1989 *Human Skeletal Remains: Excavation, analysis and interpretation.* 2nd edition. Washington: Taraxacum Press.

von den Driesch, A. 1976 *A Guide to the Measurement of Animal Bones from Archaeological Sites.* Peabody Museum Bulletin 1. Harvard: Harvard University.

von den Driesch, A. and Boessneck, J. A. 1974 'Kritische Ammerkungen zur Widderisthöhenberechnung aus Längenmassen vor- und frühgeschichlichen Tierknocken', *Säugetierkundliche Mitteilungen,* 22(4), 325–48.

van der Veen, M. 1992 *Crop Husbandry Regimes.* Sheffield: University of Sheffield Archaeological Monograph 3.

Walton Rogers, P. 1997 *Textile Production at 16–22 Coppergate.* York: Archaeology of York Fascicule 17/11.

Watt, J., Pierce, G. J. and Boyle, P. R. 1997 *Guide to the Identification of North Sea Fish using Premaxilla and vertebra.* Denmark: ICES Cooperative Research Report 220.

Weber, B. 1999 'Bakestones', in Crawford and Ballin Smith 1999, 134–8.

Wheeler, A. and Jones, A. K. J. 1989 *Cambridge Manuals in Archaeology: Fishes.* Cambridge: Cambridge University Press.

Wheeler, A. 1969 *The Fishes of the British Isles and North-West Europe.* London: Macmillan.

Wheeler, A. 1978 *Key to the Fishes of Northern Europe.* London: Frederick Warne.

Whimster, R. P. 1981 *Burial Practices in Iron Age Britain.* Oxford: British Archaeological Report 90.

White, T. D. and Folkens, P. A. 2000 *Human Osteology.* San Diego: Academic Press.

Yalden, D. 1999 *The History of British Mammals.* London: T. & A.D. Poyser (A. & C. Black).

Zohary, D. and Hopf, M. 2000 *Domestication of Plants in the Old World.* 3rd edition. Oxford: Oxford University Press.

Index